FINAL RESEARCH REPORT

THE PROJECT MANAGEMENT OFFICE (PMO): A QUEST FOR UNDERSTANDING

FINAL RESEARCH REPORT

THE PROJECT MANAGEMENT OFFICE (PMO): A QUEST FOR UNDERSTANDING

Brian Hobbs, PhD, MBA, PMP
Monique Aubry, PhD, MPM

Project Management Research Chair
University of Quebec at Montreal

The Project Management Office (PMO): A Quest for Understanding

ISBN: 978-1-933890-97-5

Published by: Project Management Institute, Inc.
14 Campus Boulevard
Newtown Square, Pennsylvania 19073-3299 USA.
Phone: +610-356-4600
Fax: +610-356-4647
E-mail: customercare@pmi.org
Internet: www.PMI.org

PMI Publications welcomes corrections and comments on its books. Please feel free to send comments on typographical, formatting, or other errors. Simply make a copy of the relevant page of the book, mark the error, and send it to: Book Editor, PMI Publications, 14 Campus Boulevard, Newtown Square, PA 19073-3299 USA.

To inquire about discounts for resale or educational purposes, please contact the PMI Book Service Center.

PMI Book Service Center
P.O. Box 932683, Atlanta, GA 31193-2683 USA
Phone:1-866-276-4764 (within the U.S. or Canada) or +1-770-280-4129 (globally)
Fax: +1-770-280-4113
E-mail: info@bookorders.pmi.org

10 9 8 7 6 5 4 3

ACKNOWLEDGMENTS

This book presents the results of a multi-method research program that was funded in part by the Project Management Institute (PMI®). Part The authors wish to express their gratitude to all those who completed surveys conducted as part of this research. They provided the essential information that was analyzed and presented in this research report. The participants responded to solicitations made by many members of the international project management research community. The invitation to participate was available on the PMI website, and the authors also solicited respondents through several project management networks, including the PMI Montreal Chapter's Community of Practice on PMOs; the PMI Southern Ontario Chapter; PMForum; American Society for the Advancement of Project Management; Human Systems and Valence, and colleagues from the University of Limerick, Athabasca University, University of Technology Sydney; and ESC-Lille. The authors wish to thank all of those who collaborated to make this project possible. The authors also wish to thank Raymond Laliberté and Carl St-Pierre who provided invaluable assistance in both the preparation of the survey instruments and the analysis of data.

Four organizations participated in the qualitative case studies in a later phase of the program. The authors thank these organizations and their employees for their time and interest. Their contributions must, however, remain anonymous.

Partial results have been presented, discussed, and enriched in many different venues during the six years this research program has unfolded. The authors thank all the participants who took part in these conversations and the reviewers of journal articles for their comments and suggestions.

TABLE OF CONTENTS

LIST OF FIGURES

Chapter 4

Chapter 5

LIST OF TABLES

EXECUTIVE SUMMARY

This book presents the results of a multi-year, multi-method research program aimed at developing a better understanding of PMOs. There were two main projects in the research program. The first project was a survey to describe the population that collected the descriptions of 502 project management offices (PMOs) worldwide. The survey was designed to answer the questions, "How are PMOs structured?" and "What functions do they fill?" The most important and influential finding from the survey is that most PMOs change every few years. This simple fact has profound consequences for practitioners, professional organizations, and researchers.

The survey showed that PMOs are extremely varied and change frequently. It is highly plausible that the internal dynamics of the organization drive the implementations and frequent reconfigurations of PMOs. The second major project in this research program was an investigation of PMOs within their organizational context. PMOs in four organizations were examined by in-depth qualitative case studies using a retrospective historical approach. The aim of the case studies was to answer the question, "How and why do organizations implement their first PMO or reconfigure existing PMOs every few years?" The qualitative study provides a rich description of PMOs embedded in their organizational context. Rather than examining the PMO as a static and isolated organizational entity, the PMO is conceptualized as an entity that plays multiple roles in multiple organizational processes.

The professional-practitioner community has been demanding best practices, guidelines, and eventually a standard on PMOs since the turn of the century. Its underlying questions are, "How should PMOs be structured?" and "What functions should they fill?" If PMOs are temporary arrangements, it is impossible to answer these questions as they are presently being conceptualized.

The best way to set up a PMO is context-specific. However, the findings from the survey show that PMOs do not vary systematically according to the classic organizational contingency factors. PMOs in different industries, different geographic regions, in large and small organizations, and in public and private organizations do not vary systematically in either the way they are organized or the functions they fill. Because these contingency factors are quite stable and PMOs change quickly, it is normal that no relationship exists between them.

When designing a PMO, an organization has a large number of choices as to how the PMO is organized and what roles it plays. This variety could be reduced and better managed if PMOs could be arranged into homogeneous groups or types. Several strategies were deployed in search of such types. The analysis of the survey data identified a cluster of two project management specific organizational characteristics (level of project management maturity and supportiveness of the organizational culture) and three PMO characteristics (decision-making authority of the PMO, the portion of projects within the PMO and the number of functions filled by the PMO) that are associated with each other and with the performance of the PMO. The choice to include a large or a small portion of projects and project managers in a PMO can be used to create four types of PMOs that differ significantly on the variables identified in this cluster and on the performance of the PMO. The functions filled by PMOs can also be used to identify types, but attempts to identify types by function were less fruitful.

The competing values framework is used as an alternative means of conceptualizing the role of PMOs. The framework employs two dimensions, internal-external and flexibility-control, to identify four concepts of organizational performance, each with a different focus. The empirical results show that different PMOs contribute to different models of organizational performance. The use of this framework to address the question, "What should the role of the PMO be?" reframes the issue as one of strategic choice.

Because the PMO is most often a temporary structural arrangement, the process that transforms the PMO becomes an object of interest. The analysis revealed that the organizational and political context in which the PMO is embedded is the most important driver of change to PMOs and thus determines to a large extent how PMOs are organized and the roles they play. The perceived performance of PMOs is determined mainly by their embeddedness in their organizational contexts, which is to say that having a mandate that is in line with the vision of senior management and that is well understood throughout the organization, having competent personnel that is recognized by others for their expertise and having cooperative relationships with other parts of the organization involved in projects are the best predictors of PMO performance.

It is important to provide a theoretical basis for PMOs. In this research program an effort has been made to do so by situating the PMO within organizational project management and the project-based organization, and by situating both of these within organization theory and innovation management. However, more work is needed.

CHAPTER ONE: INTRODU(

1.1 What is a PMO?

In recent years, many organizations have established PMOs. Dai and Wells (2004) showed that PMOs first started to become popular in 1994 and that the number of PMOs has been growing significantly since. Many books and articles on PMOs have been published in recent years, with the vast majority of the literature produced by practitioners and consultants promoting the implementation of PMOs. This literature is rational, self-evidently correct and normative, as is much of the project management literature (Williams, 2005).

Observations of PMOs in organizations contrast quite sharply with the image portrayed in the literature. The population of PMOs is characterized by very significant variation in:

- The structure of PMOs,
- The roles assumed by PMOs, and
- The perceived value of PMOs.

Prior to this research program, a reliable portrait of the population of PMOs was not available. In addition, an adequate explanation of the great variety of PMOs has yet to be found.

1.2 The Definition of a PMO

A Guide to the Project Management Body of Knowledge (*PMBOK® Guide*) defines a PMO as:

> An organizational body or entity assigned various responsibilities related to the centralized and coordinated management of those projects under its domain. The responsibilities of the PMO can range from providing project management support functions to actually being responsible for the direct management of a project. (PMI, 2008a, p. 369)

This definition is very close to the definition the authors adopted during this investigation. It highlights that PMOs are organizational entities and that their mandates vary significantly from one organization to the next. It also highlights that the creation of a PMO involves the centralization of certain project management roles and responsibilities in this organizational entity (Marsh, 2000). However, study makes a distinction between the multi-project PMO and the single-project PMO or "project office," which has responsibility for the management of one large project. The *PMBOK Guide* definition and much of the literature on PMOs include both, and both are important phenomena worthy of investigation. Multi-project PMOs and entities responsible for the management of a single project are quite different and can best be investigated separately. The scope of this investigation includes only PMOs with mandates that cover many projects or multi-project PMOs.

In part because of the great variety found among PMOs in different organizations, and in part because of the lack of both a consensus among practitioners and adequate descriptions in the literature, discussions on this topic tend to be characterized by diversity of opinion and confusion. Many people have been exposed to a limited number of PMOs and have concluded inappropriately that all PMOs are similar to the ones they have observed. The lack of consensus is understandable given that the PMO is a relatively recent phenomenon, that PMOs take on a great variety of forms and functions, and that there has been a lack of systematic investigation. This investigation employs this rather large definition of the PMO to capture the variety of form and function. For the purposes of this investigation, it is not necessary that the organizational entity be called a PMO.

1.3   A Model of the PMO

A description of a phenomenon as complex as PMOs is based either explicitly or implicitly on a model. "A research model is an instrument for linking theory with data in terms of functions, representation and learning" (Van de Ven, 2007, p. 144). The PMO model will serve to represent a portion of the reality of PMOs, what they are, and what they do. The model is a piece of knowledge that may contribute to a better understanding of the reality. The model defines what will be described and which characteristics are important to include. The model of a PMO and its context that is used in this research identifies the following five classes of variables. Figure 1.1 illustrates the model of a PMO and its context.

The description of the PMO is broken down into the following two classes of variables:

*   *Structural characteristics of the PMO*
    A PMO is a complex multi-dimensional entity. The design of a new or modified PMO is based on a large number of design choices. Likewise, the description of an existing PMO is based on a large number of variables. These could be grouped into more detailed subclasses of variables, but in this preliminary model the descriptive characteristics of PMOs have not been structured into a more detailed model.
*   *Roles and functions*
    PMOs fill many different roles or functions in different organizations.

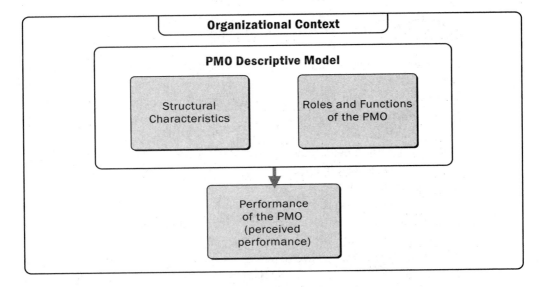

Figure 1.1. A model of the PMO in its context

The context in which the PMO operates is described in the following two classes of variables:

- *Organizational context*
  A PMO is not an isolated entity; rather, it is embedded in an organization, which in turn is embedded in a socioeconomic context. An understanding of the organizational context is key to understanding PMOs. The context could be modeled in more detail, but this has not been done in this preliminary model.
- *Types of projects in the PMO's mandate*
  Different types of projects are managed differently. This may have an impact on both the role and the structure of the PMO.

Organizational performance is very often the ultimate dependent variable in organizational studies. Considering both the performance of the PMO and its contribution to the performance of the organization is necessary.

- *Perceived value or performance of the PMO*
  The performance of the PMO can be conceptualized and measured in several ways. These include global measures of its value or its legitimacy, as well as measures of specific contributions to value.

In an exploratory study such as this, it is important to have a model that defines the borders of the object of study and serves as a basis for organizing the investigation and the data collection and treatment. The model should be open enough to allow the underlying structure to emerge from the analysis of the data and not to overly constrain the investigation of its results. This high-level preliminary model forms the basis for the empirical investigation of PMOs in their organizational context. The model will be enriched by the results of the research.

1.4 The Emergence of PMOs

The PMO is an important part of project management as it is currently practiced and is the focus of the research that is presented in this book. However, the emergence of the PMO is only a small part of important changes that have taken place during the last ten years in both the management of organizations and the professional field of project management. The PMO is not just another tool or technique in project management, it is part of the fundamental changes in the role of project management in organizations and the definition of what constitutes the field of project management.

Quite often during the last ten years, it has been observed that organizations are facing a new context characterized by increased competition, increased rates of product, service and process innovation, and an increasing emphasis on time to market. Organizations have responded to these challenges by developing new, more flexible organizational forms (Pettigrew, 2003) in which projects are both more numerous and more strategically important (Jamieson & Morris, 2004). As part of the response to the new challenges and as part of the movement to increase both the number and the strategic importance of projects, many organizations have implemented a new organizational entity, the most common name for which is the PMO. Dai and Wells (2004) showed that the number of organizations with PMOs has increased sharply since 1994, and Cosgrove Ware (2003) reported that "76% of the executives surveyed are saying they've created a PMO within the past three years." The study by Thomas and Mullaly (2008) was based on an inventory of what organizations have implemented in recent years when implementing project management. They found that the PMO is often a central component of the implementation of project management. The PMO is clearly an important part of project management practice today.

An abundance of literature has emerged and continues to develop documenting and analyzing these organizational innovations. The special issue of the *Scandinavian Management Journal,* particularly the article on projectification by Midler (1995), and the special issue of the *International Journal of Project Management* reporting on the "Rethinking Project Management" initiative, particularly the papers by Maylor et al. (2006) on programmification and by Winter et al. (2006) on business projects, are early and later milestones in this stream of writings. Within this tradition, organizations[1] have been qualified as "project-based" (DeFillippi & Arthur, 1998; Lindkvist, 2004; Lundin & Söderholm, 1995; Thiry, 2006; Turner & Keegan, 2001; Whitley, 2006), "project-led" (Hobday, 2000), "project-intensive" (Söderlund & Bredin, 2006), and "project-oriented" (Gareis & Huemann, 2003).

During the last ten years, the field of project management has undergone a fundamental transformation parallel to the mutations that have taken place in organizations. Ten years ago, the field was focused almost exclusively on the

---

1 The terms firm, company, and enterprise have also been used, but the more general term organization is used here.

"project." The publication of the *Organizational Project Management Maturity Model* (*OPM3*) (PMI, 2003, 2008b) marked the expansion of the field, which now encompasses "organizational project management," which is defined as "the alignment and systematic management of projects, programs, and portfolios to achieve strategic organizational objectives" (PMI, 2008b). *OPM3* divides the field of project management into three domains: project, program, and portfolio management, and the second edition adds "organizational enablers." The field of project management can now be seen as covering four levels of analysis: project, program, portfolio, and organizational levels. The focus is clearly at the organizational level, not just the project level. The concept of "organizational project management" and the literature references above on "project-based organizations" are clearly situated at the organizational level of analysis. The PMO is also at the organizational level of analysis. The PMO can thus be conceptualized as being an element of organizational project management.

The concept of "organizational project management" originated in the project management practitioner community, where it has been accepted very quickly. It has taken very little effort to anchor the concept theoretically. Doing so is beyond the scope of this book, which specifically addresses empirical research on PMOs. However, it is important to anchor concepts in their theoretical domain. The concept of organizational project management is clearly in the domain of management generally and organization theory specifically. Aubry, Hobbs, and Thuillier (2007) made a contribution to the theoretical anchoring of the concept and defined organizational project management as a new sphere of management where dynamic structures in the firm are articulated as a means to implement corporate objectives through projects to maximize value. The theoretical anchoring of the PMO in organizational project management, and its methodological consequences, are developed further in Chapter 4.

1.5 PMOs in the Literature

Treatment of the PMO is relatively plentiful in the professional literature (Benko & McFarlan, 2003; Bridges & Crawford, 2001; Crawford, 2002; Dinsmore, 1999; Duggal, 2001; Kendall & Rollins, 2003). These texts deal principally with three themes: the justification of the PMO's existence, its roles and functions, and steps for its implementation. The topic has received very little treatment in the scientific literature.

PMOs are envisioned by some authors as playing an active role in specific functions. Huemann and Anbari (2007) pointed out that PMOs should be more involved in audit functions, particularly in learning from audits, and Huemann, Keegan, and Turner (2007) identified the PMO as a key actor in HR management in project-oriented organizations. The descriptions of PMOs in the literature are often summarized in typologies comprised of a small number of models. Dinsmore (1999) introduced an early typology of PMOs with four types, starting with a single-project entity, in which project management services are developed and used within this single project. The three other models in Dinsmore's typology are multi-project entities: project support office, project management center of excellence, and program management office. The Gartner Research Group's 2000 study (as cited in Kendall & Rollins, 2003) proposed one of the most influential typologies of PMOs. The Gartner Group typology is comprised of three types of PMOs: project repository, coach, and enterprise. Several authors have proposed typologies since the publication of the Gartner report, some of which explicitly referenced the earlier work. Table 1.1 presents some common typologies of PMOs described in the literature, identified only by their names.

Table 1.1. Typologies of PMOs in the literature

Author	Single-project entities	Multi-project entities		
Dinsmore (1999)	Autonomous Project Team	Project Support Office	Project Management Center of Excellence	Program Management Office
Gartner Research Group		Project Repository	Coach	Enterprise
Crawford (2002)	Level 1: Project Control Office	Level 2: Business Unit Project Office	Level 3: Strategic Project Office	
Englund, Graham, & Dinsmore (2003)		Project Support Office	Project Management Center of Excellence	Program Management Office
Kendall & Rollins (2003)		Project Repository	Coach	Enterprise "Deliver Now"
Garfein (2005)	Project Office	Basic PMO	Mature PMO	Enterprise PMO

Some of the typologies identify the single-project entity of "project office," which is outside the scope of this study. Each of the typologies proposes two, three, or four multi-project PMOs, organized in an ascending hierarchy. Different authors used different properties to characterize the passage from one level to the next within their hierarchy. The following are among these properties:
• Staff functions or line functions with project managers included within the PMO
• Organizational scope: covering larger portions of the organization
• Level within the organizational hierarchy: from the lower operational level to the top level
• Influence and authority: from passive to supportive to enforcing standards to empowered
• Operational issues to strategic issues, often associated with a progression from project management to program and/or portfolio management
• Process-driven to business-driven

- Project management maturity of the organization
- Supportiveness of the organizational culture: from non-supportive to fully supportive

Each type presented in these typologies is a model of a PMO. Any model is a simplification and a reduction of the complexities of organizational reality. Models are very useful, even necessary, to support both research and practice. However, the reduction of all or even most multi-project PMOs to two, three, or four types is a radical reduction. This investigation does not use the models found in the literature as a starting point. The authors believe that it is useful and necessary to put these models aside and to investigate organizational reality directly to capture the diversity and the complexity of PMOs in practice.

1.6 The Origins and Goals of the Research

This book is the result of six years of research on PMOs. What began as a simple inquiry into the reality of PMOs has become an ongoing quest to understand a very complex organizational phenomenon. The aim of this book is to contribute to a better understanding of PMOs based on solid empirical research that can provide guidance to practitioners and establish the basis for future research.

The impetus that gave rise to this research began in 2002, when the authors were teaching in the post-graduate programs in project management at the University of Quebec in Montreal. Many of the more mature students were familiar with this new reality of a PMO from experience in their own organizations. When asking students to describe what their PMO was doing, it became apparent that each PMO was a unique setup in a unique organizational environment. Great variability among the PMOs was observed within this rather small sample. The challenge was to see if the same variety would be found in a larger sample.

During 2002 to 2005, we were involved in or witnessed many ad-hoc conversations among practitioners, often at international events organized by PMI and activities organized by PMI-Montreal. During these conversations it seemed as if each individual practitioner tended to see the *PMO truth* through the lens of his or her own experience, which was mainly limited to the PMO in his or her organization. Often one practitioner would make a statement about the characteristics of PMOs and another practitioner would disagree. There seemed to be no way of knowing who was right and who was wrong. In retrospect, both may have been right, because each was describing one of the great variety of forms that PMOs take.

By 2000, the PMO was a prominent feature of the project management landscape. One of the authors was a member of the PMI Standards Member Advisory Group (MAG) for three years, ending in 2002. The question as to whether PMI could and should produce a standard on PMOs came up on several occasions. The conclusion, although nothing official was ever published, was that the PMO was an important phenomenon but that because PMI standards are based on a consensus among practitioners and because no consensus existed, a standard could not be produced. At the time of writing this report, PMI does not yet have a standard on PMOs. In retrospect, the research reported here confirms the lack of consensus and the impossibility of producing a consensus-based standard at the present.

Consultants have answered the pressing questions from organizations with models based on a limited number of types of PMOs. The effort by researchers has been limited and has provided little help to organizations and consultants in better understanding this phenomenon. The situation described here is one in which applied research can play a very important role. What started as a survey in 2003-2004 has developed into a multi-year, multi-method research program, within which one of the authors has completed a PhD degree (Aubry, 2007). In 2003-2004, the research program on PMOs was launched at University of Quebec in Montreal to develop a better understanding of this important phenomenon. The Project Management Research Chair was created in 2007 and this program is now included among the Chair's activities (see www.pmchair.uqam.ca). The objectives of the research program are twofold. The first objective is to produce a reliable description of the present population of PMOs. The second objective is to develop a better understanding of PMOs, of why they take such a variety of forms, and of the dynamics surrounding their creation, transformation, and action in organizations.

When the research program on PMOs was initiated, the state of knowledge did not provide a reliable, empirically grounded description of the phenomena. Many research activities had to take place to develop an adequate understanding of PMOs and of their roles in organizations. The investigation of PMOs has, therefore, been organized into a multi-year, multi-phase, multi-method research program. Each phase is a separate project with its own methodological approach. Successive phases build upon the findings of previous phases. This approach is motivated by the lack of knowledge, by the great variety of forms and functions observed, and by the complexity of the organizational phenomena under investigation. The authors adopted the approach suggested by Van de Ven in his book *Engaged Scholarship: Creating Knowledge for Science and Practice* (2007), where the complexity of the subject merits looking at the problem from various angles. An overview of the research program and each of the first three phases is presented in Section 7. The global methodological strategy is discussed in Section 8.

1.7 The Research Program

The program has been organized into the phases shown in Table 1.2 (Hobbs & Aubry, 2007). Phases are presented sequentially, but in reality much work has been done in parallel, offering opportunities for cross-fertilization.

This book was produced in Phase IV and includes the results from the first three phases. Phases II to IV were funded in part by PMI. The follow-up studies in Phase V and VI also received funding from PMI. The monograph presenting the results was submitted to PMI in the first quarter of 2010. The follow-up

Table 1.2. The research program on PMOs

Phase of the research program	Period	Description	Book Chapter
I	2005-2006	Two descriptive surveys of 502 PMOs aimed at providing a realistic portrait of the population of PMOs	Chapters 2 and 3
II	2006	Development of a rich conceptual model to guide further investigation	Chapter 4
III	2006-2007	In-depth case studies of 12 PMOs in four organizations, aimed at understanding the dynamics surrounding PMOs in their organizational context	Chapters 4 and 5
IV	2008	Analysis of the data from Phases I, II, and III and production of the present book	Entire book
V	2008-2009	Follow-up study of the process by which PMOs are transformed in their organizational context	A new project underway at the time of writing
VI	2009-2010	Follow-up study of networks of multiple PMOs in single organizations	A new project initiated in 2009

study in Phase VI was ongoing at the time of writing. The monograph will be submitted to PMI by the end of 2010. The following sections present each phase in more detail.

1.7.1 Phase I: A Descriptive Survey of 502 PMOs

This phase includes two surveys. The first is referred to as the 2005 initial survey, to which 502 responses were received (Hobbs, 2007). A second survey was undertaken in 2006 to complement the initial one with a smaller number of questions. The complementary survey was sent to participants who answered the initial survey. This was done using the e-mail addresses provided in response to the initial survey. Valid responses were received for 123 PMOs. The final database, therefore, consists of the description of 502 PMOs, of which 123 are more complete. Both surveys serve the same goals: describe one PMO and its context. (Please refer to Chapter 2 for more details on the survey methodology. The survey instruments can be found in the appendices.) Each respondent described one particular PMO at a particular point in time; each is a snapshot of a PMO. The descriptions were quite rich. Data was gathered on the five classes of variables describing the PMO and its organizational context identified in the preliminary model presented in Section 1.3:

1. Organizational context
2. Scope of projects in the PMO's mandate
3. Structural characteristics of the PMO

4. Roles or functions within the PMO's mandate
5. Perceived performance of the PMO

The 502 snapshots were analyzed to:

- Provide a description of the total population and variations in PMO structure, role, and perceived value.
- Identify common configurations or models that describe significant numbers of PMOs.
- Identify relationships between the variability of PMOs and the variability of their contexts.
- Identify correlations between the characteristics of PMOs and their perceived value.
- Identify typologies of PMOs.

A descriptive survey with a large sample is an adequate methodology for describing a population. The primary result of Phase I was the production of such a description of the population, a description characterized by extreme variety. The description of the population is presented in Chapter 2.

PMOs are complex organizational entities. The data presented in Chapter 2 shows that PMOs vary considerably. An effective typology of PMOs would greatly facilitate their study, design, and management. Without a typology, it is very difficult to describe or analyze PMOs. The descriptive data presented in Chapter 2 is analyzed systematically in Chapter 3 in search of patterns that could reveal empirically grounded typologies of PMOs. The analysis was unable to reduce the great variety found among PMOs to a few simple types. However, significant and meaningful patterns were found in the data. These are presented in Chapter 3.

The survey data was largely descriptive. However, the survey instrument did include questions on the perceived value of each PMO. Statistical analysis revealed that some characteristics of PMOs are associated with more highly valued entities. The statistical associations are quite strong and provide some insight into the dynamics surrounding highly valued PMOs. This analysis is also presented in Chapter 3.

Phase I provided a description of the population of PMOs but did not provide an adequate understanding of the dynamics surrounding the PMO, nor did it identify the major sources of variability. The survey and its analysis failed to identify a direct link between organization's economic or industrial context and the particular form and function of the organization's PMO. The survey did, however, identify that most PMOs change every few years. This fact fundamentally changed the way PMOs are conceptualized: rather than being seen as permanent features of organizations, they are now conceived as temporary arrangements that are likely to be modified within a few years. This re-conceptualization had a profound impact on the subsequent phases of the research program. Phases II through IV were designed to investigate the relationship between the PMO and the internal dynamics of the organization in which it is embedded.

1.7.2 Phase II: The Development of a Rich Conceptual Model to Guide Further Investigation

In Phases II and III of the research program, the PMO is not considered as a standalone entity but rather as an important structural element of the organization in which it is implemented. The unit of analysis passes thus from the PMO to the organization that encompasses it. In this perspective, the PMO is seen as the gateway into the organization in order to study the dynamics of project management in the organizational context and the role of the PMO within these dynamics. "The critical task is to adopt and use the models, theories, and research methods that are appropriate for the research problem and question being addressed" (Van de Ven, 2007).

Given the complexity and the richness of the subject being studied and the exploratory nature of the investigation, a constructivist ontology in which the PMO is conceptualized as a dynamic constructed entity has been adopted for Phases II and III of the research program. It is not the purpose of this research to provide a complete description of the rich conceptual model that has been developed (Aubry, Hobbs, & Thuillier, 2007). The theoretical model developed in Phase II is presented in more detail in Chapter 4 and has been used as the basis for the next phase.

1.7.3 Phase III: In-Depth Case Studies Aimed at Understanding the Dynamics Surrounding PMOs in Their Organizational Context

> "Engaged Scholarship is defined as a participative form of research of obtaining the different perspectives of key stakeholders (researchers, users, clients, sponsors, and practitioners) in studying complex problems." (Van de Ven, 2007, p. 9)

This quotation from Van de Ven (2007) inspired the way the methodology for the in-depth case studies has been designed. PMOs represent a complex phenomenon not only by the variety of their expressions, but also by the number of entities to which they relate in a single organization. In matrix organizations, projects naturally form networks, which converge in one or more PMOs. Yet, within a single organization there are multiple managers and professionals in relation to the PMO, including project managers, members of the project team, portfolio managers, financial and HR managers, and so forth. How do these individuals perceive the importance of what the PMO does? How do they value PMO results? It depends on the perspective each of these stakeholders has on the PMO. The PMO often participates in different degrees in the decision-making process in projects. The implementation or renewal of a PMO changes the political games and the associated power relations. This is favorable to the emergence of tensions that sometimes degenerate into conflicts. In-depth case studies are particularly well adapted to subjects as complex as the one investigated here, especially when the study is exploratory, as is the case here.

Both the survey results from Phase I and the conceptual model developed in Phase II were drawn upon in the design of the research instruments for Phase III. These included interview guides and questionnaires. Extensive data was gathered in each of the four organizations to produce a rich description of the organization, its PMO or PMOs, and their joint evolution. In each of the four organizations, data was collected on the historical evolution of PMOs and the organization, going back to before the implementation of the first PMO.

Details on the research design for case studies are presented in Chapter 4. Three types of data were gathered:

- Company documents
- In-depth, semi-structured interviews were conducted, recorded, and transcribed with multiple respondents with different organizational roles. Each interview gathered both factual and perceptual information.
- Two questionnaires were used: one based on the survey instrument from Phase I on functions undertaken in a PMO and one addressing the issue of the contribution of PMOs to organizational performance.

The analysis of data from multiple sources provides a rich, detailed and reliable description of each organization and its PMO or PMOs in their specific context as they evolved together over time. The analysis of the data provided:

- The history of the 12 PMOs found in the four organizations
- The value of the PMOs and their contributions to the organizational performance
- Descriptions of the processes that transformed PMOs
- A typology of drivers leading to PMO transformations

This research proposes not only snapshots of PMOs as in Phase I, but a more holistic understanding of the PMO in its organizational context and of the dynamic processes that transform PMOs. Chapter 4 presents the history of the PMOs in four organizations from three different industrial sectors. The evolution of the PMOs can be observed together with the external and internal environments. Light is shed on the human side of the PMO, and on the politics and tensions that surround it. The exploration of the contribution of the PMO to organizational performance shows the diversity of values underlying the evaluation of PMOs. This chapter proposes a set of indicators that reinforce the coexistence of different but complementary perspectives on the PMO.

Chapter 5 focuses on the PMO transformation process. Under a given set of conditions, a decision is made to implement or transform the PMO to a specific configuration. This configuration generates consequences or impacts from which new conditions will emerge that will start a new transformation cycle. Data show that the drivers that lead to the transformation of PMOs are mostly internal. PMOs change and adapt to situations as part of the construction of a global response to organizational issues. The changes in the PMOs are embedded in the internal political system. From the variety of events and tensions that were identified, a typology was developed. This approach to the PMO examines why PMOs get transformed, and sometimes dismantled. The approach challenges the dominant rationalist paradigm.

1.8   The Global Methodological Strategy

Each of the different phases of the research program is a distinct project that builds upon the results of previous phases. Each project adopts a methodology that is adapted to its objectives. During the entire program, multiple methods are used in an effort to better understand PMOs. There are two major approaches to research methodologies: variance and process approaches. According to Van de Ven (2007), these approaches are used to empirically examine two different types of research questions: the *What* questions and the *How* questions. The What questions entail a variance model. Answering the What questions can provide a description of some phenomenon or its different variations. Explanations in this perspective are provided by independent variables that statistically explain variations on some dependant variables. The How questions entail a process model, are given by narratives, and refer to a sequence of events in terms of an underlying generative mechanism that has the power to cause events (Van de Ven, 2007). The overall strategy contains both approaches.

1.8.1   The Variance Approach

The objectives of Phase I was to describe the population of PMOs and to examine this population in search of regularities. This is clearly a variance approach. Chapter 2 presents descriptive statistics from the survey, where more than 502 valid questionnaires have been analyzed, from which more data was obtained on 123. Descriptive statistics serve to organize and summarize the data to make them more intelligible (Singleton & Straits, 2005). The questionnaire on the PMO contained 29 questions, the majority of which were quantitative. Chapter 2 presents a graphic representation of the distribution of the most important variables describing PMOs. This provides knowledge of the phenomenon one variable at a time.

Chapter 3 presents a search for patterns in the data, based on multi-variant analyses. Each variable has been tested for its relationship with others. Multiple regression analysis is used to explore relations between a single characteristic and several other characteristics. The sample has been divided into sub-populations forming types of PMOs and the differences between the types have been tested for level of significance. The objective is to identify regularities in the variability of the population. The variance approach is particularly well suited to describe a population and to identify and validate the statistical significance of patterns within the population. However, identifying a statistically significant relationship between two or more variables does not give the orientation of this relationship, so neither could reliably be said to be the cause or the effect. "[…] a simple correlation does not indicate which variable came first" (Shadish, Cook, & Campbell, 2002, p. 7). In addition, the variance approach is not well adapted to the study of phenomena embedded in their context or the dynamic interactions that produce change. The process approach is better suited to this end.

1.8.2 The Process Approach

"Process studies are fundamental for gaining an appreciation of dynamic social life, and developing and testing theories of 'how' social entities adapt, change, and evolve over time" (Van de Ven, 2007, p. 145). The process approach is best adapted to the study of the dynamic environment of the PMOs. Data in the process approach takes mostly the form of narratives either from people doing the real job on the ground or from researchers observing the reality on-site. The in-depth case studies presented in Chapters 4 and 5 were inspired largely by a process approach. For the case studies, data was gathered primarily from interviews with a large array of people having different roles in the PMO and its organizational context. The process approach was adopted first to describe the context in which PMOs are embedded. This is the object of Chapter 4, which presents the history of the PMOs being studied. Chapter 5 examines the transformation process in an effort to understand why PMOs change so often.

Results presented in Chapters 4 and 5 rely mostly on retrospective accounts from people interviewed, except for data on most recent events that were ongoing at the time of the interviews. One of the most important advantages of relying on retrospective accounts is that people have time to make sense of the events. When data is gathered as the event is unfolding, important elements of the situation might go unnoticed, particularly if one is personally involved in the change process (Van de Ven, 2007). On the other hand, not observing the process in real time might lead to not seeing events or elements that were not seen as meaningful at the time and are no longer available for observation (Van de Ven, 2007).

In the case studies, data was collected from both retrospective accounts and real-time observations. Retrospective accounts for the history were relied upon for the previous stage of the PMO, and real-time data was collected for the change that was underway at the time of the interviews. An example of this dynamic environment is given in one case study, where the top management was ejected and the PMO dissolved the day after all interviews were completed. In this specific case, we had a chance to observe the PMO while the change process was unfolding. Globally, the richness of this research program comes from the blending of these two research approaches, the variance and process approaches.

1.8.3 A Multi-year Program

The fact that the research program was spread over several years allowed for cross-fertilization between phases, and for discussion and validation of partial results as they became available. The program benefited from a certain amount of overlap between phases. The second "complementary survey" of Phase I was designed and carried out after the case study had been completed in the first organization.

The results from this first organization were thus able to give substance to the survey questions. In addition, the fact that the case study in one organization was virtually complete before the others were initiated also allowed the results to inform the studies in the other three organizations. Likewise, the final analysis of the statistical data from Phase I was only completed after the all the case studies had been completed and analyzed. On several occasions, insights from the case studies provided avenues for exploring the statistical data. The partial results from different parts of the program have been confronted with each other on many occasions.

The discussion and confrontation of partial results has been part of a global strategy to better understand this complex and little-understood phenomenon. This has been done at two levels of the research: internally within the research design and the research team, and externally with the participation in external venues. Partial results have been presented, discussed, and enriched in many different venues during the six years this research program has unfolded. Table 1.3 summarizes these venues and their participants.

Table 1.3. Venues where partial results have been presented, discussed, and enriched

Research Phase	Activity	Participants
Phase I	Building the model and the questionnaire	Mature students in post-graduate project management programs in Canada and the United States, practitioners, consultants, members of the PMO Community of Practice at PMI-Montreal
	Answering survey	502 practitioners
	Workshops	Practitioners, consultants, members of the PMO Community of Practice at PMI-Montreal
Phase II	Building the model	Informal discussions with PMO directors and practitioners
		Doctoral seminar: senior researchers
		Research conferences: senior researchers
		Professional conferences: practitioners
Phase III	Interviews	49 persons in different roles in relation with PMOs: executives, PMO managers, PMO employees, project and program managers, functional managers, human resources, and accounting
	Workshops	Practitioners and consultants, members of the PMO Community of Practice at PMI-Montreal
		PMO managers and PMO employees, organizations participating in the research
Phase IV	Workshops	Practitioners and consultants, members of the PMO Community of Practice at PMI-Montreal
		Researchers from other universities
		Managers and PMO managers – Australia, Europe, North America

1.9   How to Read This Book

Presenting results from a multi-phase and multi-method research project requires special attention from the researchers. Efforts have been made to translate the scientific results from several years of research into accessible wording. This represents the ultimate sense-making test: the capability to transfer the knowledge that has been gained through research for direct use in organizations. This section is intended to accompany the reader, whether a manager, a professional, a student, or a researcher in the field of project management. Now it is time for the reader to make sense of these results in his or her specific context. Research results can be descriptive or normative. The vast majority of the material in this book describes what is observed in empirical reality. An empirically grounded portrait of reality is a base upon which normative statements can be built, whether they are best practices, guidelines, or, eventually, a standard. A search for the bases for normative statements is conducted throughout. In many cases, no basis for normative statements was found. This in and of itself is useful information. On several occasions, bases for normative statements were identified. These have been clearly identified as such. However, the present state of knowledge does not provide a sufficient basis for a standard. The research goal is first to gain better understanding, and then norms and standards might be proposed on solid foundations.

Table 1.4 presents the content of this book using three different perspectives to help situate the reader: phase of the research program, methodological approach, and time perspective.

Table 1.4. Different perspectives on the book's content

	CHAPTER				
	1	2	3	4	5
Perspectives	**Context**	**Portrait of PMO**	**Typologies of PMOs**	**In-depth Case Studies**	**Transformation Process**
1. Phase of the research program	All	I	I	II and III	III
2. Methodological approach	All	Variance	Variance	Process	Process
3. Time perspective	N/A	Synchronic	Synchronic	Diachronic	Diachronic

The phases are presented in Table 1.2. The second perspective refers to the two methodological approaches, variance and process. Chapter 1 presents the overall approach. Chapters 2 and 3 adopt a variance approach, and Chapters 4 and 5 adopt primarily a process one.

The third perspective proposes to read the results using the time perspective. The synchronic perspective means looking at each of the PMOs at a point in time, describing and comparing them. The survey results presented in Chapters 2 and 3 are synchronic. The case histories presented in Chapter 4 and the transformation processes described in Chapter 5 are diachronic.

1.10 Limits of the Research

The object of study in this research has been the multi-project. Two important objects have been excluded from consideration. First, the PMO or project office that deals with a single project has not been examined. This is an important topic that future research should examine.

Second, the PMOs that have been examined during the research presented in this book and in the first of the two follow-up studies presented in Table 1.2 have each been examined in isolation from other PMOs in the same organization. The survey results presented in Chapter 2 identified that 22% of the 502 PMOs in the sample are in hierarchical or network arrangements with other PMOs. It is quite common to have multiple interdependent PMOs in one organization, particularly in large organizations. The survey identified the importance of this phenomenon but did not explore either the nature of these interdependent relationships or the impact these relationships have on PMOs. None of the four case study organizations had interdependent networks of PMOs. Two did have multiple PMOs during one specific period. In one organization, the PMOs were located in separate business units and were independent of each other. In this case, one PMO was investigated. In the other organization, multiple entities that could be considered PMOs were being created at the time the interviews were coming to a close. The situation was emerging at the time and it was not possible to study the entire set of PMOs and the relationships among them. Two of the PMOs were, however, included in the sample of 12 case studies of PMOs. Because PMOs that are interdependent with other PMOs have not been studied during the research reported here, the results should only be extrapolated to such situations with considerable caution. Interdependent groups of PMOs are the object of the follow-up study presented as Phase VI in Table 1.2, the results of which will be available in the future.

CHAPTER TWO: A DESCRIPTIVE PORTRAIT OF PMOs

2.1 Introduction

The objective of this chapter is to provide a reliable description of the population of PMOs. To accomplish this goal, web-based surveys were designed to gather descriptive data on PMOs. The questions were formulated to gather factual description more than evaluative opinion. The chapter first presents the survey instruments followed by a detailed presentation of the population of PMOs. Globally, the portrait is one of great variety. The following chapter exploits this data in search of patterns in the population of PMOs that might form the bases for types of PMOs.

2.2 The Web-based Survey Design

2.2.1 The Development and Deployment of the Surveys

The development and deployment of the surveys followed a five-step process:

Step 1 was to undertake a preliminary and systematic investigation of 30 PMOs in different organizations and different industries. This was done in 2003 and 2004. The objective was to provide a preliminary validation of the hypothesis that the structures, roles, and legitimacy of PMOs vary significantly from one organization to the next, and to gather data that would contribute to a richer and more reliable portrait of the reality of PMOs. To this end, a preliminary version of the survey questionnaire was developed and tested. Feedback sessions were held with informants from the organizations to validate and discuss these preliminary results. The preliminary investigations produced an image of PMOs characterized by extreme variety in structures, roles, and legitimacy, while at the same time validating and significantly enriching the questionnaire, which became the original survey instrument. The results from Step 1 were enlightening, but the sample was small. For this reason, it did not lend itself to statistical analysis and it is impossible to judge how representative this sample was of the general population.

Step 2 was undertaken to validate and further enrich the preliminary results from Step 1. A web-based survey instrument was designed and tested. The questionnaire had already been validated and tested in Step 1; however, three respondents from different industries tested the web-based version and a small number of minor adjustments were made. The instrument was designed so that each respondent described one PMO. The questions were descriptive until the end of the instrument, where a small number of more evaluative questions completed the instrument.

Step 3 was the data collection phase. The authors solicited respondents through several project management networks. A total of 502 usable responses were received.

Step 4 produced a follow-up survey. During the analysis of the data from the original survey, it became evident that the results were describing a very varied population and that identifying clear patterns in the population was going to be difficult. The qualitative case studies presented in Chapter 4 were also underway. From the case studies and the analysis of the results of the original survey, a series of additional characteristics of PMOs was identified. A web-based survey instrument was used to gather data. An invitation to answer this second survey was sent to the 365 respondents of the original survey who provided e-mail addresses. Valid responses were received for 123 PMOs. The final database, therefore, consists of the description of 502 PMOs, of which 123 are more complete.

Step 5 was the data analysis phase. The descriptive statistics are presented in this chapter. Factor analysis was used to group the 27 different roles or functions filled by PMOs in Section 2.5. Further analysis is presented in Chapter 3.

2.2.2 The Survey Instruments

The preliminary descriptive model presented in Section 1.3 provided the basis for elaborating the questionnaire. The model defines the major groups of variables in the questionnaire. For each PMO described, the survey instruments collected data on six categories of data: quantitative data for each of the five groups of variables in the model presented in Figure 1.1 and qualitative data from an open question. The variables from the follow-up survey are marked with an asterisk (*). As previously indicated, the sample size is smaller for these variables. The original and the follow-up survey can be found in the appendices A and B, respectively.

1. Organizational context

   A PMO is not an isolated entity; rather, it is embedded in an organization, which is embedded in a socioeconomic context. An understanding of the organizational context is key to understanding PMOs. For this reason, information was gathered on each of the following characteristics of the organizational context:
   - Economic sector
   - Public or private
   - Size of organization

- Number of projects in the organizational unit where the PMO is located
- Percentage of resources that report to the same management as the PMO manager or that are matrixed throughout the organization
- Internal or external project customers
- Single or multiple project customers
- Level of organizational project management maturity
- Supportiveness of organizational culture

2. Types of projects in the PMO's mandate
   The following indicators of project type were used:
   - Scope expressed as the number of people working on the project
   - Scope in terms of duration
   - The type of product or service delivered*
   - The primary performance criteria of the PMO's projects*
   - The inclusion of post-delivery activities within project scope *
   - Involvement in outsourcing contracts*

3. Structural characteristics of PMOs
   Each PMO was described using the following variables:
   - The name used to identify the PMO
   - Time to implement the PMO
   - Location within the organizational hierarchy
   - Relationship(s) with other PMO(s) in the same organization
   - Staff of PMO (other than project/program managers)
     - Size expressed as the number of people working on the project. This is also a measure of the size of the PMO.
     - Experience of the staff*
     - Professional background of the staff*
     - Presence of business analysts or business architects among the staff*
   - Age of the PMO
   - Percentage of projects within the mandate of the PMO
   - Percentage of project managers within the PMO
   - Decision-making authority of the PMO
   - The status of the project management methodology
     - Homegrown or brought in from outside*
     - Use is compulsory or discretionary*
     - Degree to which methods are actually followed*
   - The adequacy of funding of the PMO *
   - The means of funding, including the billing for services*

4. Roles and functions
   PMOs fill many different roles or functions in different organizations.

This survey identified the importance of 27 functions commonly assigned to PMOs.

5. Perceived performance of PMOs

   Following these descriptive variables, the survey instrument concluded with several measures of the perceived performance of PMOs. The measures were all highly correlated. This chapter presents the results for two measures of the performance of PMOs:

   - "Legitimacy" reported in response to the question, "Has the relevance or even the existence of the PMO been seriously questioned in recent years?"
   - "Performance" measured with a construct identified by a Varimax factor analysis of several measures of PMO performance and with a measure of the PMO's impact on the performance of projects and programs

6. Strong points and areas for improvement

   The survey instrument included a qualitative question in which respondents indicated in their own words what they believe are the strong points of their PMO and the areas for improvement. The responses can be allocated to the other classes of variables during the analysis.

2.3 The Respondents and the Organizational Contexts of PMOs

The information on respondent demographics and their organizational contexts was collected on the original survey instrument. The data presented here pertains therefore to the 502 responses to the original survey.

2.3.1 The Respondents

The respondents are distributed among organizational roles as follows:
- Project managers   38%
- Managers of PMOs   23%
- Professionals in PMOs   11%
- Executives and other managers 10%
- Consultants   8%
- Others   10%

The geographical distribution is as follows:
- Canada   44%
- United States   26%
- Europe   19%
- Other   11%

2.3.2 The Organizational Contexts

The organizations are from a wide variety of industries. The survey instrument identified 22 industries, which have been combined into the following groups:

- Tangible products[2]   29%
- Information technology (IT)/information systems (IS)   14%
- Telecommunications   10%
- Financial services   13%
- Other intangible products or services[3]   24%
- Other   10%

The organizations are split between the public and private sectors as follows:
- Private sector   61%
- Public sector   36%
- Not-for-profit   3%

The PMOs surveyed in this investigation are from organizations of varying size. The distribution is presented in Figure 2.1.

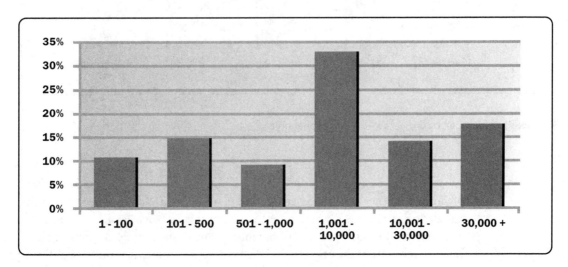

Figure 2.1. Size of the organizations expressed as total number of employees

The organizational size reported in Figure 2.1 refers to the entire organization, which may be a large organization, even a multi-national. PMOs are often active

---

2 Industries producing tangible products include manufacturing, engineering, energy, chemicals, natural resources, transportation, construction, pharmaceuticals, aerospace, and military equipment.

3 Intangible products and services other than financial include public administration, health and social services, consulting, business services, education, hotels, restaurants, tourism, military services, international aid, sport, and culture.

in only part of large organizations. For PMOs that are not active throughout the entire organization, several questions referred only to the organizational entity (department, division, or other part of the organization) in which the PMO is active. One such variable is the total number of projects undertaken simultaneously within the organization or the organizational unit within which the PMO is active. The result is shown in Figure 2.2. A large proportion of PMOs (45%) are in contexts where between 11 and 50 projects are being carried out simultaneously.

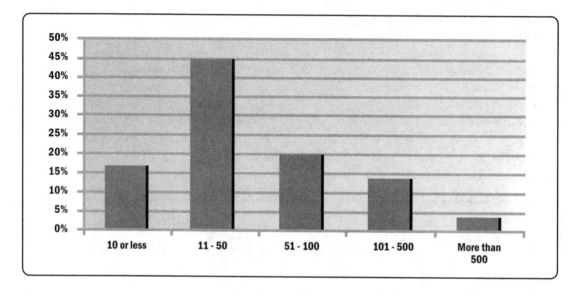

Figure 2.2. Number of projects in organizational unit

As would be expected, the number of projects is related to the size of the organization. The correlation between the two is 0.28 (p=0.000). The fact that the correlation is quite weak may be explained by two factors. First, organizational size refers to the entire organization, while the number of projects refers in many cases to only part of the organization. Second, organizations execute very different proportions of their activities by project.

In some cases, the PMO is located in the same unit as the resources that work on the projects. In other cases, the resources are located elsewhere in the organization. Figure 2.3 shows the percentage of resources working on projects that report to the same management as the manager of the PMO. A low percentage indicates a matrix relationship with resources located elsewhere in the organization. Although a high percentage indicates a non-matrix relationship, most PMOs are in one of the two extremes with respect to the location of the resources working on the PMO's projects.

Some PMOs do projects for only one customer while others do projects for many customers. Their customers can be primarily internal or external to the organization. The distributions within the sample are shown in Table 2.1. As can be seen, the vast majority of PMOs have multiple customers, but the split between those with internal customers and those with external customers is relatively even.

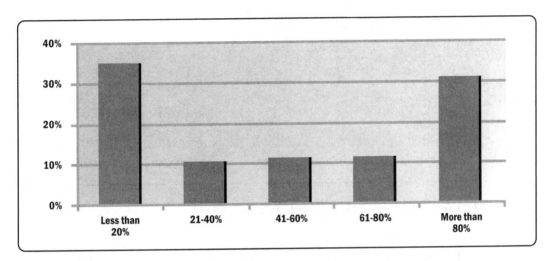

Figure 2.3. Matrixed and non-matrixed project personnel

Table 2.1. Project customer distribution

	Internal	External	Total
One	10%	6%	16%
Several	45%	39%	84%
Total	**55%**	**45%**	**100%**

The organizational project management maturity of the organizations participating in the survey was evaluated using the well-known 5-point scale. Participants rated the project management maturity of their organizations as shown in Figure 2.4. This distribution is consistent with the results reported by Mullaly (2006).

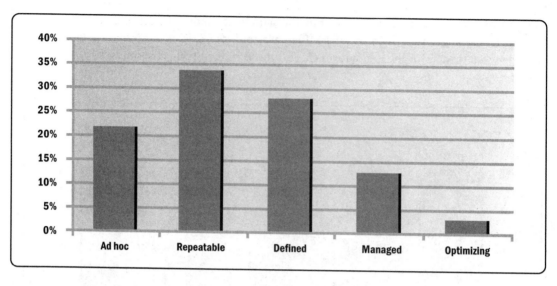

Figure 2.4. Organizational Project Management Maturity (OPM3®)

The extent to which the organizational culture was supportive of the implementation of the PMO is indicated in Figure 2.5.

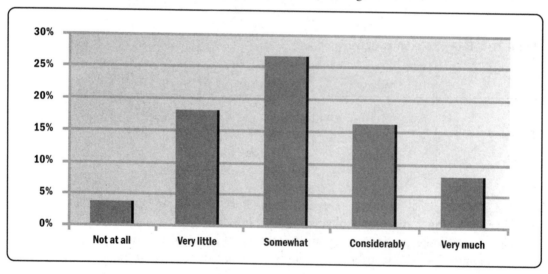

Figure 2.5. Supportiveness of the organizational culture

As can been seen from the demographic data previously provided, the sample of 502 PMOs described by this survey is drawn from a very wide range of contexts. The sample size and distributions are sufficient to identify important differences among PMOs from different contexts if any systematic differences exist. Chapter 3 explores this data in pursuit of such differences within the population.

2.3.3 Types of Project in the PMO's Mandate

Projects can be divided into types in many different ways (Crawford, Hobbs, & Turner, 2005). The survey instruments included six variables that describe the projects in the PMO's mandate and can be used to classify projects by type. The two measures of project scope were included in the original survey of 502 PMOs, while the other four measures were in the follow-up survey and therefore have smaller sample sizes.

The scope of the projects included within the mandate of the PMOs was measured first by the number of people working on typical projects and second by the duration in months. The distributions are shown in Figures 2.6 and 2.7, respectively.

There are many ways of describing and classifying the type of product or service delivered. Three measures were included in the follow-up survey. First, the respondents classified the product or service into one of the following three categories:

- Tangibles products (33%)
- IS/IT (46%)
- Other intangible products or services (21%)

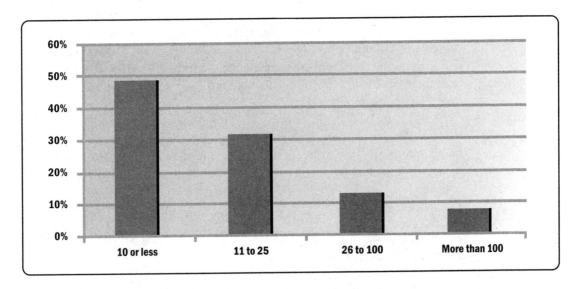

Figure 2.6. The number of people on typical projects

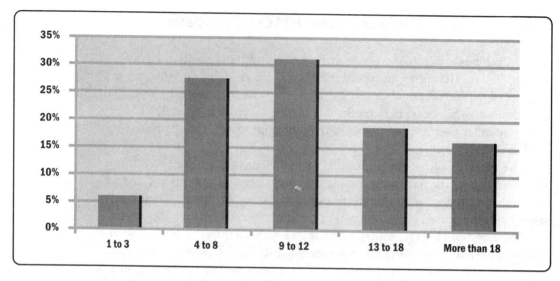

Figure 2.7. Duration of typical projects in months

All of the 123 respondents to the follow-up survey were able to classify the products or services delivered by their projects into one of the three categories. The field of project management was born in the 1950s and 1960s in industries that produce tangible products. Theses types of projects are still an important component of the population of projects. However, IS/IT has become the dominant project type and other intangible products or services have become an important part of the field. This distribution is in line with the distribution of PMI's membership by industry.

Projects for which the priority is to meet the schedule, budget, technical specifications, or business needs are managed quite differently, which may in turn have an impact on the mandate and the organization of the PMO. The follow-up survey identified the single most important performance criteria for projects as being:

- Schedule (29%)
- Budget (12%)
- Technical specifications (11%)
- Business needs (48%)

The population divides almost equally between those who report that meeting business needs is the most important project performance criteria and those who report that meeting time, cost, or technical specifications are more important. Among these three traditional measures of project performance, schedule is the most frequently reported. This is consistent with the emphasis on time to market in recent years. In tougher economic times, cost may become more important.

In some contexts, projects end with the delivery of the final product. In other contexts, project scope includes post-delivery activities. The follow-up survey gathered data on the portion of projects that ended with delivery of a product and those that included several types of post-delivery activities:

- Projects end with delivery of the final product 38%
- Project scope includes responsibility for:
  - Communication 30%
  - Commercialization 12%
  - Integration into operations 47%
  - Organizational change 22%

Percentages add to more than 100% because many projects have more than one type of post-delivery activity. Although the majority of projects include post-delivery activities within their scope, a significant minority do not. The high proportion of projects with post-delivery activities is consistent with the high proportion of IS/IT projects that very often have such activities within their scope.

Outsourcing has become a very popular strategy in recent years and projects executed through an outsourcing contract are managed differently. The data from the follow-up survey indicates that 30% of respondents are involved in outsourcing contracts on either the customer or the supplier side. Although this proportion is significant, the sample size is too small to explore the implications of outsourcing for the mandates and organization of PMOs.

2.4 The Structural Characteristics of PMOs

2.4.1 The Name Used to Identify the PMO

The majority of entities described in this study are called Project Management Offices. However, many of these organizational entities are given a great variety of other names. The distribution of names is presented in Table 2.2.

Table 2.2. Names given to the entities in the study

Name	Percentage
Project Management Office	59%
Name containing the term "project" and somewhat similar to project management office (e.g., project department)	4%
Project Support Office	7%
Project Office	2%
Program Management Office	12%
Center of Excellence	2%
No name	2%
Other (a great variety with none greater than 1%)	12%

Project Office: The number of entities bearing the title "project office" is certainly much greater than these results indicate. This label is often used to name an entity responsible for the management of a single large project. The survey instructions asked specifically that informants not describe this type of entity in responding to the questionnaire. An examination of the 2% of responses describing entities with this label indicates that these are multi-project entities similar to those labeled PMO. They have, therefore, been included in the sample.

Program Management Office: A total of 12% of responses describe entities labeled as "Program Management Offices." The program management function is more important for those labeled program management office, but the difference is not statistically significant. Program management is very often part of the role of the PMO, whether it is labeled a project or a program management office. The analysis that follows is, therefore, based on the entire sample, including both project and program management offices.

No Name: Interestingly, 2% of respondents describe entities that exist in their organizations but have no official label and, therefore, do not appear on the organizational chart. It is quite plausible that these entities have been created to fill a real need but their existence has not yet been made official. It is also plausible that because of a previous failed attempt to implement a PMO, or for some other reasons, some PMOs are maintaining a low profile. Nevertheless, they fall under the wide definition of a PMO (PMI, 2004).

Although a majority of the entities in this survey are named "project management offices," a vast array of other names are currently used in practice. In many cases, names do not clearly differentiate PMOs.

2.4.2 Time to Implement a PMO

The time it took to implement the PMOs is indicated in Figure 2.8. The mode or most common response is 1 to 2 years.

2.4.3 Number and Location Within the Organizational Hierarchy

PMOs may be located in different organizational units and at different levels in the hierarchy. However, it proved very difficult to formulate a question that would be understood in the same way in the many different organizations in which PMOs are found. The terminology used to describe organizational levels is very different in small businesses, large public bureaucracies, and multi-national firms. It also proved difficult to find names for organizational units and hierarchical levels that do not bias the responses because of social desirability issues. For example, being in a "strategic business unit" is so socially desirable that some respondents qualified their functional unit as being a strategic business unit. Likewise, when asked if the PMO reported directly to a member of senior management, most PMO managers

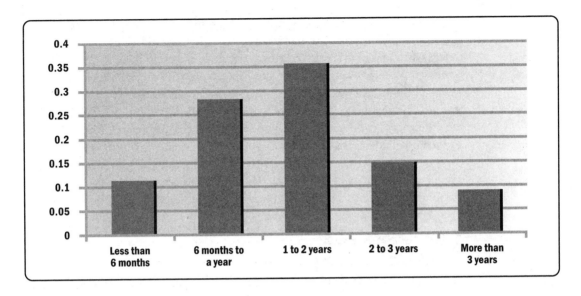

Figure 2.8. Time to implement a PMO

reported that they did. This is more a reflection of the desirability of reporting to senior management than it is an accurate description of the organizational reality.

Each respondent to the original survey described one particular PMO. However, PMOs can be placed in different locations within the organizational structure, and some organizations have more than one PMO. Table 2.3 presents the classification of the PMOs in the sample.

Table 2.3. Number and location of PMOs

	Location in the Organization	
1	Only one centrally located PMO	30%
2	Only one PMO located in a business, functional, or regional unit	23%
3	PMO located in business, functional, or regional unit; no relationship with a more central PMO	25%
4	Central PMO in a hierarchy of interrelated PMOs	8%
5	A hierarchy of interrelated PMOs. This PMO is located in a business, functional, or regional unit and is related to a more centrally located PMO.	14%

This data can be grouped in different ways to explore different aspects of the issues of number and location of PMOs.
- 54% of organizations have only one PMO (lines 1 + 2)
- 78% of PMOs operate autonomously from other PMOs (lines 1, 2 + 3)
- 22% of PMOs are in hierarchical or network arrangements (lines 4 + 5)
- 38% of PMOs are centrally located (lines 1 + 4)
- 62% of PMOs are in business, functional or regional units (lines 2, 3 + 5)

Section 1.10 identified that one of the limits to the research reported in this book is that PMOs are described and analyzed without considering relationships with other PMOs in the same organization. As can be seen from Table 2.3, 22% of PMOs in the sample have relationships of interdependence with other PMOs. The original survey distinguished between PMOs that are "centrally located" (38%) and PMOs that are "located in a business, functional, or regional unit" (62%). The analysis of the differences between these two groups of PMOs is pursued in Chapter 3. This is an incomplete description of the organizational placement of PMOs. The authors continue to believe that location within the organizational structure and hierarchy are important issues when designing or analyzing a PMO. The authors are refining the measurement instruments to capture this important aspect in future research.

2.4.4 PMO Staff

The people who staff the PMO have a significant impact on what the PMO can and will do, as well as on the status that the PMO will have in the organization. When describing the staff of a PMO, it is important to distinguish between the project managers, who may or may not be part of the staff, and the other staff members. The variables described here refer to the staff other than the project managers.

Most PMOs have very little staffing. Figure 2.9 shows the staffing levels of PMOs expressed in full-time equivalents, including the person responsible for the PMO, but excluding project managers. This staff is overhead, and organizations are very reluctant to create overhead expenses. The issue of overhead costs is a key issue for PMOs, creating a somewhat paradoxical situation in which the PMO is often asked to take on many functions with few resources.

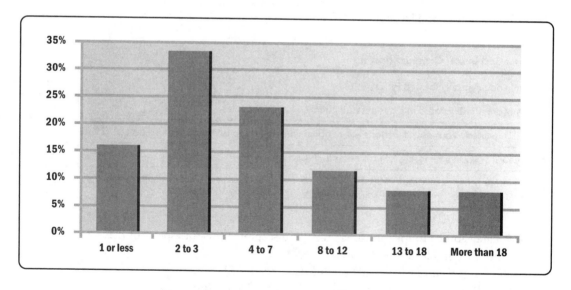

Figure 2.9. Personnel of PMO excluding project managers (full-time equivalents)

The professional background of PMO staff was investigated in the follow-up survey. The first question identified the primary background of PMO staff. The results are as follows:

- IT (43%)
- Finance or accounting (7%)
- Other technical or professional specializations (32%)
- Operations (8%)
- Business (10%)

The vast majority of the PMO staff have a professional or technical background. The large number in IT is not surprising given the large proportion of IS/IT projects found in PMOs. Few staff members have backgrounds in business or operations. However, an additional question identified that 34% of PMOs have business analysts or business architects on their staff. The final question in the follow-up survey relative to the background of the PMO staff identified past experience as project or program managers. As can be seen from Figure 2.10, most PMO staff have significant past experience as project or program managers. This experience is critical to their ability to do their work and to their credibility. For further data on the importance of staff qualifications, see the presentation of the qualitative data in Section 2.6.

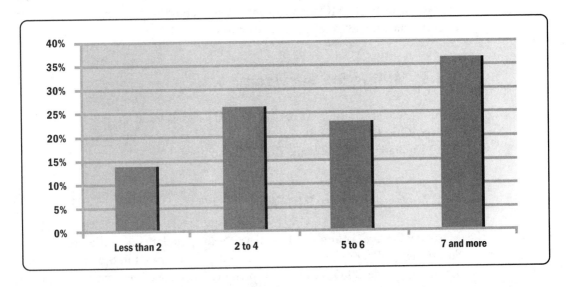

Figure 2.10. Years of PMO staff experience as project or program managers

2.4.5 Adequacy of Funding

The majority of PMOs receive adequate funding, while others complain of inadequate funding compared to the mandates they are expected to fill. Adequacy of funding was reported from the follow-up survey as follows:

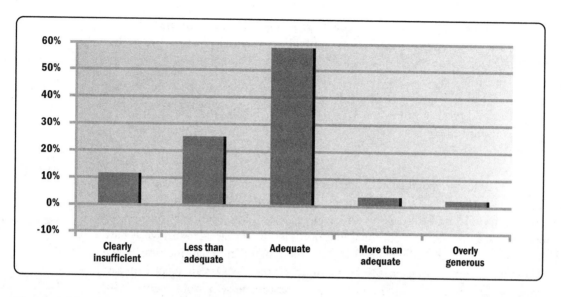

Figure 2.11. Adequacy of PMO funding

These are, of course, the respondents' perceptions. Given that people are rarely happy with the funding they receive, this data would seem to indicate that the vast majority of PMO are adequately funded, but that there exists a significant minority that are not receiving adequate funding.

2.4.6 Billing for Services

Many PMOs are considered part of general overhead and do not bill for their services. Others, however, do bill for services. The follow-up survey data shows that 34% bill for services, while the others do not.

2.4.7 Age of the PMO

Most PMOs are young. PMOs have been popular since the mid-1990s. Surprisingly, 54% of PMOs in existence today were created in the last two years, according to the 2005 survey data presented here. At least two independent surveys have shown that the average age of PMOs is approximately two years (Interthink Consulting, 2002; Stanleigh, 2005). This has not changed in recent years. The authors know of no research results that are inconsistent with these observations. Two phenomena are at work producing this result. First, new PMOs are being created at a relatively high rate. Second, PMOs are being shut down or radically reconfigured at almost as fast a rate. The result is a population dominated by PMOs that have only been in existence in their present form for a few years, as shown in Figure 2.12.

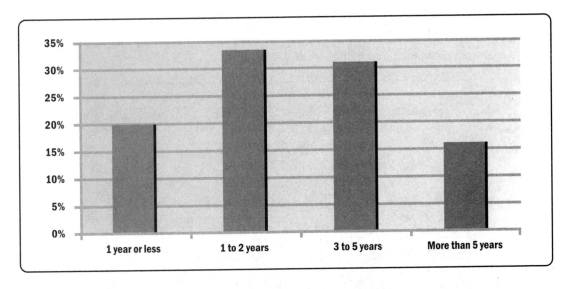

Figure 2.12. Age of PMOs

At first glance this result is interesting and possibly a little intriguing. However, this has become one of the most influential pieces of data in the effort to better understand PMOs. This finding was confirmed by the results of the case studies presented in Chapter 4. Three of the organizations in the in-depth case studies have had PMOs for several years but have reconfigured their PMOs every few years. These results have led to a fundamental change in the way PMOs should be conceptualized. If most PMOs are reconfigured every few years, then they should be considered temporary or transitory arrangements, and both studied and managed as such. If PMOs are transitory arrangements, then what would be a "best practice," if best practices are normally thought of as generally applicable and implicitly stable solutions? This conceptualization is developed and exploited in Chapters 4 and 5.

2.4.8 Percentage of Projects Within the Mandate of the PMO

Organizations are choosing two very different approaches when determining what proportion of projects and project managers to place within the mandate of the PMO. In order to grasp the reality of the situation, first it must be determined what constitutes the whole set of possible projects and project managers. The information on the location of the PMO previously presented shows that 62% of PMOs are located in business, functional, or regional units. This being the case, respondents were asked to focus on projects and project managers present in the "organizational unit in which the PMO is active," explicitly stating that this could be the entire organization, a division, a department, or any other part of the organization. The proportions of projects within the PMO's mandates are presented in Figure 2.13. As can be seen in the figure, organizations tend to place either almost all the projects within the PMO's mandate or only a small portion, creating two quite different PMOs.

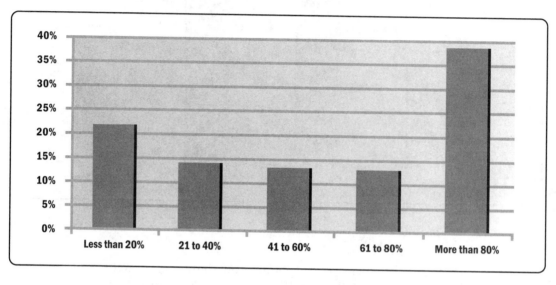

Figure 2.13. Percentage of projects within the mandate of the PMO

PMOs with less than 20% of projects may have been put in place to deliver solutions for a specific purpose or program; examples are PMOs for implementing business process reengineering or for the transition of systems to the year 2000. In these cases, only a specific group of projects is placed under the PMO's umbrella. In other situations, some other criteria are being used to determine which projects are placed under the PMO's umbrella. The choice is likely the consequence of some other organizational choices. A system for categorizing projects to determine which projects to include in the PMO's mandate is likely to be in place. Crawford, Hobbs, and Turner (2005, 2006) showed that organizations use systems for categorizing projects for many different purposes, including project portfolio management. For those PMOs that have only a portion of the organization's projects within their mandate, the identification of these projects could be a way of characterizing the PMO. The data in this survey does not contain the information that such a characterization of PMOs would require.

2.4.9 Percent of Project Managers in the PMO

The percentages of project managers within the PMO are shown in Figure 2.14. Please note the scale, which isolates the extreme responses of "all" and "none." The majority of PMOs are in one of these two extreme situations. In one case, the PMO has all the organization's project managers. In the other, it has no project managers. This again creates two very different PMOs. In the case where no project managers are within the PMO, the PMO is filling staff functions exclusively.

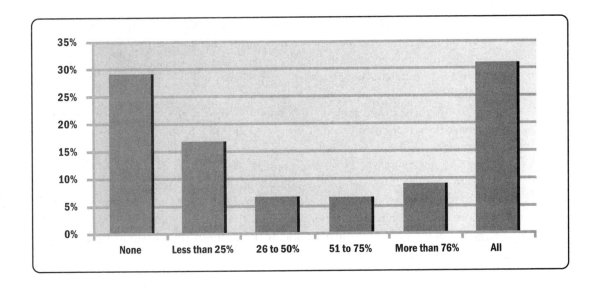

Figure 2.14. Percent of project managers in the PMO

Both the percentage of projects and of project managers within the PMO can be used to identify distinctive types of PMOs. The two variables are correlated (Pearson coefficient 0.453) but the relationship is not simple. The use of these two variables to identify types of PMOs is explored in Section 3.6.

2.4.10 Decision-making Authority of PMOs

The distribution of decision-making authority is close to a normal distribution, but with very high variance, as shown in Figure 2.15.

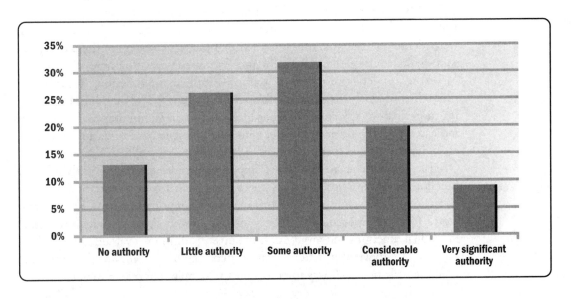

Figure 2.15. Decision-making authority of PMOs

Many PMOs are in a passive or supporting role with little or no decision-making authority, while others have considerable authority to make decisions to allocate resources, set priorities, or initiate, change, or cancel projects. These are two very different organizational roles, illustrating the great variety of roles that different organizations assign to their PMOs.

As the data presented in this section shows, the vast majority of PMOs have been recently created or restructured. Most have little staff other than the project managers. PMOs have little else in common. Quite to the contrary, great variety characterizes the population of PMOs described in this survey. On some characteristics, the population displays distributions that are close to being either normal or skewed toward one extreme. In many cases the variance is high. On other variables the distributions are almost bipolar, with most PMOs at one extreme or the other of the distribution, and few in the middle.

2.5 The Roles or Functions of PMOs

2.5.1 The Functions Filled by PMOs

PMOs fill many different roles or functions in different organizations. The interchangeable terms "role" and "function" are used here to identify the content of the PMO's mandate within the organization. The functions that are examined here are functions other than the management of projects, that is to say, "staff functions." It is assumed that if the project managers are in the PMO, then the management of projects will be part of the PMO's mandate. If they are not, then it will not be. A list of roles or functions that are part of the mandates of PMOs was derived from preliminary investigations of a smaller sample of PMOs and from a review of the literature. A large number of different functions were identified. The final list contained 27 functions. Several of these functions were added during the process of pre-testing the questionnaire. Within the survey, respondents were asked if their PMO filled any functions not included in this list. An analysis of the responses did not identify any functions important for more than a very small number of PMOs. A large number of respondents indicated that the list is complete, which can be seen as a validation of the list of 27 functions of PMOs.

The respondents to the survey reported the importance of each of these functions for their PMO using a scale ranging from 1 (not important at all) to 5 (very important). The results for this variable are reported in two ways. Average scores for the importance rating are used below to report the importance of individual functions and groups of functions. In addition, a variable called "Total number of important functions" was created. The mean score for importance of 3.5 on a scale of 1 to 5 was used to split the sample. Functions were considered important for PMOs reporting a function as 4 (of considerable importance) or 5 (very important). On average, each function was important for a third of the population of PMOs. As can been seen in Figure 2.16, the distribution of the number of important functions is skewed to the left with a mean of 12.7 and a standard deviation of 6.50.

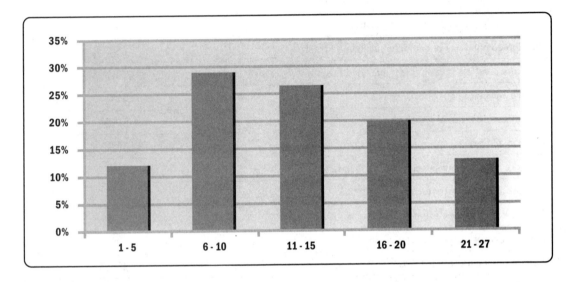

Figure 2.16. Number of important functions in the mandate of PMOs

Table 2.4 shows the percentage of PMOs in which each function was "important," being scored either *of considerable importance* or *very important.*

Table 2.4. PMO functions in decreasing order of importance

PMO Function	Percent of PMOs that rated function important
Report project status to upper management	83%
Develop and implement a standard methodology	76%
Monitor and control project performance	65%
Develop competency of personnel, including training	65%
Implement and operate a project information system	60%
Provide advice to upper management	60%
Coordinate between projects	59%
Develop and maintain a project scoreboard	58%
Promote project management within organization	55%
Monitor and control performance of PMO	50%
Participate in strategic planning	49%
Provide mentoring for project managers	49%
Manage one or more portfolios	49%
Identify, select, and prioritize new projects	48%
Manage archives of project documentation	48%
Manage one or more programs	48%
Conduct project audits	45%
Provide interface between management and customer	45%
Provide a set of tools without an effort to standardize	42%
Execute specialized tasks for project managers	42%
Allocate resources between projects	40%
Conduct post-project reviews	38%
Implement and manage database of lessons learned	34%
Implement and manage risk database	29%
Manage benefits	28%
Provide networking and environmental scanning	25%
Recruit, select, evaluate, and determine salaries for project managers	22%

In the minds of many practitioners, PMOs were associated with particular roles or functions. It is not uncommon to hear statements such as, "A PMO is an entity that develops and implements a standardized project management methodology." Table 2.4 confirms that 76% of PMOs are heavily involved in this function. Note also that reporting project status to upper management is an important role for 83% of PMOs and monitoring and controlling project performance is important for 65%. In fact, the latter function was the only one that was important for all 12 PMOs investigated in the in-depth case studies presented in Chapter 4. All 27 functions are important for significant numbers of PMOs, and 21 of the 27 are important for at least 40% of PMOs. Therefore, to define PMOs by associating them with a particular function or group of functions is out of line with organizational reality. This result again illustrates the extreme variety found among different PMOs in different organizations, and the difficulty in providing a simple and accurate description of what they are and what roles they fill.

Members of the project management community recognize most of the functions listed in Table 2.4 very easily. However, some functions have only recently come into prominence. Program management (48%) and portfolio management (49%) are shown as quite important, despite the fact that they only recently became the focus of much attention with the development of "enterprise or organizational project management." Benefits management (28%) is an even more recent phenomenon in the project management community and literature. Many members of the community are as yet unfamiliar with this practice, which may explain why it is considered relatively less important.

2.5.2 Groups of Functions

Analyzing 27 different functions is quite fastidious. Identifying groups of functions greatly simplifies interpretation and use of this data. This can be done conceptually by identifying practices that are logically related. For example, reporting project status to upper management requires that project performance be monitored, which can best be done with a project information system and a project scorecard. These four functions are thus logically related. One would expect to find that if PMOs filled one of these functions, then they would also have a tendency to fill the others.

The tendency to fill functions in groups can also be identified and measured through statistical associations. Varimax factorial analysis was used to identify such groupings. Functions that are grouped together through factorial analysis are tightly associated statistically with each other, and statistically independent from the other functions and groups of functions. These independent groups constitute the dimensions of the fundamental underlying structure. The factorial analysis identified five groups of functions and three independent functions that are not associated with the groups. Each group was examined to ensure that it was internally consistent in both conceptual and practical terms.

These groups show the structure underlying the many roles filled by PMOs in organizations. Identifying groups of functions that are both conceptually and statistically sound has very practical consequences. The long and disorganized list of functions is replaced by a simple structure of underlying high-level roles or functions. These are presented next in decreasing order of the average importance of the functions included in the group, which are indicated on a scale of 1 to 5. The average importance and the standard deviation are indicated in parentheses for each group. Within each group, the functions are presented in decreasing order of average importance.

Group 1: Monitoring and controlling project performance (3.82, 0.8746)

The group of functions related to the monitoring and controlling of project performance is the most important group. This group includes the monitoring, controlling and reporting of project performance and the management of the computer-based tools to do these tasks. PMOs with these functions are providing for the information managers' needs to maintain visibility and control the performance of projects for which they are responsible. In so doing, the PMO is supporting project governance functions. The interrelatedness of these functions was previously discussed. In addition to being conceptually consistent, this group of functions provides a reliable construct with a Cronbach Alpha of 0.762.
- Report project status to upper management
- Monitor and control project performance
- Implement and operate a project information system
- Develop and maintain a project scoreboard

Group 2: Development of project management competencies and methodologies (3.54, 0.8387)

The group of functions most traditionally associated with PMOs includes functions dealing with tools and methodologies and with competency development. This group is composed of the following functions:
- Develop and implement a standard methodology
- Promote project management within the organization
- Develop competency of personnel, including training
- Provide mentoring for project managers
- Provide a set of tools without an effort to standardize

The development and implementation of tools and methodology and the provision of project management training and mentoring are the functions many people associate with PMOs. The PMO with these functions is often in the role of promoting the use of the methodology, the development of competencies, and project management in general. Conceptually, there are two different subgroups within this group: functions related to the development of methods and tools, and functions related to competency development. These are associated statistically and in practice because training and mentoring includes instruction and support for the use of tools and methods. This group thus constitutes a coherent set of functions that reinforce one another. This reinforcement is the practical reality behind the statistical phenomenon identified by the factorial analysis. With a Cronbach Alpha of 0.769, this group of functions constitutes a reliable construct.

The follow-up survey further investigated the status of the project management methodology. The methodology can be "homegrown," brought in from outside the organization, or be a mix of both. Figure 2.17 presents the degree to which the methodology is homegrown. As can be seen from this figure, there is much customization of methodologies. Given the considerable amount of effort this requires and the overall importance of the development of methodologies, a significant portion of the work done in PMOs must be devoted to the development of tools and methods. Because the development of tools and methods is often based on the identification of tools, methods, and practices that have performed well in the past, this effort is often very closely related to organizational learning.

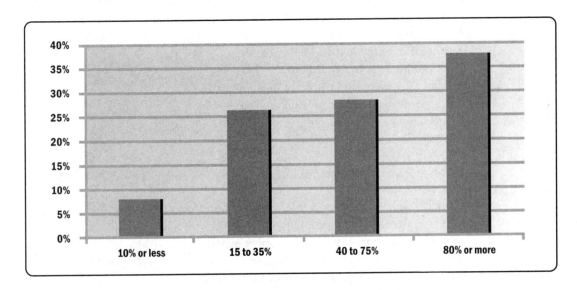

Figure 2.17. Percentage of the methodology that is homegrown

The use of the organization's methodology is discretionary in some cases and compulsory in others. The follow-up survey respondents reported the extent to which use is discretionary or compulsory as follows:

- Discretionary or encouraged but not enforced   36%
- Compulsory but weakly enforced   37%
- Compulsory and strongly enforced   27%

These three situations are very different. This illustrates the extreme variety found among many aspects of PMOs. Whether the methodology is actually used is yet another aspect of the question. The follow-up survey respondents reported the following frequencies of use:

- Never   1%
- Occasionally   24%
- Regularly   47%

- Almost always   26%
- Always   2%

As can be seen from this data, the usage rates for the methodologies are quite high. Only one quarter of respondents report using their organization's methodology only occasionally or never.

Group 3: Multi-project management (3.23, 1.0031)

Some PMOs have mandates to manage whole sets of projects in a coordinated fashion, which often involves program or portfolio management. These have become important aspects of project management, as signaled by PMI with the publication of the *Organizational Project Management Maturity Model (OPM3)* (PMI, 2003) and the publication of standards on program and portfolio management (PMI, 2006a, 2006b). The coordination of interdependences within programs and portfolios is a central issue in multi-project management, as can be seen from the functions in this group. Together they form a conceptually consistent construct with a Cronbach Alpha of 0.813.
- Coordinate between projects
- Identify, select, and prioritize new projects
- Manage one or more portfolios
- Manage one or more programs
- Allocate resources between projects

Group 4: Strategic management (3.06, 0.9333)

There has been a tendency in recent years for project management in general, and PMOs in particular, to become more involved with issues of strategic alignment and to become more closely tied to upper management. The factor analysis reveals that the following group of functions related to strategic management constitutes one of the underlying dimensions of PMO roles:
- Provide advice to upper management
- Participate in strategic planning
- Manage benefits
- Networking and environmental scanning

Involvement in these functions brings project management and the PMO closer to upper management. Networking and environmental scanning are used to keep abreast of current development so as to give up-to-date advice to upper management. With a Cronbach Alpha of 0.733, this group of functions constitutes a conceptually consistent and reliable construct.

Group 5: Organizational learning (3.00, 0.9784)

Organizational learning has been a very important topic in the management literature and practice in recent years. Some PMOs are actively involved in

organizational learning through the following group of functions:
- Monitor and control the performance of the PMO
- Manage archives of project documentation
- Conduct post-project reviews
- Conduct project audits
- Implement and manage a database of lessons learned
- Implement and manage a risk database

The last four functions in this group are very directly related to organizational learning (Huemann & Anbari, 2007; Williams, 2007). An examination of Table 2.4 shows them to be among the functions viewed as least important. From this it can be seen that, although organizational learning is of considerable importance, it is often seen as less important than other functions more directly related to operational or strategic issues.

The functions in this group form a conceptually consistent construct with a Cronbach Alpha of 0.853. The first two functions in this group are related to organizational learning, but can also be deployed in the pursuit of other objectives. Archiving project documentation has important operational aspects. The function to "monitor and control the performance of the PMO" can be seen as part of the learning feedback loop, and thus as closely related to the other organizational learning functions in this group. The in-depth case studies presented in Chapter 4 revealed that some PMOs specifically use the evaluation of the performance of their PMO in an organizational learning perspective. It is, however, conceivable that the measurement of PMO performance may also be done in response to questioning of the expenses generated by the PMO. The overall average importance of this group is influenced positively by the importance that the first two functions may have for objectives not directly related to organizational learning. Thus, the average importance of this group may slightly overstate the overall importance of organizational learning for PMOs.

The importance of this group of functions that has been labeled "Organizational learning" significantly underestimates the overall importance of organizational learning activities for PMOs, because many of the activities in the group of functions labeled "Development of project management competencies and methodologies" are intimately related to organizational learning. Organizational learning is, therefore, important for many PMOs. Project management in general and PMOs in particular are participating in the general trend toward the increased importance of organizational learning in the knowledge economy.

Additional functions not included in the groups of functions

The factorial analysis produced these five groups of functions. Three functions not included in these groups complete the list of 27 functions identified in this study. These three functions are excluded from the groups previously listed, not because they are not important, but because their presence is neither statistically nor conceptually related to these groups. The remaining functions are presented here in decreasing order of importance.

Execute specialized tasks for project managers (e.g., prepare schedules) (3.05, 1.338)

Many PMOs provide specialized services to project managers and project teams. To execute these tasks, PMOs maintain specialized resources on their staff. The preparation of schedules is a common example, but such services can include many other tasks, such as contract and risk management.

Manage customer interfaces (2.84, 1.369)

Some PMOs have the responsibility for managing customer interfaces. Responsibility for this activity depends to a great extent on the type of customer. Not all PMOs are in a position to fill this role. A PMO responsible for all the projects for a given customer may play an important role in managing this customer interface. A PMO responsible for an outsourcing contract is an example of this.

Recruit, select, evaluate and determine salaries for project managers (2.35, 1.290)

This is the least important function for PMOs, but it remains important for 22% of PMOs. The human resources (HR) department in most organizations carries out these HR activities, but the involvement of a number of PMOs in these activities is considered important in some contexts. The PMOs fit into very different organizational realities regarding HR management relative to project managers (Crawford & Cabanis-Brewin, 2006; Huemann, Keegan, & Turner, 2007).

The five groups of functions form a set of constructs that are conceptually internally consistent, statistically reliable, and independent from one another. Together with the three independent functions not included in the five groups, they form a set of eight concepts that constitutes the structure that underlies the list of 27 functions. The set was further validated during the case studies presented in Chapter 4. Furthermore, as part of 10 additional case studies conducted by the authors as part of research presented as Phase V in Table 1.2, it was confirmed that the eight presented a good overview of the functions filled by PMOs and that no significant functions are missing. This structure of eight is further exploited as one of the bases of the analysis presented in Chapter 3.

2.6 The Performance of PMOs

At the end of the survey instrument, after having described their PMO, respondents were asked questions related to the performance of their PMO. First the respondents were asked, "Has the relevance or even the existence of the PMO been seriously questioned in recent years?" We refer to the answer to this question as a measure of the PMO's legitimacy. As shown in Figure 2.18, 42% of the respondents answered "yes." The reality of PMOs in organizations is even darker than this result indicates. A survey of this type has a positive bias, particularly on evaluative questions such as this. People who are interested enough to respond to the invitation to participate in the survey tend to have a positive attitude on the topic of the survey. Those unfavorable and strongly opposed tend not to respond. In this survey, there is an additional positive bias created by the fact that organizations that have shut down their PMO or have decided not to implement one have not responded to this questionnaire, in which respondents are asked to describe an existing PMO. The extent of the bias is difficult to estimate, but it is not unreasonable to think that about half of organizations are critical enough of PMOs to decide not to implement one, or if they have one, to seriously consider shutting it down or significantly modifying it. The data on the age of PMOs, shown in Figure 2.12, indicates that PMOs are being shut down or radically restructured almost as fast as they are being created.

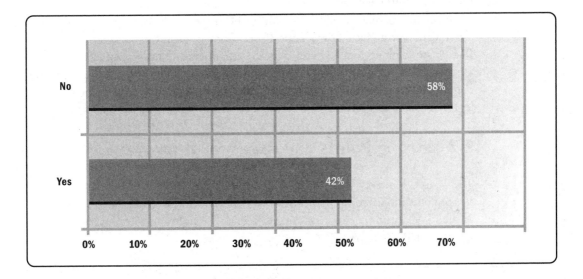

Figure 2.18. Legitimacy of PMOs

This result clearly identifies a lack of consensus in the project management community. About half of PMOs are seen as legitimate within their organizational context. This level of strong support for PMOs, combined with the large number of PMOs currently in existence, underscores the importance of PMOs in project management practice today. On the other hand, the very existence of the other half of PMOs is being questioned.

The performance of a PMO is multidimensional. The performance of the PMOs was also measured by questions asking respondents to what extent they agreed with the following eight statements:

- The PMO's mission is well understood by those who deal with the PMO (0.769).
- The PMO works in close collaboration with other project participants (0.832).
- Those who deal with the PMO recognize the PMO's expertise (0.812).
- The PMO is perceived as having a significant impact on the performance of projects and programs (0.833).

- The PMO's reporting level is too low in the organization.
- The PMO is fully supported by upper management.
- The PMO is relatively useless and costly.
- The PMO is perceived as controlling too much.

A Varimax factor analysis identified the first four statements as forming a reliable construct of PMO performance, with a Cronbach Alpha of 0.845, a mean of 3.46 on a scale form one to five, and a standard deviation of 0.9317. The weightings of the four statements in the factor are indicated in parentheses above. The average scores of these four questions is used as a measure of PMO performance and is referred to as "the performance construct." As would be expected, the two measures "legitimacy" and "performance" are correlated. The level of correlation is moderate (coefficient 0.392, p=0.000). Both are measures of performance but are not measuring exactly the same thing. Both measures of the performance of PMOs are exploited in Chapter 3 in an attempt to identify characteristics that are associated with high- and low-performing PMOs. Note that throughout, the correlations with the performance construct are stronger that the correlations with legitimacy. The analysis therefore provides a better explanation of the former.

2.7 Strong Points and Areas for Improvement

The original survey instrument included a qualitative question in which respondents indicated in their own words what they believed are the strong points of their PMO and the areas for improvement. The eight most important elements are presented in Figure 2.19.

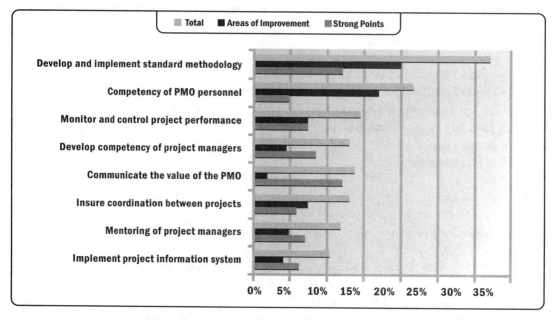

Figure 2.19. Strong points and areas for improvement

In many cases, the same issue was mentioned as a strong point for some PMOs and as an area for improvement for others. This indicates that this issue is considered critical by respondents. There are two different types of issues shown here. Most of the issues are functions that either the PMO is doing well and that contribute to its value, or that PMOs are doing poorly and that are critical to improve. These functions are among the most important functions presented in Table 2.4.

Some of the issues are not functions but issues that are critical to success. The most important of these is the ability to attract competent personnel to the PMO. Those respondents who have competent personnel see this as a strong point and those who do not have competent personnel see this as a critical area for improvement. Note that the recognition of the PMO's expertise is an item in the performance construct presented in Section 2.6, which is exploited in Chapter 3. The results of the qualitative case studies presented in Chapter 4 confirmed that this is an important issue and that many PMOs are having difficulty attracting competent personnel. In many organizations a position in a PMO is not seen as a good career move. The ability to attract good people to the PMO depends on the organizational culture and personnel management practices, but also on the reputation and the ability of the manager of the PMO.

Communicating the value of the PMO is also an important issue. Interestingly, it is mentioned as a strong point of several PMOs, but not mentioned as an area of improvement. It may be that those that do this well recognize the benefit, while those that do not, don't see the value of doing so.

Implementing a project information system is one of the functions included as part of the group of functions related to monitoring and controlling project performance. However, the project information system is also a facilitating factor for many of the PMO functions. A strong project information system supports not only project monitoring activities but also program and portfolio management functions. In another ongoing research project on the implementation of portfolio management, the authors have identified this as a critical success factor. Having a good project information system in place is thus a facilitating factor, similar to having competent personnel. The qualitative data from the survey confirms some of the quantitative results and makes significant additions. Much more qualitative data is presented in Chapter 4.

2.8 Conclusion

The data presented in this chapter describes a population that is characterized by extreme variety in the value, form, and function of PMOs. The variation in the perceived value of PMOs confirms the lack of consensus among practitioners on their value, which in turn confirms the impossibility of producing a consensus-based standard on PMOs. All of the variables describing the structural characteristics and the functions of PMOs in the descriptive model presented in the Section 2.1.2 are practical, meaningful ways of describing different features of PMOs. The variability of all the structural characteristics is extremely high in all cases except two: the age of the PMO and the size of the staff. The young age of most PMOs is particularly meaningful. It signifies that PMOs are most often temporary and transitory arrangements that will likely change in the next few years. The conceptualization and the strategies for both the study and the management of PMOs should reflect this reality.

Apart from being young and having small staffs, most PMOs have little in common. The variability on all the other structural characteristics is high. On some characteristics the population displays distributions that are close to being either normal or skewed toward one extreme. On other variables the distributions are almost bipolar, with most PMOs at one extreme or the other of the distribution, and few in the middle.

The analysis of the survey data revealed that all 27 functions investigated are important for significant numbers of PMOs. The variety can therefore not be reduced by removing some functions from the list. The analysis did reduce the list by identifying eight independent groups of functions. However, the fact that the selection of one function to be included in the mandate of a PMO is independent from the choice of other functions means that the population of PMOs is likely to contain a large number of different combinations of functions filled by PMOs. The next chapter further explores this population in search of patterns that could lead to a better understanding of PMOs and form the bases for types of PMOs.

CHAPTER THREE: AN EMPIRICALLY GROUNDED SEARCH FOR A TYPOLOGY

3.1 Introduction

The population of PMOs was described in Chapter 2 based on survey data. The main conclusions were that a PMO in its organizational context constitutes a complex entity that cannot be described with just a limited number of characteristics and that the population of PMOs is extremely varied. This chapter further explores this data in search of patterns that might form the basis of one or more typologies of PMOs. A typology would be very useful for describing and managing PMOs, but it would need to be empirically grounded to be reliable and useful.

Typology is "the branch of knowledge that deals with classes with common characteristics" or "a classification of especially human behavior or characteristics according to type" (*Canadian Oxford Dictionary*, 2004, p. 1864). Typologies are useful when dealing with complex phenomena, such as human behavior. Typologies have also been very useful in the study of organizations. Mintzberg (1979) reviewed the abundant literature on this complex topic and concluded that organizations could be grouped into five internally consistent and clearly differentiated configurations. Miller and Friesen (1984) showed empirically that the vast majority of organizations could be grouped into types very similar to Mintzberg's configurations. The reduction of the complexity of organizations to a small number of types has enormous advantages for those who study, design, and manage them. This is exactly the process reported in this chapter: an attempt to reduce the great variety of PMOs to a reasonable number of types based upon empirical data.

Without a typology, it is very difficult to describe or analyze PMOs. Typologies for PMOs are proposed in the literature (Crawford, 2002; Dinsmore, 1999; Englund, Graham, & Dinsmore, 2003; Kendall & Rollins, 2003; Light, 2000). These typologies present two problems. First, they are of a very limited number of types, usually three or four. It is difficult to reduce the great variety found among PMOs to the limited number of types found in the literature. Second, these typologies have not been empirically validated, or their empirical basis is not in the public domain.

This chapter aims to identify an empirically grounded typology of PMOs. It is based primarily on the analysis of descriptive data on the 502 PMOs presented in Chapter 2, enriched by the results from the qualitative case studies presented in

Chapter 4. The identification of characteristics that can form the basis for creating types of PMOs can be of use to those studying, designing, or managing PMOs or organizations containing PMOs. The identification of characteristics that do not show a strong relationship with the characteristics of PMOs is useful for two reasons: first, it identifies avenues of investigation that are likely to be less fruitful, and second, it provides a basis for questioning typologies found in the literature based on these same characteristics.

3.2 Methodology and Chapter Structure

3.2.1 The Data

The vast majority of the results presented in this chapter are based on the original sample of 502 PMOs. Variables from the follow-up survey have a smaller sample size (n=123) and are marked with an asterisk (*). Different subsets of the data are analyzed successively in a search for patterns in the data that could provide an empirical basis for one or more typologies of PMOs. The four classes of descriptive variables that are examined are presented in Table 3.1.

Table 3.1. Four classes of descriptive variables

Organizational context of the PMO	Type of project	PMO structural characteristics	Roles or functions of a PMO

• Geographic region
• Economic sector
• Private or public
• Organizational size
• Number of projects in organization
• Internal or external project customers
• Level of project management maturity
• Location relative to project personnel
• Supportiveness of organizational culture
• Single or multiple project customers
	• Project size, the number of people working on the project
	• Project duration
	• The type of product or service delivered*
	• The primary project performance criteria*
	• The inclusion of post-delivery activities within project scope*
	• Involvement in outsourcing contracts*
		• The PMO's name
		• Location within organizational structure
		• PMO staff
		  o Size of staff
		  o Experience*
		  o Background*
		  o Presence of business analysts or business architects*
		• Percent of projects within mandate
		• Percent of project managers within PMO
		• Decision-making authority of PMO
		• Age of PMO
		• PM methodology
		  o Homegrown?*
		  o Compulsory?*
		  o Actual use?*
		• Adequacy of funding*
		• Billing for services*
			• Monitoring and Controlling
			• Development of PM competencies and methodologies
			• Multi-project management
			• Strategic management
			• Organizational learning
			• Specialized tasks
			• Client interface management
			• Recruit, select, evaluate, and determine salaries for project managers

In addition to these descriptive variables, the survey instrument included measures of the perceived performance of PMOs. This chapter investigates the relationships between the descriptive characteristics presented in Table 3.1 and the two measures of PMO performance, "legitimacy" and "the performance construct," presented in Section 2.6, with the objective of identifying characteristics that are associated with high- and low-performing PMOs.

3.2.2 The Analysis of Data

The objective of the analysis is to identify patterns in the data that can be used to create types of PMOs and variables that are not good candidates for creating types of PMOs. Figure 3.1 illustrates the data analysis strategy.

If contextual variables are associated with certain characteristics of PMOs, then these contextual variables could be the basis of a typology. For example, if PMOs differ between public and private organizations or if PMOs in different industries differ systematically, then these could be bases of typologies. The first step in the analysis is therefore to test for relationships between the context (organizational context and project type) on the one hand and the characteristics of PMOs on the other. This identifies the contextual variables that are and are not good candidates as bases of typologies of PMOs. This approach is inspired by the contingency approach, which has been well established in organization studies for a long time (Donaldson, 2001). Those that are good candidates are examined further to determine if relationships exist among contextual variables that could form the basis of an organizational configuration analogous to Mintzberg's (1979) configurations. The performance data will also be analyzed in this step to determine if PMOs perform better in certain organizational contexts. This approach is represented as Step 1 in Figure 3.1. The results are presented and discussed in Section 3.3.

If one structural characteristic of PMOs is strongly associated with others, this could be the basis of a typology. For example, if PMOs in a particular location within the organizational structure are similar, then this information could be the basis of a typology of PMOs. Likewise, if a strong relationship were found between the size of the PMO and the level of its decision-making authority, then this pair of characteristics might form the basis of a typology. The more characteristics that are associated together, the more likely the group is to form the basis of a typology. The second series of analyses tests, therefore, for relationships among the characteristics of PMOs. This is presented as Step 2 in Figure 3.1. The results are presented and discussed in Section 3.4. The performance data is also analyzed in this step to determine if PMOs with specific characteristics perform better.

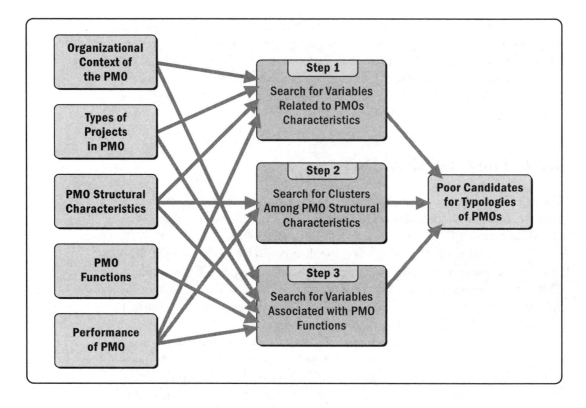

Figure 3.1. Data analysis strategy

If PMOs that fill a particular role or function have similar structural characteristics or are found in similar organizational contexts, then the PMOs filling this function could constitute a type of PMO. This analysis is presented as step 3 in Figure 3.1 and is presented in Section 3.5. Section 3.6 brings together the results from all three steps of the data analysis strategy and develops a typology based on these results.

3.2.3 Statistical Methods

The primary approach of the investigation was to identify whether two variables varied together in a systematic fashion. The primary tool used was the Pearson correlation coefficient. The vast majority of correlations between pairs of variables are very weak. However, because the sample size is relatively large, several of the weak correlations are statistically significant. None of the correlations is above 0.50, but there are several between 0.20 and 0.35. Please note that the square of the correlation coefficient provides an estimate of the portion of variability of one variable explained by variation in the other. Thus a correlation of 0.20 explains only 4% of the variability and a correlation of 0.35 explains 12%. The decision as to what level of correlation to report in this document is somewhat arbitrary. In order to provide maximum information to the reader, all correlations greater than or equal to 0.20 are reported. The correlations are identified so that the reader can appreciate the strength or weakness of the relationship. All correlations are significant at the level of p=0.0000. The pattern of the relationship between each pair of variables was also examined in the accompanying cross-tabulation. Relationships between variables that were neither continuous non-decreasing nor continuous non-increasing were considered as irregular relations and were not considered in the analysis and are not presented in this chapter. For example, a u-shaped relationship between two variables is neither continuous non-decreasing nor continuous non-increasing and was not reported here. In Step 3 of the analysis presented in Figure 3.1, multiple regression analysis was also used. The analysis is discussed further in Section 3.4.

3.3 Organizational Context and Project Type as Bases for Typologies of PMOs

3.3.1 Variables not Showing Significant Relationships with PMO Characteristics

This section presents the first part of Step 1 of the data analysis strategy shown in Figure 3.1.

3.3.1.1 Regional Differences

Some of the most intuitively obvious ways of creating typologies of PMOs do not show significant relationships with the characteristics of PMOs when tested against the data. Two of the most obvious are characterizations by geographic region and by industry. The sample can be divided into the following four sub-samples to test for regional variability: Canada, United States, Europe, and others. Testing for regional variability is more difficult than testing for relationships between continuous variables, partly because regional variability is a set of categories that can be regrouped and compared in many different ways. The comparisons are also limited by the fact that the sample does not contain sufficient data on many regions. The comparisons between regions were not explored exhaustively, but several comparisons were made and none showed any significant relationships across regions. This lack of relationship across regions is illustrated in Figure 3.2, which shows the percent of project managers who are located in the PMO. This variable is an important design choice when establishing a PMO. The same variability is found in each region. The search for a typology based on geographic region is not pursued further.

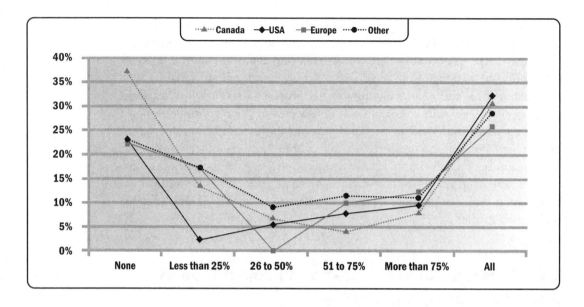

Figure 3.2. Variations in percent of project managers in PMOs in different regions

3.3.1.2 Differences Between Industries

Likewise, *industry* differences are an intuitively obvious way of creating typologies of PMOs. Here again, the data does not support the creation of such typologies. The sample can be divided into 22 different industries, which can be grouped in different ways. Figure 3.3 shows the variability found on the same important PMO design variable found in six product groups.

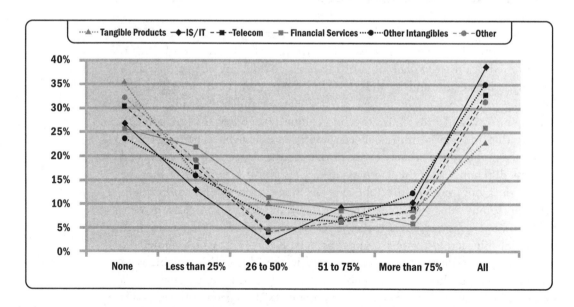

Figure 3.3. Variations in percent of project managers in PMOs in different industries

This lack of systematic differences seems counterintuitive. However, the data presented in Figure 2.11 and the data from the qualitative case studies in Table 4.5 show that most PMOs are reconfigured every few years. If companies stay in the same industry and the same region for decades but reconfigure their PMOs every few years, this would explain the variability found in the population of PMOs in any one industry or region at any point in time, as shown in Figures 3.2 and 3.3. The search for a typology based on industry is not pursued further.

3.3.1.3 Public and Private Sector Organizations

It is generally recognized that public and private sectors are different in many ways. It is plausible that PMOs may vary significantly between the two sectors. The sample of 502 PMOs is split relatively evenly between the two: 40% public and 60% private. Public organizations showed lower project management maturity (correlation 0.207), more internal customers (correlation 0.237), and longer duration projects (correlation 0.291). The focus of the chapter is, however, on ways to differentiate among PMOs, not on ways to differentiate between public and private organizations. The results show that PMOs in public organizations differ little from those in private organizations. The only significant difference was that PMOs in the private sector bill for their services in 71% of the cases, compared to only 29% in the public sector (n=119). This difference is not meaningful enough to form the basis of a typology of PMOs.

3.3.1.4 Organization Size

The size of the organization is among the variables most often cited in organizational studies (Mintzberg, 1979). Few characteristics of PMOs are related to the size of the organization. Variations among PMOs in different-sized organizations are rather intuitive. Larger organizations have more projects (correlation 0.280) and PMOs with more staff (correlation 0.245). Very small organizations are too small for the concept of a centrally or a non-centrally located PMO to be meaningful. Very small organizations have a greater proportion of projects with external customers. Organizational size does not have the potential to be a meaningful basis for a typology of PMOs.

3.3.1.5 Project Type

An analysis of the variables describing project scope (project size and duration) revealed only one relationship with PMO characteristics. Project size is related to the size of the PMO staff; the correlation of 0.358 is the strongest identified between the characteristics of organizations and PMOs and explains 13% of the variance. Here again, the fact that larger PMOs tend to manage large projects is not surprising. Obvious results such as these are reassuring, because they indicate that the data is of good quality. This relationship is not meaningful enough to form the basis of a typology of PMOs. The characteristic of PMO size is examined further in Step 2 of the analysis.

The follow-up survey examined several other project characteristics: type of product or service, primary performance criteria, inclusion of post-delivery activities, and involvement in outsourcing contracts. No systematic relationship was found between any of these variables and any of the structural characteristics of PMOs.

3.3.1.6 Location Relative to Project Personnel

Figure 2.2 shows that project personnel tend to be located either in the same part of the organizations as the PMO or spread throughout the organization, which can be referred to as being matrixed throughout the organization. This might be considered a characteristic of the PMO or of the organization. We feel that the location of project personnel throughout the organization is more an organizational characteristic. In either case, this characteristic is not related to other characteristics of the PMO.

Not only did the design of PMOs in different industries or region, in public and private sectors, in different-sized organizations, co-located with project personnel or not, and managing different types of projects, not vary significantly, but the performance of the PMOs in these different contexts did not vary significantly either. The lack of differential performance confirms that these five variables can be excluded from further consideration as bases for typologies of PMOs.

3.3.2 Organizational Characteristics Showing Significant Relationships with PMO Characteristics

This section presents the final part of Step 1 of the data analysis strategy shown in Figure 3.1. The following three organizational characteristics show significant relationships with PMO characteristics and are therefore explored further:
• Internal or external project customers
• Level of project management maturity
• Supportiveness of organizational culture

3.3.2.1 Internal or External Project Customers

The distinction between internal and external project customers has been used for creating taxonomy of projects (Andersen, 2006; Archibald, 1992; Thomas & Mullaly, 2008; Turner & Keegan, 2001). This characteristic is often linked to the *raison d'être* (or essential purpose) of the organization. Organizations have been classified in two types: organizations that offer a service of project management for external clients (type 1) and organizations where project management is not their *raison d'être* and where projects are a means for other business objectives (Type 2) (Archibald, 1992). In the latter type, clients are usually internal to the organization. Companies in construction or engineering and companies offering consulting services in IT or in project management are of Type 1. These types of companies deliver products and services to customers through projects. Type 2 organizations use project management primarily to develop new products or services or to manage internal change projects to modify the organization and its business processes. The use of project management in Type 2 organizations is related to the intensity of innovation or change. Examples of Type 2 organizations are found in many industries, including manufacturing, telecommunication, and banking, among others. Their primary *raison d'être* is to offer products or services to their final clients that are represented by internal intermediaries within the organization, precisely the ones that are called internal clients. In this type of organization, projects are means that contribute to specific business objectives. Table 3.2 shows the PMO structural characteristics for which significant differences are found between organizations of Types 1 and 2.

Table 3.2. Differences between organizations with internal and external project customers

	Variables	Correlation coefficient
Organizational context	Public or private	0.237
PMO characteristics	Decision-making authority	0.231

As was previously noted, *public organizations* are more often of type 2. The analysis also reveals that most small organizations are of type 1. This latter result is not surprising; many small organizations deliver customized products and services on a project basis but are too small to invest heavily in internal change projects.

The level of decision-making authority is the only structural characteristic of PMOs shown to vary significantly between organizations with internal and external project customers. On the average, PMOs with external project customers hold more *decision-making authority* than those with internal project customers. Implementing a PMO has an impact on the internal system of power (Crawford & Cabanis-Brewin, 2006). For organizations having internal clients, the case studies have shown how the PMO and both business and functional units clash in struggles for control over projects. For organizations having external clients, it may be easier to exercise authority on projects because they are less embroiled in the internal political systems. This difference may not be sufficient to form the basis of a typology of PMOs, but it is certainly noteworthy that PMOs with internal customers have more difficulty establishing decision-making authority. No significant difference in the perceived performance of PMOs was found between organizations of Type 1 and Type 2.

3.3.2.2 Supportiveness of Organizational Culture

A *supportive organizational culture* is identified as a major success factor for project management (Henrie & Sousa-Poza, 2005). It must be noted that only 370 of the 502 respondents answered this question on the survey. This fact poses two problems. First, it is not clear if the variation in response rate is related to some other consideration that is relevant to the discussion here. Second, with fewer responses, it is more difficult to identify statistically significant relationships. The analysis identified a stronger relationship with one other organizational characteristic than with one characteristic of PMOs, as presented in Table 3.3.

Table 3.3. Differences in organizations with a supportive organizational culture

	Variables	Correlation coefficients
Organizational context	Level of project management maturity	0.353
PMO characteristics	Decision-making authority	0.264

The supportiveness of the organizational culture is related significantly to only one other element of the organizational context, the level of project management maturity of the organization. This variable is discussed in the next section. PMOs with little or no support from the organizational culture tend to be situated at a lower level of maturity. It may be that in an organization where project management is valued, the culture is supportive, the project management practices are well implemented, and the PMO is valued as well. The cause-and-effect relationships may be impossible to ascertain.

The supportiveness of the organizational culture is related to the decision-making authority of the PMO. The results show that the more supportive the organizational culture is, the more decision-making authority the PMO will have. The supportiveness of the organizational culture is related with both measures of perceived PMO performance, the performance construct (correlation 0.436), and legitimacy (correlation 0.269).

3.3.2.4 Level of Project Management Maturity

The level of project management maturity has been evaluated by respondents using the well-known scale from the Capability Maturity Model (CMM) that was developed by the Software Engineering Institute of Carnegie-Mellon University between 1986 and 1993 (Cooke-Davies & Arzymanow, 2003). It proposes five levels through which an organization is expected to progress: initial level, repeatable level, defined level, managed level, and optimized level. As shown in Figure 2.4, the distribution of the population in the survey shows that very few organizations have reached the highest level (less than 3%). Most organizations are at the lower levels of maturity (57% at levels 1 and 2).

As previously mentioned, the level of project management maturity is related to the supportiveness of the organizational culture and is higher in private organizations. Project management maturity is related to many other variables, as indicated in Table 3.4.

Table 3.4. Variables associated with project management maturity

	Variables	Correlation coefficients
Organizational context	Supportive organizational culture	0.353
	Private or public	0.207
PMO characteristics	Age of the PMO	0.385
	Decision-making authority	0.323
	Percent of project managers within PMO	0.258
	Size of PMO staff	0.245
	Percent of projects within mandate	0.215

The level of project management maturity is associated with the age of the PMO. A statistical association does not indicate the nature of the causal relationship. However, if the mature project management environment causes the PMO to survive longer, one would expect to find a relationship between the supportiveness of the organizational culture and the age of the PMO, but this relationship was shown to be extremely weak. The PMO being in place longer may explain the relationship between maturity and age. The analysis of the survey data and the results of the case studies have shown that most organizations that have PMOs restructure them quite frequently. Organizational maturity is associated with stable project management processes. A more mature project management environment is thus more stable. This may explain the tendency to change the PMO less often. It may also be that organizations that are mature in project management have set up PMOs earlier and thus have older PMOs. As can be seen from this discussion, there are several possible explanations for the association between project management maturity and the age of the PMO.

The size of the PMO staff is related to the maturity level. The results of the analysis show that PMOs that have one employee, often not full-time, are concentrated at maturity levels one and two. Thus, having a small staff is associated with lower levels of maturity. While still significant, the relationship between maturity and PMO size is not as clear-cut for larger PMOs.

The level of project management maturity is related to three PMO characteristics that are related to one another: the decision-making authority of the PMO, the percent of projects in the PMO's mandate, and the percent of project managers located within the PMO. This cluster of PMO characteristics is discussed beginning in Section 3.3.4. The level of organizational project management maturity is related to both measures of perceived PMO performance, the performance construct (correlation 0.310) and legitimacy (correlation 0.209).

3.3.2.5 A Pattern in the Data

The maturity in project management varies with many other variables. Project management maturity seems to somehow transcend many other important variables. It has the potential of capturing a great deal of the variance between PMOs and is by far the organizational contextual variable that correlates with the largest number of characteristics of PMOs. In addition, it is correlated with the supportiveness of the organizational culture and both correlate with the PMO's decision-making authority. A pattern seems to be emerging from the data. However, before exploring this emerging pattern any further, the relationships among the structural characteristics of PMOs are examined in the next section.

However, caution should be taken in interpreting this relationship, as the identification of a statistical relationship does not indicate the direction of influence among variables. The relationships among the supportive culture, the level of project management maturity, and the perceptions of PMO performance may be circular.

3.4 Structural Characteristics of PMOs as Bases for Typologies

This section presents Step 2 of the data analysis strategy shown in Figure 3.1.

The characteristics of PMOs also serve as bases for types of PMOs. A single characteristic of a PMO is not likely to be a good basis for a typology of PMOs unless this characteristic is related to others to form configurations analogous to Mintzberg's organizational configurations (Mintzberg, 1979). The focus here is therefore on scrutinizing the data, looking for the most significant relationships among the characteristics of PMOs. The aim of this approach is to identify clusters of characteristics that reveal potential typologies of PMOs. The variables describing the characteristics of PMOs are listed in the third column of Table 3.1. An examination of the relationships among these variables identified five potential bases for typologies of PMOs: location within organizational structure, size of PMO staff other than project managers, decision-making authority of PMO, percent of projects within mandate of PMO, and percent of project managers within the PMO. Each is discussed here.

The other structural characteristics in the third column of Table 3.1 are not good candidates for forming typologies of PMOs because they are not related to other characteristics. Interestingly, the name that is given to the entity is not a good basis for identifying its characteristics. As can be seen in Table 2.2, the names given vary considerably and only two names have sufficiently large sample sizes to compare them statistically: Project Management Office and Program Management Office. There was no statistically significant difference between entities with these two names.

3.4.1 PMO Types Based on Location in the Organizational Structure

PMOs can be located at different levels in the hierarchy and in different parts of the organization. The original survey of 502 PMOs identified PMOs as being "central" or "located in a business, functional or regional unit." Somewhat surprisingly, few systematic differences between PMOs of these two types were identified. Centrally located PMOs showed no systematic variations with respect to organizational contextual variables or structural characteristics of PMOs, except that centrally located PMOs bill for their services less often (correlation 0.259, p<0.004). Centrally located PMOs are not perceived globally as better or worse performing than PMOs located in a business, functional, or regional unit.

Overall, the location in the organizational structure has not been as powerful a means of identifying types of PMOs as might have been expected. One of the case studies provides a good illustration of the possible lack of relationship with the location in the organization: in this case study the PMO is located in the IT unit but has a mission that covers all the projects of the firm. Most of the differences that have been identified by the analysis are intuitively sensible. In addition, the results for the second survey can only be considered indicative of possible differences because of the small sample size. Location within the organizational structure is therefore excluded from further consideration in the analysis. However, because of the intuitive appeal of location within the organization and because of methodological issues discussed in Section 2.3.3, this issue deserves further consideration in future research efforts.

3.4.2 Size and Characteristics of PMO Staff Other than Project Managers

The size as measured by the number of full-time equivalents other than the project managers was the only staff characteristic that was found to be associated with other characteristics of PMOs. None of the characteristics examined by the follow-up survey, such as level of experience or professional background, varied systematically with other characteristics of PMOs or with the perceived performance of the PMO.

The size of the PMO staff is rarely used solely as a criterion for identifying types of PMOs. It is often the consequence of other organizational choices. Nevertheless, one important issue PMO managers are facing is justifying the number of human resources needed to do the great variety of tasks expected of the PMO. They are often asked to benchmark their mandate and their size with other PMOs. The size of PMO staff has numerous relationships with other variables, as shown in Table 3.5.

Table 3.5. Variables related to size of PMO staff

	Variables	Correlation coefficients
Organizational context	Size of the organization	0.245
	Number of projects in organization	0.295
	Level of project management maturity	0.195
Project scope	Size of projects	0.358
PMO characteristics	Age of PMO	0.275
	Decision-making authority	0.274

PMOs with a very small staff are associated with low levels of project management maturity. However, the correlation between the two variables is very weak for the entire sample: only 0.195, which is below the level reported elsewhere in this report. The size of the PMO staff correlates with both the size of the organization and the number of the projects in which it is involved. It is not at all surprising to find that bigger PMOs are involved in more projects and larger projects, and are located in larger organizations. In addition, older PMOs tend to have more staff.

The association between the percent of project managers in the PMO with the size of the PMO staff is very weak for the overall sample. However, PMOs with a large staff and no project managers are rare; of the population of 502, only 7 PMOs have a staff of 13 or more and no project managers. PMOs are often under pressure to justify the costs they incur. A large staff with no project managers is a very visible overhead expense. The overhead expense of the same staff with a large number of project managers would be much less visible. This may explain the rarity of large PMOs with no project managers.

There is a relationship between the size of the PMO staff and the decision-making authority. This is discussed in the next section. Interestingly, there is no statistical relationship between the size of the PMO staff and perceptions of its performance. Larger PMOs are perceived as generating enough value to justify the expense, but not more. The funding of larger PMOs tends to be viewed as more adequate, while the funding of smaller PMOs tends to be judged as less than adequate (correlation coefficient 0.255, p<0.005). The meaning of this negative relationship between adequacy of funding and the size of the PMO staff may indicate that large PMOs are difficult to maintain without adequate funding, but that smaller PMOs do exist that do not have adequate funding.

3.4.3 Decision-making Authority of the PMO

One approach to categorize PMOs is to differentiate by level of authority (Bridges & Crawford, 2001). When a PMO holds authority, it is said to be empowered, and if without authority, as passive. As shown in Figure 2.15, the distribution of this variable in the sample is close to a normal distribution but with very high variance: 41% of the sample has a passive or supporting role while 29% have considerable or very significant authority. Table 3.6 presents the variables that are related to the decision-making authority of the PMO. The relationships with the characteristics of the organizational context, project management maturity, internal or external project customers, and supportive organizational culture, have been presented and discussed in previous sections of this chapter.

Table 3.6. Variables related to the decision-making authority of the PMO

	Variables	**Correlation coefficients**
Organizational context	Level of project management maturity	0.323
	Supportiveness of organizational culture	0.264
	External project customers	0.231
PMO characteristics	Percent of project managers within PMO	0.345
	Percent of projects within mandate	0.289
	Size of PMO staff	0.274

The size of the PMO staff is related to the decision-making authority of the PMO. This creates the image of powerful PMOs with a larger staff, although PMO staffs are generally rather small. It also creates the image of very small PMOs with little or no authority. The relationship with the percentage of projects and project managers is discussed in the next section. The level of the PMO's decision-making authority is correlated with both measures of PMO performance, the performance construct (0.287) and legitimacy (0.187). Note that this later correlation is very weak.

3.4.4 A Trilogy of PMO Design Variables

The percentage of project managers placed within a PMO, the percentage of the organization's projects included in its mandate, and the decision-making authority that is given to the PMO are three very important variables in the design of a PMO. All three are strongly related to one another. The relationships among these variables is discussed following the analysis of the percentage of project managers placed within a PMO and the percentage of the organization's projects included in its mandate, each presented separately.

3.4.5 Percentage of Project Managers Within the PMO

One major decision to be made regarding the structure of a PMO is its line or staff position. This makes the difference between being accountable or not accountable for project results. This decision goes hand in hand with the inclusion or exclusion of project managers in the PMO. The project manager is the person ultimately accountable for project results (PMI, 2004).

As was shown in Figure 2.14, most organizations are choosing between two radically different designs for their PMOs: some are placing all of their project managers within the PMO and others are placing no project managers within their PMO. The presence or absence of project managers in the PMO is related to several other variables, as shown in Table 3.7. The relationship with the organizational contextual variable level of project management maturity is noteworthy and is discussed in the following sections of this chapter. The weak relationship with the size of PMO staff was discussed in Section 3.4.2.

Table 3.7. Variables related to the percentage of project managers within the PMO

	Variable	Correlation coefficients
Organizational context	Level of project management maturity	0.258
PMO characteristics	Percent of projects within mandate	0.426
	Decision-making authority	0.345

A PMO with a high percentage of the organization's project managers would quite naturally also have a high percentage of the organization's projects within its mandate. The fact that the percentages of projects and project managers located within PMOs are correlated comes as no surprise. However, the correlation of 0.426, which is the strongest found among the relationships between PMO characteristics, only explains 16% of the variance. This relationship is examined further in Section 3.6.2. The percentage of project managers in the PMO is only very weakly related to the performance construct.

3.4.6 Percentage of Projects in the PMO's Mandate

The variation among PMOs as to the percent of projects within their structure is a bipolar distribution, as shown in Figure 2.13. Thirty-nine percent of organizations have chosen to place most or all of their projects within the mandate of the PMO. Another 22% have chosen to place only a select group (less than 20% of their projects) within the PMO. The relationships with other variables presented in Table 3.8 have been discussed in previous sections. The percentage of the organization's projects within the PMO's mandate is correlated with the performance construct (0.293).

Table 3.8. Variables related to the percentage of projects within the PMO's mandate

	Variable	Correlation coefficients
Organizational context	Level of project management maturity	0.215
PMO characteristics	Percent of project managers within PMO	0.426
	Decision-making authority	0.289

3.4.7 A Cluster of Characteristics

The three structural characteristics of PMOs—decision-making authority, percentages of projects within the mandate, and percentage of project managers within the PMO—are all related to one another. In addition, these three characteristics are not related to other characteristics of PMOs, except for the relation of decision-making authority with PMO size previously discussed. This means that organizational choices relative to these three characteristics are highly interdependent, but largely independent from other choices relative to the PMO. The three may be related for several reasons. Having more of the organization's projects and project managers within their structure can certainly be seen as a source of influence for the PMO. Inversely, a more powerful PMO may have the influence necessary to bring more projects and project managers into its mandate.

All three PMO characteristics are correlated with one organizational characteristic: the level of project management maturity. This is the only organizational characteristic correlated with the percentages of projects and project managers. The level of decision-making authority is also correlated with the supportiveness of the organizational culture, which is in turn correlated with the level of maturity. It is also correlated with external project customers. With these exceptions, project management maturity is the only organizational characteristic with which the three PMO characteristics are related. This means that the choices made relative to these three PMO characteristics are not only independent of choices related to other PMO characteristics, but are also largely independent of organizational contextual variables other than the level of project management maturity and possibly the supportiveness of the organizational culture with which they are associated. These five variables form a cluster of variables that are highly interdependent, but largely independent from other organizational design choices relative to PMOs. This cluster of variables is illustrated in Figure 3.4. All five variables are correlated with the performance construct, although the correlation with the percentage of project managers is very weak. This cluster of variables is exploited in the development of a typology in Section 3.6.

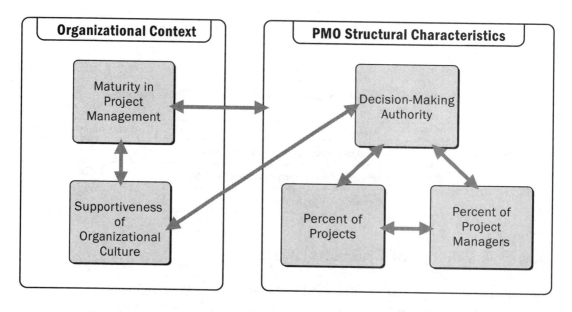

Figure 3.4. The cluster of organizational contextual variables and PMO structural characteristics

3.5 PMO Functions as Bases for Typologies of PMOs

This section presents Step 3 of the data analysis strategy shown in Figure 3.1.

Previous sections of this chapter have examined the variables describing the organizational context and the structural characteristics of PMOs in the search for relationships that might constitute a basis for one or more typologies of PMOs. In addition to these variables, each respondent was asked to assess the importance of each function within the mandate of the PMO using a scale from 1 (not important at all) to 5 (very important). If there are associations between variables describing the organizational context or the structural characteristics of PMOs on the one hand, and the functions filled by PMOs on the other hand, then these associations could form the bases of typologies. Likewise, if PMOs filling a particular group of functions had similar structural characteristics or are found in similar organizational contexts, then the functions filled by PMOs could be the basis for a typology. For example, if PMOs, for which standardized methodology is an important function, had specific characteristics or were found in specific contexts, then PMOs heavily involved in methodology would be a type of PMO. However, if the characteristics and contexts of these PMOs are not specific, then this would be a poor basis for a typology. These avenues of investigation are pursued in this section.

The survey collected data on the importance of the functions in the mandates of the 502 PMOs. This data was presented in Section 2.5. One important outcome from the analysis of the survey data is the identification of eight groups of functions (three groups containing one single function) (see Section 2.5.2). The reduction from 27 individual functions to eight groups simplifies the manipulation and the interpretation of the data and ultimately makes the results easier to use in practice. The analyses presented here are therefore based on the eight groups of functions.

The fact that the eight groups were identified by a Varimax factorial analysis indicates that they are statistically independent. This means that the fact that an organization chooses to include one group of functions within the mandate of a PMO is unrelated to the choice of which other groups of functions to include in its mandate. Because organizations are making independent choices from a "menu" of eight possible groups of functions and, because as was shown in Figure 2.16, most organizations are assigning multiple functions to their PMOs, the number of possible independent combinations of functions found within the mandates of PMOs is quite large. Consequentially, it is highly unlikely that the classification of PMOs by the functions they fill will produce clearly defined groups or types. The analysis does, however, identify some meaningful patterns.

3.5.1 Associations Between Pairs of Variables

The initial analysis of the relationship between organizational context and PMO structural characteristics on the one hand, and functions within the PMO's mandate on the other, is based on relationships between individual pairs of variables. There are many such relationships, some of which are not particularly strong. Note that with a large sample such as the one here, a relationship between two variables may be significant at a level of p=0.000 and yet have a very low correlation coefficient, indicating a significant but weak relationship. The objective at this point in the analysis is to identify relationships, including weak relationships that indicate possible patterns in the relations with the PMO functions. These relationships are exploited in Section 3.5.2. An overview is presented in Table 3.9. The variables are presented in three groups: organizational context, project scope, and PMO characteristics. Relationships with a level of significance of p < 0.05 have been included to give an overview of the whole set of associations. Associations with a level of significance of p < 0.005 are highlighted. A minus sign (-) indicates a negative correlation between the variables. The variables from the follow-up survey have not been included in order to simplify the presentation and because few of the relationships with the functions were statistically significant and meaningful.

As can be seen from the table, large numbers of functions are associated with several of the characteristics in the left column of Table 3.9. In other words, several of these characteristics are associated not only with a single function but with the total number of functions within the PMO's mandate as well. The associations between the total number of important functions within the PMO's mandate and characteristics are shown in the right column of Table 3.9. The bottom rows of Table 3.9 show the association between each of the eight groups of functions and the measures of PMO performance, the performance construct and legitimacy.

The first observation is that interpreting this table will be difficult for two reasons. First, the table contains a great deal of information. And second, no simple and obvious relationship that might form the basis of a typology of PMOs stands out: none of the groups of functions is associated with a specific set of contextual or PMO structural characteristics, and few of these characteristics are associated with specific groups of functions. An alternative way of analyzing this data is proposed in Section 3.5.2. However, several interesting observations on Table 3.9 can be made before doing so:

Observations on the relationships with performance:

- As can be seen in the bottom rows of Table 3.9, the importance of all eight functions is correlated with the performance construct, as is the total number of important functions. The correlation coefficients vary from 0.284 to 0.438 for the eight functions. These are as strong as and in some cases stronger than the correlations between this measure of performance and the contextual variables and the characteristics of the PMOs. The strongest correlation with the performance construct is that of the total number of functions, which is 0.516. The importance of the functions being filled would seem to be at least as good a predictor of PMO performance as other variables, if not better. These functions represent the roles filled by PMOs in organizations. It is reasonable, then, that the more roles a PMO fills, the better it is perceived. This might form the basis of a best practice: PMOs should seek to be useful by filling multiple roles. The relationship with performance is further investigated in Section 3.7.

- During the last several years, the authors have often been asked which functions a PMO should fill or which functions are "best practices." Because all eight functions are correlated with performance with coefficients in a relatively small range, it is not possible to state that PMOs filling specific functions are "better" than others. The decision as to which functions a PMO might fill in a specific context will most likely be influenced by this context. The analysis in Section 3.2.5 explores the relationships between organizational context, PMO characteristics, and the functions filled by PMOs.

- As can also be seen from the bottom roles of Table 3.9, there are few significant relationships with legitimacy, the other performance measure, and those that do exist are very weak, as was the case with the contextual variables and the PMO characteristics. The relationship with performance is further investigated in Section 3.7.

Observations on the number of functions being filled by PMOs:

- Some aspects of the organizational contextual and some PMO characteristics are associated with the importance of large numbers of functions. This can be seen both in the number of significant relations in a particular row and by the scores in the right column. The five variables that form the pattern presented at the end of the previous section in Figure 3.4 are all associated with PMOs filling more functions. The variable *total number of important functions* is employed along with these five variables in the development of a model in Section 3.6.

- As would be expected, the size of the PMO staff is associated with the total number of important functions being filled. PMOs with larger staffs are able to fill more functions.
- The supportiveness of the organizational culture is associated with all the groups of functions and thus with the total number of functions. The supportiveness of the organizational culture may be a general facilitating factor that allows PMOs to be more active in all of their roles. The level of project management maturity of the organizations is associated with six of the eight groups of functions, with the total number of important functions, and with the supportiveness of the culture. It is possible that a circular relationship exists whereby a PMO in a mature and supportive project management organization is able to fill many functions and thus contribute to its perceived value, to the level of project management maturity, and to the support it receives.
- When project personnel are not matrixed throughout the organization but share a common manager with the PMO, the PMO fills many more functions. This may be because a common superior is mandating the PMO to fill more roles in his or her organization. He or she has both the incentive and the means to set up a PMO and to give it several mandates to fill. Note that this effect of a common superior is present in all cases except when the percentage of project personnel reporting to this common superior decreases below 20%. In other words, only when more than 80% of project personnel is matrixed throughout the organization is a decrease observed in the importance of the functions filled by the PMO.
- The PMO's decision-making authority is associated with the total number of important functions and six of eight groups of functions. But interestingly, the level of authority is not related to monitoring and controlling project performance. The results of the case studies provide an explanation. Some PMOs with little or no decision-making authority are monitoring project status but exercising little or no influence, while other PMOs are exerting significant control over projects and are able to do so because of their level of decision-making authority. The functions of monitoring and controlling should be separated. Most PMOs are monitoring but only some of them are controlling.

Poor bases for typologies of PMOs:

- Previous sections of this chapter showed that the organizational contextual variables public/private sector and organizational size, number of projects in the organization, and project scope were not associated with PMO structural characteristics. The lack of association with the functions filled by PMOs confirms that these variables are poor candidates for creating typologies of PMOs.
- Likewise, the lack of association between the age of the PMO and the functions it fills confirms that the age of the PMO is a poor candidate for creating typologies of PMOs.

The following Section explores an alternative approach to the analysis of the associations presented in Table 3.9.

Table 3.9. Variables associated with the importance of groups of functions in PMO mandates

	FUNCTIONS								
	Monitoring and controlling	Development of PM competences and methodologies	Multi-project management	Strategic management	Organizational learning	Specialized tasks	Client interface management	HR	Total number of important functions
Organizational context									
Public sector				0.023					
Size of the organization							-0.017		
Number of projects in organization						-0.000	-0.008		
External project customers									
Multiple project customers	0.010	0.000	0.013	0.002	0.012	0.001	0.002	0.015	0.000
Non-matrixed project personnel	0.000		0.000	0.000	0.000	0.000	0.000	0.001	0.000
Supportiveness of organizational culture	0.008	0.008	0.032	0.000	0.000	0.000	0.003	0.001	0.000
Organizational PM maturity	0.001		0.027	0.002	0.000	0.001	0.027	0.000	0.000
Project scope									
Project size				0.047	0.004	0.009		0.008	0.001
Project duration			0.006			0.004	0.041		0.020
PMO descriptive characteristics									
Central location within organization		0.001		0.000					0.013
PMO staff size			0.000	0.011		0.000	0.021	0.000	0.002
Percent of projects within mandate	0.000		0.000		0.003	0.000	0.000	0.000	0.000
Percent of project managers in PMO	0.010	0.047	0.000	0.015	0.002	0.001	0.000	0.000	0.000
Decision-making authority			0.000	0.000	0.000	0.000	0.000	0.000	0.000
Age of PMO									
Correlation with performance construct	0.399	0.438	0.363	0.326	0.458	0.440	0.333	0.284	0.516
P	0.0000	0.0000	0.0000	0.0000	0.000	0.0000	0.0000	0.0000	0.0000
Correlation with legitimacy	0.115	0.102	0.181	0.109	0.088	0.141	0.115	0.088	0.110
P	0.0280	0.0480	0.0000	0.0420	0.0500	0.0100	0.0340	0.1000	0.0220

3.5.2 A Search for the Best Explanations of the Importance of Groups of Functions

One of the difficulties in interpreting the information in Table 3.9 is that large numbers of characteristics of the organizational context and the PMOs are associated with the importance of several of the functions in the PMO's mandate. For example, 10 descriptive variables are associated significantly (p <0.005) with the "specialized tasks" function. A subset of this group of 10 variables is likely to provide a more parsimonious description of PMOs and organizational contexts where this function is important. Multiple regression analysis (backward selection method with exit probability >0.1) was used for this purpose. In this analysis, the importance of a group of functions is considered as a dependent variable to be explained while the other descriptive variables are considered as possible sources of explanation or independent variables. A regression model was produced for each of the groups of functions into which only the variables with an association shown in Table 3.9 were included.

A regression analysis requires a large sample size. Because of their sample size (n=123 or less), all the variables from the follow-up survey were excluded from the regression analysis. Before undertaking the multiple regression analysis, the independent variables must be checked for multicollinearity, or the degree of association among the independent variables. A high level of collinearity can cause unreliable results when performing regression analysis. A correlation matrix was used to detect collinearity. Collinearity is a question of degree (Aczel, 1996). When a pair of variables shows a Pearson correlation superior to 0.35, one of the variables is removed from the analysis. The following variables were removed:

- Level of project management maturity and the supportiveness of the organizational culture are strongly correlated (Pearson coefficient 0.353). Because there are several responses missing for supportiveness of organizational culture (n=370), this variable was removed from all the models.
- The percent of projects within the mandate of the PMO is correlated with the percent of project managers within PMO (Pearson coefficient 0.426). Six of the eight groups of functions show associations with both variables. For these six groups of functions, two regression analyses were run, one with each of these variables. The regression models are very stable. Substituting percent of projects for percent of project managers did not change the other variables in the models and did not change the weightings appreciably. In one case, one variable changed. In each case, the model with the highest percent of variance explained (R^2) is shown in Table 3.10 and discussed.
- Project size and project duration are correlated as well (Pearson coefficient 0.340). In only one case are both of these variables associated with a group of functions, specialized tasks. In this case, only the project duration was used in the regression analysis, because of its tighter association with the function.

The fact that a variable is removed from this analysis does not mean that it is not important. It means only that its ability to predict the importance of PMO functions is captured by other variables with which it is correlated. For example, when interpreting the results for organizational project management maturity, it should be remembered that this variable is correlated with the supportiveness of the organizational culture. Likewise, it should be remembered that the percentages of projects and projects managers are also correlated.

The independent variables are listed in the left column of Table 3.10. They are presented in three groups: organizational context, project scope, and PMO characteristics. Each column in Table 3.10 presents the best regression model for each group of functions, the one using the least number of independent variables for a maximum of fit with the data (R^2). "[...] a good statistical model fits the data well but is also parsimonious, that is, it has as few parameters as possible" (Aczel, 1996, p. 471). Loadings in the factors are indicated in the rows next to the variable names. A minus sign indicates a negative correlation between the variables.

The second-to-last line of the table presents the adjusted R2, which gives the percentages of the total variance in the importance of the function explained by the regression models. The percentage of variance explained varies from 21.5% to 7.2%. (All of the regression models are significant at a level of p=0.000.) The importance of a group of functions can be used to characterize a PMO if a high percentage of the variability in the importance can be explained by the organizational contextual and the structural characteristics of the PMO. This could, therefore, constitute the basis for a type of PMO. On the other hand, if a very small percentage of the variance is explained, the importance of the group of functions is not a good basis for identifying types of PMOs.

The last line of the Table 3.10 indicates the maximum value of the Variance Inflation Factor, which is a measure of the multicollinearity of the regression models. A high score indicates a high level of multicollinearity. A value below 10 is generally considered acceptable. The scores are all close to the minimum score of 1, indicating that the regression models contain almost no multicollinearity among independent variables.

A further examination of the R2 scores reveals that the regression models can be divided into three groups (the percentage of variance explained is indicated in parentheses):
1. The best models:
- HR functions (21.9%)
- Multi-project management functions (20.1%)

2. The regression models of four other groups of functions that have similar but weaker explanatory power (17.4% to 15.0%):
- Specialized tasks (17.4%)
- Strategic management (16.1%)
- Client interface management (16.1%)
- Organizational learning (15.0%)

3. The regression models for the final two groups of functions that have quite limited explanatory power (9.7% and 6.7%):

Table 3.10. Multiple regressions with individual groups of functions as dependant variables

Dependant variable		FUNCTIONS						
	Monitoring and Controlling	Development of PM competences and methodologies	Multi-project management	Strategic management	Organizational learning	Specialized tasks	Client Interface Management	HR
Independent variables:								
Organizational context								
Public sector				0.15				
Size of the organization								
Number of projects within mandate						-0.24	-0.15	
External project customers						0.09	0.08	0.10
Multiple project customers	0.10	0.22	0.07	0.14	0.10	0.09	0.13	
Non-matrixed project personnel	0.11		0.16		0.16	0.09		
Organizational PM maturity	0.10				0.19	0.10		
Project Scope								
Project size					0.10	0.12		
Project duration			0.11					
PMO descriptive characteristics								
Central location within organization		0.14		0.13		0.17	0.10	0.17
Size of PMO	0.22			0.11		0.09	0.10	
% of projects within mandate			0.13					0.26
% of project managers in PMO								
Decision-making authority			0.30	0.29	0.15	0.10	0.22	0.21
Age of PMO								
N	446	454	439	431	444	439	438	439
F-statistic	12.91	17.34	23.12	17.56	16.66	12.56	14.96	31.81
Adjusted R-squared	0.097	0.067	0.201	0.161	0.150	0.174	0.161	0.219
Variance Inflation Factor (max)	1.112	1.008	1.192	1.197	1.216	1.341	1.227	1.186

- Monitoring and controlling (9.7%)
- Development of project management competencies and methodologies (6.7%)

The functions within the first group with the highest scores may reasonably constitute bases for characterizing PMOs and thus for identifying types of PMOs. The functions within the third group with the lowest scores are not good bases for characterizing PMOs. The four functions of the second group are in between. In the search for a better understanding, identifying characteristics that can and cannot be used to identify types of PMOs are both important.

In the text that follows, each column of Table 3.10 is examined successively to analyze and interpret the regression models for each of the groups of functions. The regression models have identified the characteristics that provide the best explanation of the variations in the importance of each group of functions. The groups of functions are examined in decreasing order of the explanatory power of the regression model as shown by the adjusted R^2 in the second last row of Table 3.10.

3.5.3 PMOs That Recruit, Select, Evaluate, and Determine Salaries for Project Managers

The roles of recruiting, selecting, evaluating, and determining salaries for project managers were grouped in the survey instrument into one overall HR function (mean importance 2.54). As shown in Table 2.4, this was the least important of all the functions on average, but remained important for 22% of PMOs. These PMOs that provide HR functions for the project managers are therefore quite specific and can be considered a type of PMO. Crawford and Cabanis-Brewin (2006) explored this function in more detail and stated that it is increasing in importance in PMOs. Its importance is modulated depending upon the role of the HR department (Huemann, Keegan, & Turner, 2007). The regression model based on the four variables shown in Table 3.11 explains 21.9% of the variance in the importance of this function.

Table 3.11. Variables related the HR function

	Variables	Weightings
Organizational context	Multiple project customers	0.10
	Percent of project managers in the PMO	0.26
PMO characteristics	Decision-making authority	0.21
	Size of PMO staff	0.17

The percent of project managers in the PMO is the characteristic with the largest weighting. The distribution of this variable is u-shaped, with most PMOs having either all the project managers located in the PMO or none at all. PMOs with all or most project managers are in a much better position to fill the HR functions.

The second heaviest weighting is for the decision-making authority of the PMO. To recruit, select, evaluate, and determine salaries for project managers means making decisions on these subjects. To do so requires decision-making authority. An example of this is seen in one of the case study organizations. When the company went through a bad period with negative financial results, top management questioned the performance of their project managers, because almost none of the projects respected their delivery dates. The PMO managers, together with the HR expert, went through a process of identifying the best profile for their project managers. Mapping the desired profile against the profiles of current project managers showed major gaps. It took a high level of authority to manage the layoff of certain project managers, while having others take training in project management.

The third heaviest weighting is for the size of the PMO staff. The functions to recruit, select, evaluate, and determine salaries for project managers generates considerable work, for which the PMO must have competent staff. Given that PMOs generally have small staffs, three to four people on average, it is not surprising that filling these functions requires a larger staff.

PMOs tend to fill these functions in contexts where their projects are executed for multiple customers. If all the projects are for one customer, that customer organization may be managing the HR functions for the project managers. This variable has less weight in the explanation of the importance of HR functions in the mandate of the PMO. The importance of the HR functions, together with these characteristics, constitute a type of PMO that is quite specific. Although not the most common type, it is nonetheless descriptive of a significant number of PMOs.

3.5.4 PMOs That Do Multi-project Management Functions

Multi-project management functions refer to PMOs that have mandates to manage whole sets of projects in a coordinated fashion, which includes program and portfolio management. With 20.1% of the variance in the importance of this group of functions explained by five variables, as shown in Table 3.12, this is the second most powerful of the regression models.

Table 3.12. Variables related to multi-project management functions

	Variable	Weightings
Organizational context	Non-matrixed project personnel	0.16
	Multiple customers	0.07
Project scope	Project duration	0.11
PMO characteristics	Decision-making authority	0.30
	Percent of project managers in PMO	0.13

The most important variable in the model is the PMO's decision-making authority. This is not surprising, as activities that relate to multi-project management need the capacity to make decisions, such as selecting and prioritizing projects and allocating resources. Inversely, less powerful PMOs are less likely to be involved in this group of functions.

As would be expected, PMOs involved in multi-project management functions have a larger percentage of projects and project managers within their structures. These two variables are correlated and the regression model with percent of project managers is slightly more powerful. Multi-project management deals with multiple projects and it is not surprising that the PMOs that have a higher percentage of the organization's projects and project managers are more involved in the coordination and prioritization of projects.

In non-matrix environments where the PMO and the resources working on projects report to a common superior, the PMO is more often involved in multi-project management. The common superior likely has both the authority and the responsibility for selecting, prioritizing, and allocating resources among projects. Many such managers are giving their PMO the mandate to be involved in these functions.

Project duration is also part of the model. It is plausible that multi-project management may only be feasible with medium- to long-duration projects. In the sample of this study, one third of PMOs reported have projects with an average duration of less than nine months. Program and portfolio management may have decision cycles that are longer than the life cycles of some of these projects, making multi-project management less practicable.

Multi-project management is also more common among PMOs doing projects for several customers. It is plausible that when all the projects are for a single customer, the customer organization manages selection and prioritization, and gives mandates to execute projects to the PMO. This would explain why PMOs doing projects for a single customer are less likely to be involved in multi-project functions. However, the contribution of this variable is weak.

In addition, PMOs involved in this group of functions are better perceived on average than those filling other functions, as can be seen in the last line of Table 3.9, showing the relationship with perceived legitimacy. However, the correlation is weak (0.181). A PMO filling multi-project functions and having the characteristics discussed here is, therefore, a type of PMO for which characteristics can be clearly identified.

3.5.5 PMOs That Perform Specialized Tasks for Project Managers

The regression models for the next four groups of functions are less powerful than the two previously discussed. However, the percent of variance explained in non-negligible. The function *execute specialized tasks for project managers* refers to services offered by PMOs to project managers and project teams (mean importance 3.05). In the survey instrument, this function was a single function, not a group of functions identified by factor analysis. As was observed in Table 3.9, many of the variables in the regression analysis show significant associations with the importance of this function. The regression analysis has identified a model based on eight variables, as shown in Table 3.13. The model explains 17.4% of the variance in the importance of this function. With eight variables explaining 17.4% of the variance, the weighting of several of the variables is quite small. A good model for a type of PMO would have the opposite characteristics: it would have few variables each with a significant weighting that together explain a large portion of the variance. PMOs filling this function therefore do not constitute a type with clearly identified and distinctive characteristics.

Table 3.13. Variables related to filling specialized tasks

	Variable	Weighting
Organizational context	Number of projects in organization (negative)	-0.24
	Organizational PM maturity	0.10
	External project customers	0.09
	Non-matrixed project personnel	0.09
Project scope	Project duration	0.12
PMO characteristics	Size of PMO staff	0.17
	Decision-making authority	0.10
	Percent of projects within mandate	0.09

It is worth noting, however, that PMOs filling this function operate in contexts in which there are fewer projects being executed simultaneously. When there are fewer projects to serve, the PMO is in a better position to offer specialized services. In addition, filling this role requires that the PMO acquire and maintain specialized resources that are not part of project teams. This is reflected in the larger staff found in PMOs filling this function. The size of the PMO is measured by the number of staff other than project managers. The project duration is a way of assessing the scope of a project. It makes sense that larger projects are more likely to have the PMO execute specialized tasks for the project managers.

3.5.6 PMOs Involved in Strategic Management Functions

The strategic management group of functions includes involvement in strategic planning activities and having close ties with upper management (mean importance 3.06). In the importance of this group of functions, 16.1% of the variance can be explained by the five variables shown in Table 3.14.

Table 3.14. Variables related to strategic management

	Variable	Weightings
Organizational context	Public sector	0.15
	Multiple project customer	0.14
PMO characteristics	Decision-making authority	0.29
	Central location within organization	0.13
	Size of PMO staff	0.11

The PMO's decision-making authority is the most important variable in this regression model. Activities undertaken within this group of functions deal directly with upper management and it is not surprising that those PMOs that deal directly with upper management have a high level of decision-making authority. Authority is needed to make decisions related to strategic planning or to benefits management.

Not surprisingly, more centrally located PMOs have a tendency to be more active in strategic management. Proximity to upper management and having a higher-level view of the whole organization are necessary to fill strategic management functions.

Having projects with only one customer does not favor PMO involvement in this group of functions. If all the projects are for one customer, the customer often manages strategic planning without any PMO involvement. Conversely, when projects have multiple customers, the PMO is more likely to have an important role in strategic management.

The importance of this group of functions is also related to the size of the PMO staff. Involvement in strategic planning requires qualified personnel. As most PMOs have very few members of staff in addition to their project managers, it is not surprising that those PMOs involved in this group of functions would have more staff.

This group of functions is more important in public organizations. As was shown in Table 3.9, the association with this variable is not particularly strong but is present nonetheless. This result is somewhat surprising but indicates that PMOs in public organizations are more often closer to the strategic planning activities of upper management.

3.5.7 PMOs That Manage Client Interface

The function *client interface management* refers to the role of the PMO to assume responsibility for the relationship with the clients of projects (mean importance 2.84). This is a single function in the survey instrument, which is important for 45% of PMOs. The regression model comprised of the five variables shown in Table 3.15 explains 16.1% of the variance in the importance of this function.

Table 3.15. Variables related to client interface management

	Variables	Weightings
Organizational context	Number of projects in organization (negative)	-0.15
	Non-matrixed project personnel	0.13
PMO characteristics	Decision-making authority	0.22
	Percent of projects within mandate	0.10
	Size of PMO staff	0.10

With five variables explaining 15.5% of variance, several of the variables have rather small weightings. This group of variables is not likely to form a type with distinctive characteristics. However, some of the characteristics of PMOs filling this function are noteworthy.

The decision-making authority is once again the most heavily weighted variable in the model. The case studies showed that the management of the customer interface is an issue and a source of tension in several organizations. It is an issue related to power and organizational status. Involvement in this interface requires status and, at the same time, is a source of influence. This is captured by the heavy weighting of the decision-making authority, which is a measure of the PMO's power within the organization.

As can be observed in Table 3.9, there is a negative correlation between the importance of this function and both the size of the organization and the number of projects within the PMO's organizational context. As would be expected, these two variables are correlated (Pearson coefficient 0.280). Because the two are correlated, only one is found in the regression model, the number of projects with the PMO's mandate. Smaller organizations would presumably have fewer projects and the management of customer interfaces would have more of a tendency to be centralized in a PMO. This is captured by the negative association between the importance of this function and the number of projects in the PMO's organizational context.

3.5.8 PMOs Involved in Organizational Learning

Organizational learning functions (mean importance 3.00) are an important topic in the management literature (Huemann & Anbari, 2007; Nonaka & Ahmed, 2003; Williams, 2007). The five variables shown in Table 3.16 can explain 15.0% of the variance in the importance of this group of functions.

With five variables explaining 15.0% of the variance, several of the variables have rather small weightings. This group of variables is not likely to form a type with distinctive characteristics. However, some of the characteristics of PMOs filling this function are noteworthy.

Table 3.16. Variables related to organizational learning

	Variables	Weightings
Organizational context	Organizational PM maturity	0.19
	Non-matrixed project personnel	0.16
	Multiple project customers	0.10
Project scope	Project size	0.11
PMO characteristics	Decision-making authority	0.15

The organizational project management maturity and organizational learning are associated. Improving the level of maturity requires systematic learning from past experiences and implementation of these lessons learned. Williams (2007) showed that a formal process for supporting organizational learning has a positive effect only in the organization's level of project management maturity. Decision-making authority is critical for the implementation of organizational learning. Otherwise, the good intentions often do not translate into effective implementation. Examples can easily be found of lessons learned that are not documented at the end of a project when the project team is dismantled and the project manager is already on a new project. It takes a high level of authority to get people to document and share what has been learned on a project. Huemann and Anbari (2007) describing the project auditing process, suggested that this authority should be exercised to encourage a cooperative culture of communication, not to act ruthlessly.

The functions of organizational learning have naturally more impact when projects deal with multiple customers. The need for organizational memory and transfer of knowledge are less critical when dealing with a single customer.

Project scope, measured by the number of people working on projects, is associated with a greater emphasis on organizational learning. Post-project reviews, which are an important vehicle for learning, are more easily justified on larger projects. Transferability and reusability of knowledge are more critical on these types of projects as well. Formally organized organizational learning activities are less prevalent on small projects.

Organizational learning takes place in particular organizational contexts. The level of project management maturity is an element of this context. This is correlated with the supportiveness of the organizational culture for project management. In situations where project personnel is not matrixed but is located in the same organizational unit as the PMO, the manager of the unit has the incentive and authority to support organizational learning activities and the implementation of their results. It would seem that this incentive is stronger when all the projects are not for a single customer. In this situation, the customer organization may have the incentive.

The functions grouped together under organizational learning are important for less than half of the PMOs in the sample. This makes this function more specific to certain PMOs than other more popular functions. They, therefore, are a better basis for characterizing PMOs. However, with only 15% of the variance explained by five variables, this group of characteristics does not constitute a distinctive type of PMO.

3.5.9 Functions That Are Poor Bases for Types of PMOs

The last two groups of functions examined in this section are also the most commonly observed among PMOs. Monitoring and controlling project performance is the most important function assumed by PMOs (mean importance 3.82 on a scale of 1 to 5), while development of project management competencies and methodologies is the second most important (mean importance 3.54). As was shown in Table 2.4, the function to report project status to upper management was important for 83% of PMOs. This function is the only one that is performed by all the 12 PMOs presented in the case studies in Chapter 4. The function to develop and implement a standard methodology was important for 76% of PMOs. Because the majority of PMOs fill these groups of functions, it is unlikely that the presence of these functions could be used as the basis for discriminating among types of PMOs. As would be expected, the regression models for these two groups of functions provide the weakest explanatory power.

Monitoring and controlling project performance is the most important function assumed by PMOs. The results from the multiple regression analysis show that the model has rather weak explanatory power, explaining only 9.7% of the variance in the importance of this group of functions, with four independent variables, as shown in Table 3.17.

Table 3.17. Variables related to monitoring and controlling project performance

	Variables	Weightings
Organizational characteristics	Non-matrixed project personnel	0.11
	Multiple project customers	0.10
	Organizational PM maturity	0.10
PMO characteristics	Percent of projects within mandate	0.22

The absence of an association with the PMO's decision-making authority is particularly noteworthy. It is generally recognized that controlling project performance leads to corrective actions, but bringing those actions into play requires decision-making authority. The results from one of the case studies can shed some light on this apparent paradox. In this organization, the PMO had little or no decision-making authority but had the mandate to report on project status to upper management. Because other more powerful parts of the organization had effective control of the projects, the PMO's role was reduced to monitoring and reporting status but explicitly excluded even suggesting any corrective action. Thus for some PMOs, monitoring project status is divorced from control of the projects. The absence of a strong association between monitoring and control functions and the decision-making authority of the PMOs indicates that PMOs with the mandate to monitor projects may or may not have control over projects. As is shown in Table 2.4, reporting project status to upper management is an important part of the mandate of most PMOs (83%), but it seems that a significant number of PMOs are doing a data-gathering exercise divorced from effective project control, while other PMOs are exercising effective control of projects. Or in other words, most PMOs monitor project status, but some have a role in project control and some do not.

The variable having the most explanatory power in this model is *the percentage of projects within the PMO's mandate.* Monitoring and reporting project status makes more sense when the PMO is involved in a large percentage of projects. For the reasons previously discussed, the importance of this group of functions is not worth pursuing as a basis for typifying PMOs.

Development of project management competencies and methodologies is a group of functions traditionally associated with PMOs. It is the second most important group of functions (means importance 3.54). As shown in Table 3.9, there are few variables that are associated with the importance of this function in PMOs. The absence of an association with decision-making authority is again noteworthy. The development of standardized methodologies is important for most PMOs (76%). However, as shown in Figure 2.14, some PMOs with little authority are in more of a consultant role, offering methodology, tools, training, and so forth as services from which project managers can choose depending on their particular needs or tastes. On the other hand, some PMOs have the authority to implement mandatory methods and training. Although this group of functions is important for most PMOs, there are marked differences in how it is being implemented.

The regression analysis retained two variables, as shown in Table 3.18, in the model that explain only 6.7% of the variance in the importance of this group of functions among PMOs. It is interesting to note that centrally located PMOs more often have the mandate to standardize methodology and competences over multiple units of the whole organization. These PMOs are thus providing a common language and approach for managing projects across the organization. For the reasons previously discussed, the regression analysis did not provide an explanation for the presence or absence of this group of functions in a PMO mandate and thus does not provide a good basis for a typology.

Table 3.18. Variables related to development of project management competencies and methodologies

	Variables	Weightings
Organizational characteristics	Multiple project customers	0.22
PMO characteristics	Central location within the organization	0.14

3.5.10 Functions as Bases of Types of PMOs

The regression analyses have identified two potential types of PMOs, those filling HR functions for project managers and those filling multi-project management functions. They have also identified functions that are very poor bases for discriminating among PMOs because most PMOs fill these functions; these are functions of monitoring project performance and developing project management competencies and standards. PMOs filling the remaining four groups of functions possess some characteristics more often than a random distribution would predict. Although these observations are enlightening, they do not constitute viable bases for the identification of types of PMOs.

3.6 A Synthesis of the Analysis to Form a Model of Types of PMOs

3.6.1 An Augmented Cluster of Variables Forms a Model of a PMO

Steps 1 and 2 of the analysis identified five interrelated variables, two describing the organizational context and three describing structural characteristics of PMOs forming the cluster presented in Figure 3.4. Step 3 has added one variable, the total number of important functions, to this group. The analysis of the variables associated with the PMO's functions revealed that the total number of functions that are important for a PMO is associated with all the variables in the cluster except the percentage of project managers in the PMO. The total number of important functions is a characteristic of the PMO, bringing the number of PMO characteristics to four. Only relationship with a correlation coefficient superior to 0.20 and p=0.0000 are reported here. The relationships among the variables are as follows:

- The total number of important functions is related to all of the other variables except the percentage of project managers in the PMO
- Project management maturity is related to all four of the characteristics of PMOs
- Supportiveness of organizational culture is related to the decision-making authority of the PMO and the total number of important functions
- Supportiveness and project management maturity are related to each other

The cluster of variables presented in Figure 3.4, augmented with one additional variable, is represented in Figure 3.5. This cluster can form a model of a PMO, because the characteristics are interrelated and largely independent of other characteristics of both the PMO and the organizational context. The model can also form a typology with two types, those with this group of characteristics and those with the opposite characteristics.

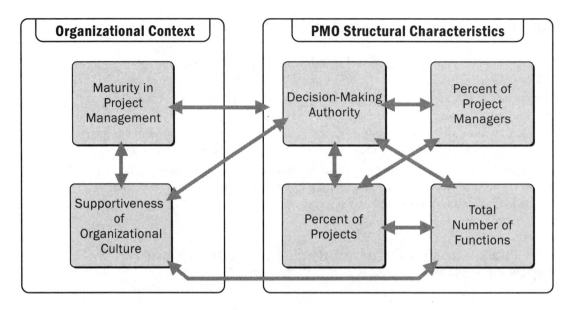

Figure 3.5. The augmented cluster of organizational contextual variables and PMO characteristics

3.6.2 Pursuing the Typology Further

As almost all of these variables are associated with one another, any subset might form the basis for typifying PMOs. However, variables with bipolar or u-shaped distributions are better candidates for dividing the population into distinct groups. The percentages of projects and of project managers are two such variables. Most organizations are choosing to put either a very large or a very small percentage of their projects and/or project managers in their PMOs. The distributions have been presented in Figures 2.13 and 2.14. There is a strong statistical association between the two variables (Pearson coefficient 0.426) but the relation is not simple. The relationship between the percentage of projects and the percentage of project managers is presented in Table 3.19. In this table, the middle values for each variable have been excluded. Doing so has removed 25% of the sample, but has the potential of creating very distinctive groups. Each of the cells in the table has been identified with a label: types 1, 2, 3, and 4. The percentages of the sample of each type are indicated. A total of 75% of PMOs fall into one of the four types. This is a powerful starting point for a typology.

Table 3.19 illustrates both the nature of the relationship between these two important design variables and the proportions in which organizations are making each of the four combinations of choices (χ^2 = 96.043, p=0.000). The Kendall's Tau-b test indicates a strong positive relationship (0.503, t=11.496, p=0.000). As can be seen on the right half of Table 3.19, organizations that choose to place all or most of their project managers within the PMO are also likely to choose to put all or most of the organization's projects within the mandate of the PMO. This association is quite intuitive; if all the project managers are within the PMO, then one would expect to find all of the organization's projects within the mandate of

Table 3.19. Four types based on the percent of project managers and the percent of projects within the PMO's mandate

		Percent of project managers within PMO	
		Less than 25%	More than 75%
Percent of projects within mandate	Less than 40%	Type 1 26%	Type 2 5%
	More than 60%	Type 3 14%	Type 4 30%

the PMO. Surprisingly, a small number of organizations are choosing to place most of their project managers but only a small portion of their projects within the PMO's mandate. These may be PMOs that allocate their project managers to manage projects that are under the responsibility of other organizational entities. PMOs in this situation would be playing the role of a "body shop," lending out their project managers to other parts of the organization.

As can be seen on the left half of Table 3.19, organizations that choose to put few or no project managers within their PMO are choosing between placing many and placing few projects within the mandate of the PMO, with more organizations choosing the latter of these options. The choice to put a few project managers with their projects in a PMO is easily understandable; this is a PMO with a specialized mandate limited to a specific set of projects. These may be one or more programs. These may be projects of the same type: for example, projects in one particular market or projects using a particular technology. They may also be the large or strategically important projects.

The choice to put a few project managers and most, if not all, the organizations' projects in the PMO was observed in one of the case study organizations. In this case, large strategic projects and their project managers were placed in the PMO, but the PMO also had a portfolio management function to monitor and report on all the organization's projects, including those managed elsewhere in the organization.

The types are based on the percent of projects and the percent of project managers. Because the percent of projects is associated with all the other variables under consideration here, while the percent of project managers is associated with all the other variables except the supportiveness of the organizational culture and the percentage of project managers within the PMO, it is reasonable to expect that differences might exist between the four types on several of these other variables. Upon further examination, a clear pattern became apparent; type 1 has the lowest score and type 4 has the highest score, while types 2 and 3 have scores between those for types 1 and 4. This pattern holds for all the other variables in the model presented in Figure 3.5, as well as the organizational context variables co-location or non-matrix relationship with project personnel. The scores are shown in Figure 3.6.

Typologies are often used to discriminate between types that are of equal value. For example, neither the introvert nor the extravert personality type is intrinsically superior. However, one may be better adapted to some specific situations. The typology formed by the model and its opposite are quite different because two of the organizational contextual variables (organizational project management maturity and supportiveness of the organizational culture) and three of the PMO characteristic are related to the performance construct.

The scores for all the variables except the number of important functions are shown with the scale on the left. These were from Likert scales from scores between 1 and 5. The scale on the right shows how many of the 27 functions are important within the mandate of each PMO. Types 1 and 4 are the extremes for both percent of projects and project managers and have been placed at either end of the scale. The scores for types 2 and 3 have been grouped for ease of presentation. The differences between types 1 and 4 are statistically significant for all variables shown in Figure 3.6.

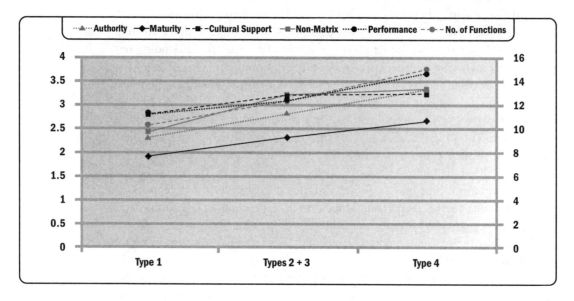

Figure 3.6. Differences among the types of PMOs

The pattern is clear, simple and statistically significant. However, types 2 and 3 are quite different PMOs. Grouping them has facilitated the presentation, but they must be separated if they are to be considered as viable types of PMOs in their own rights. A Mann-Whitney non-parametric pair-wise test was performed on the group of four types. The results are shown in Table 3.20. All significant relations show a progression from type 1 through type 4 except one. There is a decrease in the decision-making authority of the PMO when going from type 2 to type 3. The relationship is not particularly strong ($p < 0.033$). This has been indicated by putting the statistic in parentheses in Table 3.20.

As previously stated and as can be seen from column 3, all the differences between types 1 and 4 are significant. The scores for type 3 were between those for types 1 and 4 on all variables. As can be seen from the first two columns of Table 3.20, the score for type 3 is significantly greater than that for type 1 for all variables but the difference on legitimacy is less significant. The scores for type 3 are all less than for type 4 but the differences are statistically significant in only two cases.

Table 3.20. Level of significance of pair-wise comparisons among the four types of PMOs (numbers in the cells represent the level of significance of the associations)

Column number	1	2	3	4	5	6
	Types 1 & 3	Types 3 & 4	Types 1 & 4	Types 1 & 2	Types 2 & 3	Types 2 & 4
Authority	0.040	0.000	0.000	0.000	(0.033)	ns
Maturity	0.013	0.019	0.000	ns	ns	ns
Cultural support	0.022	ns	0.001	0.046	ns	ns
Non-matrixed project personnel	0.000	ns	0.000	0.086	ns	ns
Performance	0.004	ns	0.000	ns	0.001	0.000
Legitimacy	0.073	ns	0.002	ns	ns	ns
Number of functions	0.002	ns	0.000	ns	ns	0.030

The small sample size for type 2 (n=27) explains why few of the comparisons involving type 2 are statistically significant. The scores for type 2 were between those of types 1 and 4 on all variables. This forms a consistent pattern. However, the scores for types 2 and 3 do not vary consistently, on some variables type 2 scores higher and on others type 3 scores higher. It would be dangerous to draw any conclusion on the relative position of types 2 and 3 except possibly for the superior average performance of type 3. However, this difference is not particularly strong.

The pattern found among these four types of PMOs shows a set of mutually reinforcing characteristics found in the general population of PMOs. The four types are quite distinct both in conceptual as well as practical terms. Together they represent 75% of the total population of PMOs found in the sample. The fact that there is a relationship between the types and the performance of PMOs makes the typology more powerful.

3.6.3   Use and Interpretation of the Typology

Thy typology contains variables describing both the organizational context and the characteristics of the PMO. The organizational context is much less amenable to rapid change than the PMO. The variables on the organizational side of the model can only be changed very slowly and/or with significant effort. The organizational variables in the model can have two practical uses. First, the level of project management maturity and the supportiveness of the organizational culture are related to the performance of the PMOs and as such are predictors of the performance of PMOs in these contexts, or inversely, are predictors of difficulties with the performance of PMOs in contexts that do not have these characteristics. Second, organizations that have these characteristics tend to have PMOs with greater authority, higher percentages of both projects and project managers within their structures and performing a great number of functions. They can thus be predictors of the types of PMOs likely to be found in these contexts. Inversely, organizations with the opposite characteristics tend to have PMOs with the opposite characteristics.

The characteristics of the PMO in the model are, however, quite readily amenable to managerial control. They, therefore, represent more readily available design choices. As the decision-making authority of the PMO, the portion of projects in the mandate and the total number of important functions are related to the performance of PMOs, independent of the organizational context, then managers might consider whether their PMO should be designed to incorporate these design choices. However, considerable caution must be exercised, because the model is based on relations that may be statistically significant within a large sample such as this, but organizational reality is varied, complex, and multi-facetted. Statistical relationships can only provide guidance based on general trends in the population. Management needs to exercise considerable judgment when designing a PMO to fit the specific organizational context and the business objectives of the organization.

3.7 The Performance of PMOs

3.7.1 Explanations of PMO Performance Based on the Organizational Context and the Characteristics of PMOs

Two measures of the perceived performance of PMOs were introduced in Section 2.6: the performance construct and the legitimacy of the PMO. Throughout Chapter 3, the relationships between the two measures of PMO performance and the four classes of variables presented in Table 3.1 have been explored. Table 3.21 presents a summary of the relationships with PMO performance. All relationships with p=0.000 are reported in this table.

The examination of Table 3.21 reveals that the number and the strength of the correlations with the performance construct are greater than the correlations with legitimacy. The examination also reveals that the strongest correlations with performance are with the importance of the functions and the weakest are with the structural characteristics of the PMO. In addition, a large number of variables describing the organizational context and the structural characteristics of the PMO were included in the survey, but only a very small number of these variables were correlated with performance.

To further explore the relationship between these variables and the performance of the PMO, four regression analyses were performed using the measures of performance as the dependent variables Two regressions were done for

Table 3.21. Correlations with performance

Variables	Correlation with the performance construct	Correlation with legitimacy
Organizational context		
Project management maturity	0.310	0.202
Supportiveness of the organizational culture	0.436	0.269
PMO structural characteristics		
Percentage of projects within mandate	0.293	
Decision-making authority	0.287	0.187
PMO functions		
Total number of functions	0.516	
Organizational learning	0.458	
Development of PM competencies and methodologies	0.438	
Executing specialized tasks for project managers	0.440	
Monitoring and controlling project performance	0.399	
Multi-project management	0.363	0.181
Client interface management	0.333	
Strategic management	0.326	
HRM for project managers	0.284	

each measure of performance, one with all eight functions and one with the total number of important functions but no specific functions. The rationale is that either specific functions or the total number may explain the performance of the PMO. The organizational contextual variables, project scope and the structural characteristics of the PMO were included among the independent variables using the backward selection method with exit probability >0.1. The supportiveness of the organizational culture was excluded from the analysis because of the small sample size for this question. The maximum Variance Inflation Factor indicates that there are no problems of multicollinearity in the four regressions models. All four regressions are significant at a level of p=0.0000. The results of the four regressions are presented in Table 3.22.

The regressions with the performance construct as the dependent variables on the left are multiple regressions. The adjusted R squared indicates the percentage of the variance explained. The Betas and the probabilities indicate the significance of each variable in the explanation of performance. All of the relations are positive.

The regressions with legitimacy as the dependent variables are logistic regressions, a method used when the dependent variable is dichotomous (yes/no). The pseudo R squared gives the percentage of variance explained. With logistic regressions the Wald statistic replaces the beta of the multiple regressions. Where the associations with performance are negative, the Wald statistic is presented in brackets.

The most powerful model explains 39.2% of the performance construct. When the eight functions are replaced by the total number of important functions, the model remains powerful, explaining 30.3% of the performance construct. In this second model, the total number of important functions (beta = 0.444, p=0.0000) provides by far the largest portion of the explanation of performance. In the model with all eight functions, performance is also explained primarily by the functions. One should not conclude that the four functions in the model are necessarily those that provide the best explanation of performance. Regression models remove variables that are correlated and there are correlations among the functions. Table 3.20 provides a better indication of which functions are correlated the most with performance. The conclusion is that filling multiple important functions is the best predictor of performance.

Project management maturity is the only organizational contextual variable in the models. With p=0.0000, its contribution is significant. Note that the supportiveness of the organizational culture, which is correlated with maturity, was excluded from the regression analyses. One structural characteristic of PMOs provides a small contribution to the explanation of performance, the percentage of projects in the PMO's mandate. And in the case of the first model, the level of decision-making authority provides a very small contribution. The models indicate that having multiple important functions is the best predictor of performance, but does not indicate which particular functions are important in the general population. The models also indicate that organizational project management maturity provides a significant contribution to PMO performance. The structural characteristics may be important in each specific case, but these characteristics provide a very weak contribution to performance when examining the general population. So what does this mean in terms of best practices?

- Fill multiple functions that are viewed as important in the specific organizational context.
- PMOs are likely to perform better in project management mature organizations.
- Chose the structural characteristics of the PMO to suit the specific organizational context. There is a weak indication that PMOs with a large percentage of the projects within their mandates and more decision-making authority perform slightly better on the average, but the relation is too weak to be considered a best practice.

Table 3.22. Multiple regressions with performance as dependent variables

	Performance Construct				Legitimacy			
	With 8 functions		With total		With 8 functions		With total	
	Beta	P	Beta	P	Wald	P	Wald	P
Organizational context								
Organization size					(3.560)	0.0590	(2.934)	0.0870
PM maturity	0.132	0.0000	0.164	0.0000	12.579	0.0000	10.563	0.0010
Number of projects					(10.372)	0.0010	(11.455)	0.0010
Non-matrixed project personnel					4.021	0.0450	3.397	0.0650
PMO characteristics								
Percentage of projects	0.175	0.0260						
Decision-making authority	0.064	0.0790	0.128	0.0030	3.105	0.0780	5.977	0.0140
Functions								
Monitor and control	0.123	0.0090						
Methods and competency	0.289	0.0000						
Multi-project management	0.085	0.0720			3.515	0.0610		
Specialized tasks	0.244	0.0000						
Total number of functions			0.444	0.0000				
N	432		435		388		395	
R^2 en % / pseudo R^2 en %	40.20		30.80		11.20		9.50	
Adjusted R^2 / Chi-squared	39.20		30.30		45.890		39.234	
F statistic / Degrees of freedom	37.961		60.211		6		5	
Variance Inflation Factor (max)	1.4830		1.091		1.4830		1.091	

As was expected given the weaker correlations shown in Table 3.21, the regression models provide a much more powerful explanation of the performance construct than of legitimacy. The regression models on legitimacy explain only 11.2% and 9.5% of legitimacy. The explanation of legitimacy is provided primarily by the organizational context. The most important contributions are from project management maturity, as was the case for the performance construct. PMOs are perceived as more legitimate in smaller organizations with fewer projects, variables that are correlated (coefficient 0.280, p=0.0000). PMOs are also perceived as more legitimate in organizations that have at least 80% of project personnel reporting to the same management as the PMO: in other words, resources that are not matrixed throughout the organization. However, the contribution is weak. The level of decision-making authority is the only structural characteristic of PMOs that contributes to legitimacy, and its contribution is weak. The importance of the PMO's functions contributes very little to legitimacy. Since the total variance explained is low and because several of the variables make only weak contributes to the explanation, the only conclusions that can be drawn from all the analyses of relations with legitimacy are that:

- Legitimacy remains largely unexplained by the analyses.
- PMOs in project management mature organizations are perceived as more legitimate.

Assuming that best practices regarding PMOs would first and foremost be based on the characteristics of PMOs, the evidence shown here does not identify an adequate basis for such best practices.

3.7.2 Performance Reconsidered

The performance construct presented in Section 2.6 is based on a Varimax factor analysis that identified a construct comprised of four of the eight variables, indicating the level of agreement with the following statements:

1. The PMO's mission is well understood by those who deal with the PMO.
2. The PMO works in close collaboration with other project participants.
3. Those who deal with the PMO recognize the PMO's expertise.
4. The PMO is perceived as having a significant impact on the performance of projects and programs.
5. The PMO's reporting level is too low in the organization.
6. The PMO is fully supported by upper management.
7. The PMO is relatively useless and costly.
8. The PMO is perceived as controlling too much.

Two of these statements, 4 and 7, are clearly measuring perceptions of the performance of PMOs. The other statements could easily be considered as factors having an impact on the performance of PMOs. The fourth statement, "the impact on the performance of projects and programs," has been used elsewhere as a measure of PMO performance (Kendall & Rollins, 2003). In the present section, this variable is exploited as a measure of PMO performance, and statements 1, 2, 3, 5, 6, and 8 are considered as factors potentially contributing to the explanation of PMO performance. They are referred to as the "PMO's embeddedness in the organization." The advantage of doing so is to better exploit the information contained in these statements. The disadvantage is that instead of being measured by a construct with a high Cronbach Alpha, performance is measured by one question on a Likert scale.

Many analyses were done using both the performance construct and the impact on the performance of projects and programs. These two measures of performance are highly correlated (Person coefficient 0.832, p=0.0000). The associations between these two measures of performance on the one hand and other variables on the other hand are remarkably similar. Table 3.23 presents the variables that are correlated with these two measures of performance at a level of p=0.0000. The four statements describing the PMO's embeddedness in the organization that are correlated with the impact on the performance of projects and programs are presented in Table 3.23.

An examination of Table 3.23 shows that the performance construct and the impact on the performance of projects and programs are correlated with the same variables and at similar levels. It also reveals that the variables describing the PMO's embeddedness in the organization are more strongly correlated with performance than the other variables and may provide a better explanation of PMO performance. In order to explore the explanations for PMO performance, several multiple regressions were done using the backward selection method with exit probability >0.1. The maximum Variance Inflation Factors for all of the regression models indicate that there is no problem of multicollinearity. All of the models are significant at the level of p=0.0000. Table 3.24 presents the results of the regression with impact on the performance of projects and programs as the dependent variable and the variables describing the embeddedness of the PMO in the organization as the independent variables.

An examination of Table 3.24 shows that with 47.9% of the variance in PMO performance explained, this regression model is more powerful than those previously presented. The model retains three of the four variables describing the embeddedness of the PMO in the organization. The fourth variable has been excluded because it is correlated with the others, not because it is unrelated to performance as shown in Table 3.23. For the purpose of comparison, the regression presented in the left side of Table 3.22 has been redone substituting the impact on the performance of projects and programs as the dependent variable instead of the performance construct. The results are presented in Table 3.25.

Table 3.23. Correlations with two alternative measures of performance

Variables	Correlation with the performance construct	Correlation with the impact on the performance of projects and programs
Organizational context		
Project management maturity	0.310	0.260
Supportiveness of the organizational culture	0.436	0.303
PMO's embeddedness in the organization		
PMO's mission well understood		0.514
Collaboration with other project participants		0.623
Recognition of the PMO's expertise		0.606
Support by upper management		0.448
PMO structural characteristics		
Percentage of projects within mandate	0.293	0.246
Decision-making authority	0.287	0.293
PMO functions		
Total number of functions	0.516	0.475
Organizational learning	0.458	0.404
Development of PM competencies and methodologies	0.438	0.312
Executing specialized tasks for project managers	0.440	0.442
Monitoring and controlling project performance	0.399	0.312
Multi-project management	0.363	0.418
Client interface management	0.333	0.383
Strategic management	0.326	0.330
HRM for project managers	0.284	0.327

Table 3.24. PMO performance explained by the PMO's embeddedness in the organization

	Beta	P
Collaboration with other project participants	0.364	0.0000
Recognition of the PMO's expertise	0.334	0.0000
Support by upper management	0.151	0.0000
R^2 en %	48.30	
Adjusted R^2 en %	47.90	
F statistic	125.914	
Variance Inflation Factor (max)	1.531	
N	413	

Table 3.25. Multiple regressions with the impact on the performance of projects and programs as the dependent variable

	With 8 functions		With total	
	Beta	P	Beta	P
Organizational context				
PM maturity	0.143	0.0010	0.119	0.0120
Single project customer	0.079	0.0660	0.092	0.0360
PMO characteristics				
Percentage of projects	0.120	0.0060	0.127	0.0050
Decision-making authority			0.119	0.0140
Functions				
Methods and competency	0.181	0.0000		
Multi-project management	0.2.13	0.0000		
Total number of functions			0.383	0.0000
N	406		411	
R^2 en %	35.80		28.90	
Adjusted R^2	34.60		27.80	
F statistic	29.868		25.916	
Variance Inflation Factor (max)	1.4620		1.246	

The regressions with the impact on the performance of projects and programs as the dependent variable are remarkably similar to those with the performance construct as the dependent variable, but the percentage of variance explained is slightly lower. The interpretation of this regression is very similar to that provided for the regression on the performance construct and is not repeated here. These results confirm that the PMO's embeddedness in the organization provides a better explanation of the PMO's performance than all the other variables combined. Final regressions were performed with the impact on the performance of projects and programs as the dependent variable and the organizational contextual variables, project scope, the structural characteristics of the PMO, the importance of the PMO's functions, and the PMO's embeddedness in the organization were included among the independent variables. The supportiveness of the organizational culture was excluded from the analysis because of the small sample size for this question. The results are presented in Table 3.26.

Table 3.26. Multiple regressions with the impact on the performance of projects and programs as the dependent variable, including all independent variables

	With 8 functions		With total	
	Beta	P	Beta	P
Organizational context				
Organization size	-0.059	0.0920	-0.062	0.0840
Single project customer	0.078	0.0290	0.087	0.0170
Embeddedness of PMO in organization				
Collaboration with other project participants	0.243	0.0000	0.280	0.0000
Recognition of the PMO's expertise	0.323	0.0000	0.332	0.0000
Support by upper management	0.141	0.0010	0.098	0.0180
PMO characteristics				
Percentage of projects	0.078	0.0370	0.083	0.0290
Decision-making authority			0.118	0.0030
Age of the PMO	0.062	0.0790		
Functions				
Multi-project management	0.173	0.0000		
Specialized tasks	0.132	0.0010		
HRM for project managers	0.084	0.0330		
Specialized tasks	-0.089	0.0310		
Total number of functions			0.117	0.0070
N	406		409	
R^2 en %	56.40		52.40	
Adjusted R^2	55.10		51.40	
F statistic	42.986		51.550	
Variance Inflation Factor (max)	1.8390		1.693	

These regression models that include all the variables from the present study, including the embeddedness of the PMO in the organization, provide powerful explanations of the performance of PMOs. The regression model on the left that includes the eight functions explains 55.1% of the variance in PMO performance, while the one on the right that includes the total number of functions explains 52.4% of PMO performance. An examination of the betas and the probabilities reveals that in both models recognition of the PMO's expertise provides the strongest contributions to PMO performance. The qualitative data presented in Section 2.7 revealed that the competency of the PMO's personnel is critical. Having competent personnel whose expertise is recognized by the rest of the organization is a powerful determinant of the PMO's performance.

Two other measures of embeddedness, collaboration with other project participants and top management support, are also strong predictors of PMO performance. Performing important functions also contributes to PMO performance but to a lesser extent. The other variables make very small contributions to PMO performance. In terms of best practices, the following conclusions can be drawn from this analysis:

- The strongest contributors to PMO performance are:
  - Recognition of the PMO's expertise
  - Collaboration with other project participants
  - PMO's mission being well understood (included here because this is correlated with the two previous statements and with PMO performance)
- The following make smaller but significant contributions to PMO performance:
  - Upper management support
  - Filling multiple important functions
- The characteristics of the organizational context and the structural characteristics of the PMO contribute less to PMO performance.

3.8 Conclusion

PMOs are an important aspect of project management practice. Their design and management is complicated by the great variability found among PMOs in different organizations. Having a typology of PMOs can make the great variability much more manageable. However, the typology should be grounded in reality. The aim of this chapter has been to exploit a rich database of descriptions of PMOs, to identify patterns among PMOs, and to identify the bases of one or more typology of PMOs. Data on the organizational context, the characteristics of PMOs and the performance of PMOs were explored.

Identifying what works and what does not work can both contribute to understanding and guide practice. The analyses presented in this chapter have contributed to a better understanding of PMOs by first identifying that the following characteristics are a poor basis for discriminating among PMOs:

- Organizational contextual factors:
  - Geographic region
  - Industry
  - Organizational size
  - Public vs. private sector
- Structural characteristics of PMOs:
  - The entity's name
- Roles or functions filled by the PMO:
  - PMOs that monitor project performance
  - PMOs that develop project management competencies and methodologies

The analysis showed that the functions filled by PMOs are generally not associated with their specific structural characteristics or their organizational context.

The name given to the entity does not provide a reliable means of discriminating among PMOs in the general population. The fact that the analysis did not find an association between the name and other characteristics may be a methodological artifact. A large variety of names are given to this entity, but only two were used often enough to provide a sample size sufficiently large enough to be able to test for systematic differences. It is quite plausible that subtle differences exist among the entities that are captured, in part by their names, but that these differences cannot be tested for statistically. One should not conclude that the name does not have any meaning and is unimportant in a particular organizational context. Quite to the contrary, it can be important to choose a name that is appropriate to the specific history, culture, and politics of the organization and is a good label for describing how the PMO is set up, what it does, and how those that are setting it up would like it to be perceived.

Contingency theory has been prominent in the field of organizational analysis since the mid-1970s (Donaldson, 2001). The idea that organizations adapt to their context has become part of the common sense of studying and managing organizations. However, the general organizational contextual variables that are found in the contingency theory literature show little or no systematic variation with the characteristics of PMOs. The explanation of this apparent paradox may be quite simple; organizational contextual variables are quite stable, while PMOs are changing quite quickly. If one variable is changing quickly and the other is changing slowly or remaining stable, one would not expect to find any association between them.

Although general organizational characteristics drawn from the classic literature on organizational studies did not show a direct relationship with PMO characteristics, two project-specific organizational characteristics were shown to be good predictors of some of the important characteristics of PMOs and their perceived performance. In addition, these two characteristics are associated with one another. These organizational characteristics are:

- The organization's level of maturity in project management
- The supportiveness of the organizational culture

The structural characteristics of the PMOs form a loosely coupled network or system. Many characteristics are related to only a very small number of other characteristics and many of the associations are quite weak. Most pairs of characteristics are unrelated. However, a nucleus formed by the following four tightly interrelated characteristics was identified:

- Percentage of organization's projects within the mandate of the PMO
- Percentage of organization's project managers within the mandate of the PMO
- The PMO's level of authority
- The total number of functions filled by the PMO

The analyses have also shown that the two project-specific organizational characteristics and the four PMO characteristics form a close-knit group of variables. Further analysis showed that these six variables could be used to create a typology that allows the great variety of the population of PMOs to be reduced to four types, as follows:

- Type 1: A small percentage of the organization's projects and project managers
- Type 2: A small percentage of the organization's projects and a large percentage of its project managers
- Type 3: A large percentage of the organization's projects and a small percentage of its project managers
- Type 4: A large percentage of the organization's projects and a large percentage of its project managers

These types of PMOs were shown to vary systematically with the three project-specific organizational contextual variables, with two other characteristics of PMOs (the level of authority and the total number of functions filled), as well as with the perceived performance of the PMOs.

However, because of the extreme variability found among PMOs and because the results presented here are based on statistical associations that are far from being absolute, the statistical results can only provide guidance. They are not strong enough to form the basis for prescriptive statements on PMOs.

An examination of the factors that are associated with PMO performance revealed that:

- The strongest contributors to PMO performance are:
  - Recognition of the PMO's expertise
  - Collaboration with other project participants provides the strongest contributions to PMO performance
  - PMO's mission being well understood
- The following make smaller but significant contributions to PMO performance:
  - Upper management support
  - Filling multiple important functions

- The characteristics of the organizational context and the structural characteristics of the PMO contribute less to PMO performance.

These results bring the search for best practices based on the characteristics of PMOs into question.

There are limits to the study presented here. The data is comprised of 502 snapshots of PMOs. Information on the dynamics surrounding PMOs in their organizational contexts is largely missing. The case studies that form the second phase of this multi-phase multi-method research program confirmed that PMOs are very much influenced by the organizational dynamics in which they are embedded. These are presented in the following chapters.

CHAPTER FOUR: THE IN-DEPTH INVESTIGATION OF PMOs

4.1 Introduction

Chapters 2 and 3 showed the great variety of PMOs without being able to propose an adequate understanding of the phenomena. Taking these results as a starting point, this chapter proposes a different but innovative and promising approach to the study of PMOs, one based upon their position within the organization. The focus will be on their context and their evolution, instead of on their characteristics. This approach requires taking the richness of the internal and external context into account. It also recognizes the value of the history of the organization.

In this approach the PMO is considered as one particular feature of organizational project management. Organizational project management has been defined as a new sphere of management, where dynamic structures in the firm are articulated as means to implement corporate objectives through projects in order to maximize value (Aubry, Hobbs, & Thuillier, 2007). Centering on the organizational level offers the opportunity to renew research approaches by opening the door to organizational theory and getting away from traditional research, where project management is centered at the project level and treated in a positivist approach (Bredillet, 2004). Organizational project management refers to management decisions in complex environments, where multiple programs and portfolios are realized in parallel along with operational activities. Strategizing/structuring depict the dynamic relationship between strategy and structure (Pettigrew, 2003). These dynamic structures are seen as means to implement corporate objectives through projects. Organizational project management delivers value for the organization. The concept of value allows for multiple conceptualizations of project and organizational performance.

Looking at the PMO within its wider context of organizational project management leads to better understanding of the PMO phenomenon. Answering a *why* type of question in academic research calls for different methodological and empirical frameworks than when answering a *what* type of question. The latter is often based upon a variance model and its source of data is mostly from surveys. The former is based upon a process model, and data comes from qualitative approaches, such as observation, interviews, and the like. After delivering results from a quantitative approach in chapters 2 and 3, this chapter is based on in-depth investigations of PMOs in four organizations.

The rest of the chapter is organized in five sections. The first section presents a review of the literature on related concepts. The second section proposes a basic framework that will support the exploration of organizational project management using the PMO as the gateway into the organization. As suggested by Van de Ven in *Engaged Scholarship* (2007, p. 7), "The critical task is to adopt and use the models, theories, and research methods that are appropriate for the research problem and question being addressed." The framework is bold, as it draws from three complementary theoretical fields: innovation theory, organizational theory, and the PMO descriptive model presented in Chapter 1. The framework is built on the concepts of social innovation systems and coevolution drawn from the field of innovation management. These take into account the history and context of the PMO at both the organizational level and at the micro-level. The PMO as a concept rests on the structural characteristics and functions it is performing. The conceptualization of organizational performance and of the value of the PMO is drawn from the competing values model that allows for the coexistence of a plurality of perspectives for evaluating organizational performance. Together, these concepts open up new avenues for the study of organizational project management. This approach offers a new perspective contributing to the revitalization of the field of project management.

The third section presents the methodological framework. The global strategy is based upon both qualitative and quantitative data, but to a greater extent on the former. Selection of organizations responded to a research design that mixes similarities and divergences. This empirical work focuses on organizations that do projects for themselves rather than for external customers. These organizations have implemented PMOs as part of their strategy for managing projects and for dealing with the issues relative to organizational project management. The study of organizational project management is facilitated in these organizations because project management activities tend to be concentrated and more easily visible in organizations that have implemented PMOs. The discussion that follows and the theoretical model are relevant, however, in other contexts. In the fourth section, the PMOs in organizations are described synthetically. The fifth section bears specifically on the question of performance, based on the competing values framework (Cameron & Quinn, 1999).

4.2 Literature Review

The literature review is intended to provide an understanding of the founding fields on which the conceptual framework is based, and to identify its limitations. The PMO is the central notion of this book. For this reason the literature review on PMOs has been placed in the first chapter. Four other fields are discussed in the next sections: strategic alignment, program and portfolio management, project-based organization, and organizational performance.

4.2.1 Strategic Alignment: A Need That Becomes a Function

The issue of alignment is associated with the need to join together portfolios of disparate, proliferating projects into an efficient, coherent whole (Gareis, 2002). This need for strategic alignment becomes a function within the organization. Organizations must adapt their strategic processes to face changes in their environment and they must adjust themselves quickly (Pettigrew, 2003). Project management at the strategic level (including program and project portfolio) is considered a means to implement corporate strategy. The translation of strategy into programs and projects is recognized as a core process (Jamieson & Morris, 2004). However, these authors recognize that project strategic management is not sufficiently explored in the business and project literature. Other recent empirical research shows that not all organizations succeed in the linkage between projects and strategy (Dietrich & Lehtonen, 2004). A paradox seems to exist between the organizational desirability of linking strategy and projects, and the concrete actions that organizations take to achieve such linkage (Van den broecke, De Hertogh, & Vereecke, 2005).

A second facet of strategic alignment bears on the synergy created by the management of the relations between projects. In other words, the performance of the whole goes beyond the sum of the performance of the individual projects. The identification of benefits related to the management of these relations can be found in the specific literature related to the platform approach (Fernez-Walch & Triomphe, 2004; Nobeoka & Cusumano, 1997) and to programs and project portfolios (Kendall & Rollins, 2003; Thiry & Matthey, 2005; Van den broecke et al., 2005). Benefits management puts emphasis on the final steps of a strategy cycle. Alignment of the benefits from projects is difficult to actualize, as projects are temporary organizations that often end with the delivery of the product (Cooke-Davies, 2004). From the survey results, 28% of PMOs answered that benefits management is an important function. But this result doesn't confirm what they are actually doing. For the moment, benefits management may well be wishful thinking, since it has not yet been verified by solid empirical research.

A third facet focuses on preparation for the future and rarely appears in a specific way in the project management literature. The future is often envisioned from an operational rather than a strategic viewpoint, for example, in relation to the evolution toward project management maturity (Cooke-Davies, 2004) and the development of resource competencies in project management (Crawford, 2002). But interestingly, the results from the survey of 502 PMOs show that nearly half of the PMOs have indicated that the function of participating in the strategic planning process is important. Again, this doesn't tell us much about their level of involvement. Results from the case studies reveal that very few are directly involved in strategic planning processes.

The current literature provides models for the link between corporate strategy and projects. Some empirical results confirm the role of project management in facilitating the implementation of corporate strategy. However, the literature related to business and project management lacks empirical studies to describe in detail the processes of strategy translation from the corporate level down to the execution of the project. In summary, the current project management literature only partially covers the breadth of strategic alignment.

4.2.2 Program and Portfolio Management

It is not surprising to note some confusion in the definition of new concepts, as is the case in most of the existing studies of programs and project portfolios. The confusion in this literature stems from a semantic gap between the meanings given to the concepts of program and project portfolio (Van den broecke et al., 2005). The preceding section showed that in the project management literature, strategic alignment is generally considered to be a function within the organization. The confusion is related to the identification of processes responsible for this function, and whether they are program or portfolio processes. Consequently, their roles differ, depending on the definitions adopted by each author.

Authors who place the project portfolio as the major interface with corporate strategy propose a cascade from global strategy down to portfolios, from portfolios down to programs, and then from programs down to individual projects (Gareis, 2004; Jamieson & Morris, 2004). In this sense, programs are at the heart of the project portfolio. *The Standard for Portfolio Management*[4] adopts a hierarchical viewpoint on portfolio management, where the overall project portfolio of an organization is linked to the top level of the organization (PMI, 2006a). This standard recognizes that a change in the organization's strategy should lead to a change to its project portfolio. It does not, however, recognize emergent strategies nor portfolio change management processes between major redefinitions of strategy.

Other authors who present program management as the major process linking strategy and individual projects attribute a secondary role to project portfolio management, namely that of project selection and support (Pellegrinelli, 1997; Thiry, 2004). This approach confers a direct connection between strategy and program management. The standard for program management also confirms the strategic dimension of program management but puts less emphasis on a direct connection with the organizational strategy, adopting rather the program's strategic benefits and objectives (PMI, 2006a, 2006b).

Portfolio management refers also to an instrumental approach. Several methodologies have been proposed to balance a portfolio of projects (Cooper, Scott, & Kleinschmidt, 1997a, 1997b). In this portfolio management perspective, the project portfolio context contains an essential structural component that shows up through the categorization system of the project portfolio (Crawford et al., 2005).

The human side of program management has been recently explored, showing that the specificity of program management competencies. Being a competent

---

4   At the moment of writing this report, the new editions of program and portfolio standards were not yet available.

project manager does not suffice to be *ipso facto* a competent program manager (Partington et al., 2005). This HR trend in research also points out impacts of program and portfolio management on middle managers (Blomquist & Müller, 2006).

It is essential to link projects to organizational strategy, and it is clear from the literature that processes such as program and portfolio management are central to this issue. While studying a PMO as an entity participating in organizational project management, clarification of the semantic context of program and portfolio management is necessary. Confusion between these concepts prevents conceptual leadership from occurring and paving the way toward solid foundations. Program and portfolio management both have a role to play in strategizing. Program and portfolio standards published by PMI (2006 a, b) start to play this role of leadership in the definition of these concepts. However, it still is too early to confirm the mobilization of the project management community around the formalization given by PMI.

4.2.3 Project-based or Project-oriented Organization

The terms *project-oriented* or *project-based organization* and the more generic term of *managing by projects* can be applied to organizations whose strategic business objectives rely on results from projects or programs (Gareis, 2004). This approach goes beyond the classic view of project management structures that answer the question, "How should we manage this project within our organization?" (Hobbs & Ménard, 1993; Larson, 2004). The classic project organization literature proposes three possibilities: functional organization, matrix organization, and organization by project (Larson, 2004; Project Management Institute, 2004).

A contrario, the concept of project-oriented organization relates to a global structural approach for more effective project delivery. This question goes beyond the examination of the strict project structure and the position of a given project in the organization to address the structural problem from the point of view of the organization. This leads to research agendas that reflect different schools of thought. Among others, Turner and Keegan (1999) proposed looking at the versatile project-oriented firm as a dual set of functions, one of governance and one of operational control.

Dinsmore (1996) proposed a corporate view of project management, where the organization is seen as a portfolio of projects, and introduced the idea of managing organizations by projects. In more recent research, Lampel and Jha (2004) explored the relationship between projects and the corporate environment, using the construct of project orientation. Their initial findings concluded that this interface is a locus of tension. The lack of understanding of the causes and dynamics of tension between projects and organizations leads to friction and failure. This insight confirms the necessity to shed light on the global organization, where projects are realized in a dynamic environment often alongside operations.

The research and development (R&D) literature also provides a complementary discussion on project-based organizations for dealing with the development of complex products and services (Hobday, 2000). Case studies presented by Hobday concluded that "one size doesn't fit all." In certain circumstances functional or matrix structures deliver better results than those of project-based organizations, particularly in coordinating resources across projects and in organization-wide learning. Hobday (2000) proposed a new type, the project-led organization, to overcome the problems inherent to project-based organization.

The literature on project-based organization has two limitations. First, there is a tendency to focus strictly on the structural problem instead of seeing structure as part of a global organizational process. Second, apart from those adopting an economic perspective, many of the papers on the subject propose models that lack theoretical foundations.

The literature from innovation also describes new forms of organization that go beyond the hierarchical structure and take various names, such as networking (Powell, 1990), N-Form (Hedlund, 1994), molecular (Morabito, Sack, & Bhate, 1999), and cellular (Miles, Snow, Mathews, Miles, & Coleman, 1997). It recognizes that operations and projects coexist, thus adding to the complexity of their dynamics (Hagström, Sölvell, & Hedlund, 1999). It is essential to go back to a basic understanding of the nature of an organization and address the new issues related to strategic alignment, program, and portfolio management and project-oriented or project-based organizations. By doing so, new foundations will emerge.

4.2.4 Organizational Performance

Performance is nearly always the ultimate dependent variable in the literature on organizations in general, and on the subject of project management in particular. The problems are to establish both a clear definition as to what constitutes performance and a reliable relationship between performance and other variables at a comparable level of analysis. After more than half a century of history in the management of projects, its contribution to the performance is still not acknowledged outside the group of professionals who believe in project management. At the time of writing, a large international research project to answer the question, "What is the value of project management?" has recently been completed (Thomas & Mullaly, 2008).

Performance has its origin in the old French *parfournir* and is defined today as "something accomplished" (Merriam-Webster, 2007). The etymology brings us straight to the point: What indeed is accomplished by project management and how should we evaluate it?

Two conceptions of success are dominant in the project management literature: economic and pragmatic. In the first conception, researchers try to demonstrate the direct economic contribution of project management to the bottom line (Dai & Wells, 2004; Ibbs, Reginato, & Kwak, 2004). Interestingly, none of these researchers has been able to convincingly demonstrate the economic value of investment in project management. Results of the research by Ibbs et al. (2004) were not statistically significant (Thomas & Mullaly, 2008). The clear demonstration of the direct influence of project management on return on investment (ROI) is not easily accomplished, as discussed by Thomas and Mullaly (2008). In addition, the reduction of project management value exclusively to financial indicators underestimates major contributions that project management brings to organizational success: for example, innovation (Turner & Keegan, 2004), process (Winch, 2004), and people (Thamhain, 2004). Furthermore, the multifaceted concept of project success is acknowledged by several authors (Dietrich & Lehtonen, 2004; Shenhar, Dvir, Levy, & Maltz, 2001). The balanced scorecard falls under this economic conception. The balanced scorecard approach has been proposed to assess project management performance (Norrie & Walker, 2004; Stewart, 2001). It has the advantage over the traditional economic vision of project performance of encompassing four complementary perspectives. However, the foundation of this approach rests on ROI. It structures the creation of value hierarchically, with financial value at the top (Kaplan & Norton, 1996; Savoie & Morin, 2002).

The second conception of project performance found in the literature is pragmatic. It focuses on proposals aimed at indicating the way to succeed in the implementation and management of the PMO (Benko & McFarlan, 2003; Crawford, 2002; Kendall & Rollins, 2003). Titles sometimes foster hope for rapid economic results linked to the PMO: for example, *Advanced Project Portfolio Management and the PMO, Multiplying ROI at Warp Speed* (Kendall & Rollins, 2003). And yet it still seems difficult to demonstrate the value of the PMO.

Several authors have encompassed the problem of performance in an approach that seeks to identify success factors (Jugdev & Müller, 2005). Cooke-Davies (2001, 2004) examined the empirical evidence supporting the many best practices and success factors found in the literature. He concludes that most of the contributions have been based on the opinion of members of the project management community and that only a small number have been empirically validated. Based on the empirically validated data, Cooke-Davies (2004) proposed a set of 12 factors related to three distinct ways of looking at performance: project management success (time, cost, quality, etc.), project success (benefits), and corporate success (processes and decisions to translate strategy into programs and projects). It is noteworthy that the success factors are different at each level of analysis. Cooke-Davies (2004) argued that these three groups are intimately linked; corporate project and program practices create the context for individual project and program practices. Although the research on success factors has identified some conditions in organizational project management that are associated with performance at different levels of analysis, the understanding of performance and the *a priori* conditions that contribute to performance remains limited.

There is no consensus on the way to assess the value of performance in project management. The financial approach alone cannot give a correct measure of the value of project management for the organization. Project success is a vague approximation, and as such, a rather imperfect system for measuring results. New approaches are needed to extricate the field from what looks like a dead end. Organizations are multi-faceted, leading to a variety of evaluation criteria. The international research on the value of project management draws similar conclusions overall when reviewing the literature on the subject (Thomas & Mullaly, 2008). An alternative conceptualization is examined in Section 4.5.

From the review of the literature, it appears that not only specific shortcomings were identified in each of the five specific themes, but that there is a need to anchor the PMO within the organization and not isolate this entity as a stand-alone component. In this perspective, the PMO is one of the features associated with organizational project management. The study of the PMO when taken in a contextual approach should be analyzed as such. In addition, the few promising theoretical initiatives that can be found on the subject must be integrated into a more holistic view of the organization. The following is the conceptual framework build in order to overcome the shortcomings of the current state of the research on PMOs.

4.3 The Conceptual Framework

A theoretical framework that has the potential to embrace the complexity and richness of the subject is required. Three theoretical fields have been mobilized to contribute to the understanding of the PMO: social innovation system, the PMO descriptive model, and organizational performance. The resulting conceptual model is shown in Figure 4.1. This section covers two theoretical fields, the social innovation system and organizational performance. The PMO model has already been presented in Section 1.3.

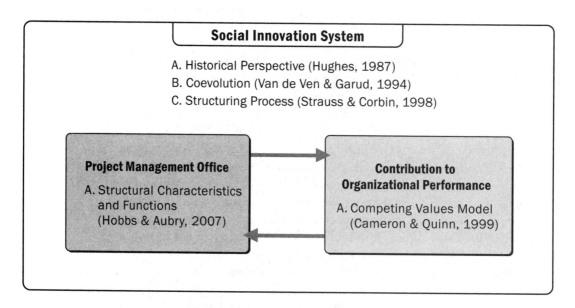

Figure 4.1. The conceptual framework

4.3.1 The Social Innovation System

Innovation plays an important role in the emergence of multi-project environments. Growth of a firm is associated with its capacity to constantly renew its product portfolio. At the same time, there is economic pressure to reduce the time to market. Both lead to a rise in the number of projects undertaken simultaneously within firms and consequently to the complexity of managing them (Fernez-Walch & Triomphe, 2004). Innovative forms of organizing are emerging (Pettigrew, 2003) and not surprisingly, quite a few concepts related to multi-project management have emerged within the project management literature: program and portfolio management (Pellegrinelli, 1997; Thiry, 2004), project-based or project-oriented organization (Gareis, 2004; Turner & Keegan, 2001), and project management office (Crawford, 2002).

For many years, innovation theorists have taken the social system dimension of innovation into consideration (Hughes, 1987). Organizations do not exist in a vacuum. They are part of a large number of complex interrelated systems, such as the social system, the economic system, and the like, in which history plays a dynamic role. The PMO is seen here as a constructed entity that is part of a social innovation system. Taking this approach provides a completely new vision of the PMO. Instead of having a picture frozen in time, the evolution of this entity, along with the evolution of its mother organization, is the focus. This study examines innovation systems from two complementary perspectives: the historical perspective and the coevolutionary perspective.

The historical context is taken into account at two levels of analysis: the organization and the PMO. The history of the organization provides information about its origin, its evolution in its specific economic sector, and the evolution of its organizational structure. The history of the PMO brings information on project management practices and internal PMO structures. Globally, history informs on how an organization has adapted itself to changes in the business environment. This historical perspective on PMOs has already been published (Aubry, Hobbs, & Thuillier, 2008).

Describing the PMO's history is not enough to bring a comprehensive understanding of why changes occur. The events that delimitate periods must be examined. Evolutionary theory helps understand the evolution of one entity, the PMO, while a coevolutionary perspective helps us understand the PMO's evolution within the social system of an organization (Van de Ven & Garud, 1994). The coevolutionary perspective highlights interconnections between events that happen at different levels in the organization. Events occur and coevolve over time to facilitate or to constrain the development and commercialization of an innovation that could be radical or incremental. In the PMO context, events are related to its legitimacy to make rules (methodology, standards, etc.) and having others follow them (rulemaking). Rulemaking can give rise to situations of tension between the PMO and other functional units, or between the PMO and the project and program managers. The issue is to determine who will impose the rules of the game.

Rule-following events confirm process standardization. Indeed, if rules are followed and accepted, they indicate a relative stability until a new event shatters them. This process continues over and over again with the alternation between initiation, expansion, and stabilization periods.

The transformation process is a notion borrowed from the two well-known researchers in social sciences, Strauss and Corbin (1998). The notion of process is interwoven with the grounded theory methodological approach. In short, the grounded theory is a way of letting concepts and categories emerge from the particular context being studied. The process is seen as having a greater capability to capture the complexity of a situation and to understand a phenomenon in relation to many other elements that would otherwise escape the attention of the researchers (Van de Ven, 2007). The notion of pattern is central to this grounded approach. The researcher looks for patterns that repeat themselves and tries to identify the driver of these patterns. The survey results presented in Chapter 2 show that PMOs change quite frequently. The process framework from Strauss and Corbin (1998) is used here to study the processes that transform the PMO. Chapter 5 bears specifically on this part of the conceptual framework.

In addition, the concept of a social system of innovation influences choices in the methodological strategy to more accurately take into account the history of the organization and the PMO. This strategy entails a longitudinal study of the evolution of dynamic structures as suggested by the definition of organizational project management (Aubry et al., 2007). The next section examines the second key concept, organizational performance.

4.3.2 Organizational Performance of the PMO

The question of performance is of great importance in the PMO professional literature. In a positivist approach, performance is a dependent variable resulting from the PMO structural choices (Kendall & Rollins, 2003). This is based on the assumption that one best PMO structure exists and it leads to best results that can be assessed with ROI. In a constructivist approach, the PMO and its organizational contribution are built up together during their evolution. From this perspective, the organizational contribution of the PMO is as much a concept describing the role played by the PMO in the organizational context as a dependent variable describing the effect of the PMO.

There is an assumption that structure has an effect on organizational performance. Galbraith (1995) suggested that structures should lead organizations to be more effective, and that effectiveness can be assessed by market performance indicators. The structure of organizations influences their organizational performance (Galbraith). For Galbraith, interest in the structure of organizations can be explained first of all by the economic situation. Organizations in developed nations, on the one hand, must integrate greater complexity to manage the new factors related to knowledge and, on the other hand, they must expand beyond their country so as to cover fixed costs coming from R&D, in addition to facing greater competition on their territory. This complexity is reflected in the structure of organizations.

The evaluation of the way in which an organization works is a question that has been addressed for quite some time. It could even be said that the main purpose of Weber, Taylor, and Barnard was to develop efficient organizational models (Boyne, 2003). Ultimately, nearly all organizational and management theories are concerned with efficiency, at least implicitly (Rainey, as cited in Boyne, 2003; Goodman and Pennings, as cited in Quinn & Rohrbaugh, 1983).

Structure must be regularly questioned so that the organization maintains or increases its organizational efficiency; the design of an organization is a dynamic process (Galbraith, 1995; Jelinek, 1993; Pettigrew, 2003). Different strategic choices lead to different organizations (Galbraith, 1995, Pettigrew, 2003). Galbraith interpreted the verb *organize* as an action verb (1995), recalling its etymology. The environment (physical, social, or human) is in constant motion, as are the economic stakes. The organizational process is a process that implies action and organizational evolution. In the same spirit, Pettigrew (2003) preferred to use *organizing* as an action in the dual expression of strategizing/structuring. This dynamic process has consequences for the study of organizational performance, which should be considered within this dynamic pattern.

What Is Organizational Performance?

The concept of organizational performance is not new. At the end of the 1950s and in the early 1960s, sustained efforts were made to understand the success of organizations. This literature developed significantly in the 1960s and 1970s, and after 1980 narrowed down to concepts like quality (Boyne, 2003). Several words are used almost as synonyms for organizational performance: for example, efficiency, output, productivity, effectiveness, health, success, accomplishment, and organizational excellence (Savoie & Morin, 2002). In this research the term *organizational performance* has been adopted, which is more appropriate in the context of organizational project management. Providing a clear definition of organizational performance is not an easy task. The conceptual clarification of organizational performance is approached here using two types of definitions: by its components and semantic.

First, a definition of the concept by the identification of its characteristics is explored. This type of definition is called a *definition of components*, where a term, here organizational performance, is given in reference to its constituent parts or its characteristics (Van de Ven, 2007). Organizational performance has been approached in the literature using different sets of characteristics or variables. A first difficulty with this type of definition is the uniformity of both the conceptual and the operational levels among the characteristics. (Cameron & Whetten, 1983; Quinn & Rohrbaugh, 1983; Van de Ven, 2007). There are other difficulties with this type of definition: it is inherently subjective (Cameron, 1981). It can be difficult, even impossible, to reconcile the multiplicity of points of view from different stakeholders. Preferences change over time in keeping with social values and the life cycle of the organization or of the unit. It can be difficult even for individuals to identify their own preferences for an organization. There exist simultaneously in the same organization a variety of contradictory preferences that this type of definition can't capture. This type of definition doesn't allow an exact definition of the concept of organizational performance.

The second approach to definition is based on the identification of limits/borders; this is a semantic definition. A semantic definition describes the meaning of a term by its similarities (positive semantic definition) or by its differences (negative semantic definition) with other terms (Van de Ven, 2007). Addressing the question, "What is organizational performance?" also comes back to trying to define the scope of the total construct by delimiting the components located inside its borders. Cameron (1981) discussed this question from two viewpoints: the theoretical border and the empirical border. Practically speaking, the theoretical border of organizational performance doesn't exist. No theory is completely satisfying and the research undertaken so far is made up of a collection of individual essays that lack integration (Cameron, 1981). It is difficult to grasp the construct when approaching it theoretically, and still today, there is no clear definition of theoretical border (Savoie & Morin, 2002). Cameron (1981) observed that few authors have tried instead to define an empirical border. Moreover, this inductive approach is appropriate when there is a high level of complexity, which is the case here (Patton, 2002). This being the case, each study has been done as in a "silo," each author observing in an isolated fashion a particular type of organization. Therefore, approaching a definition of organizational performance by the identification of a border has not determined convincingly what is inside the border; theoretical research is insufficient and empirical studies are varied and lack integration.

To overcome the problem of definition, Cameron (1981) suggested that organizational performance be defined as a subjective construct anchored in values and preferences of the stakeholders, the definition adopted in this research. This construct occupies a variable space according to the concepts that comprise it. This definition offers a great potential for adaptation to organizational situations and offers the possibility of acknowledging that there can exist a variety of evaluation models. This construct is coherent with the choice of the constructivist perspective, which properly recognizes the existence of several competing logics. What is at stake for researchers is not to find the sole model that integrates the others, but rather the model that best explains a given organizational situation in a given context.

The Competing Values Framework

Once organizational performance has been defined as a construct, the next question is how it should be operationalized. Several models have been developed over the years. Cameron (1986) proposed a classification of models by grouping them according to the meaning given to organizational performance. Table 4.1 presents eight models, each of which covers a different part of organizational performance, corresponding to a particular organizational situation. For example, the "rational goals" model evaluates efficiency according to criteria that correspond to the productivity goals of the organization. If the annual goal is to increase profits by 5%, monitoring this indicator can track how the organization is evolving toward this goal. Measures can be taken to correct the projection. Of the eight models, "competing values" is the only one that allows for several models, meaning that it integrates several concepts within its scope.

Table 4.1. Models of organizational performance

Model	Definition	When Useful
	An Organization is effective to the extent that ...	*The model is most preferred when ...*
Goal model	It accomplishes its stated goals.	Goals are clear, consensual, time-bound, and measurable.
System resource model	It acquires needed resources.	A clear connection exists between inputs and performance.
Internal processes model	It has an absence of internal strain, with smooth internal functioning.	A clear connection exists between organizational processes and performance.
Strategic constituencies model	All strategic constituencies are at least minimally satisfied.	Constituencies have powerful influence on the organization, and it has to respond to demands.
Competing values model	The emphasis on criteria in the four quadrants meets constituency preferences.	The organization is unclear about its own criteria, or changes in criteria over time are of interest.
Legitimacy model	It survives as a result of engaging in legitimate activity.	The survival or decline and demise among organizations are of interest.
Fault-driven model	It has an absence of faults or traits of ineffectiveness.	Criteria of effectiveness are unclear, or strategies for improvement are needed.
High-performing systems model	It is judged excellent relative to other similar organizations.	Comparison among similar organizations is desired.

One problem when selecting a model is that a certain number of fixed criteria are selected within a single way of looking at the organization (Cameron & Whetten, 1983). However, the competing values model maintains a diversity of models at the same time as it develops watchfulness on the part of researchers in the choice of the best model to fit the situation (Cameron & Whetten, 1983). The competing values model goes beyond the recognition of the existence of several independent models. It proposes an approach that integrates existing models in a single view (Quinn & Rohrbaugh, 1983; Morin et al., 1994). This approach allows for multiple perspectives within the organization combined in a single approach. With this approach, the values underlying the evaluation become obvious and the changes in the way these values are exerted are also identified (Quinn & Rohrbaugh, 1983; Morin et al., 1994). The competing values approach has the potential to grasp the dynamic of organizations by creating a dialogue between people having different, sometimes opposite, values underlying their evaluation of organizational performance.

In the competing values approach, organizational contribution is seen as a subjective construct rooted in values and preferences of stakeholders (Cameron & Quinn, 1999; Morin, Savoie, & Beaudin, 1994; Pettigrew, 2003). The model includes four representations intended to provide an overview of organizational performance in general, and in the specific case here, the contribution of the PMO to organizational performance. The rational goals representation integrates economic value to measure profit, project management efficiency, and ROI. The open system representation contains variables that measure growth and consider project benefits. The HR representation introduces considerations of HR development, cohesion, and morale. The internal process representation captures the measures related to corporate processes linked to project management, such as project management methodologies, program and portfolio processes, and knowledge management processes. This approach examines the performance aspect directly instead of approximating it with success factors.

The model of competing values is appropriate to describe the contribution of the PMO as it participates in multiple networks and is in contact with projects, programs, portfolios, corporate strategy, and many functional units. It is ideally used to encompass multiple perspectives on organizational contribution. This model captures internal paradoxes and sheds light on competing values around PMOs. It makes it possible to highlight the predominant value ascribed to each stakeholder within the PMO network throughout the different periods of its evolution. The competing values approach is described in more detail in Section 4.5.

Is there an underlying pattern to this coevolution? The conceptual framework using these three basic concepts offers the potential to uncover the pattern and, in addition, to construct a theory for understanding the PMO and its contribution to organizational performance.

4.4 Case Study Methodology

This research is based upon a constructivist epistemology; it represents a major change relative to the more traditional and positivist approach to project management research (Bredillet, 2006; Williams, 2005). In this epistemology, the phenomenon is in the reality and the researcher in part of the interaction that takes place between him/herself and the object of study. It modifies the more traditional researcher role of "listening" to the reality (Midler, 1994). In the case of PMOs, this position is worthwhile, as theories are almost inexistent and the complexity found in the reality cannot be explained using existing simple models and a positivist approach. Just as organizations are complex social entities, so too are the specific organizational project management structures that encompass PMOs. In this perspective, the PMO can be seen as a socially constructed entity that is part of a complex organizational system. Taking this approach will give a completely new vision of the PMO. The methodology proposed here is based on following the evolution of this entity along with the evolution of its parent organization from an historical coevolutionary perspective.

Van de Ven (2007) proposed the concept of engaged scholarship, defined "as a participative form of research for obtaining the different perspectives of key stakeholders (researchers, users, clients, sponsors, and practitioners) in studying complex problems." Inspired by Van de Ven (2007), the methodology proposed here brings together the different points of view of key people involved with PMOs using a combination of qualitative and quantitative instruments that permit to uncover some of the essential elements and properties of organizational project management. A true interplay between qualitative and quantitative methods is necessary for the emergence of dense, well-developed, integrated, and comprehensive theory (Strauss & Corbin, 1998; Van de Ven, 2007).

4.4.1 Strategy for Data Collection

The global strategy for data collection in this part of the research on PMO is based on case studies. The power of such an approach is its capacity to capture holistically a complex phenomenon in its context (Patton, 2002). In this specific case, the unit of analysis is the PMO, and data to be collected is focused around this entity: interviews, documents, and the like. The conceptual framework determines the nature of data to be collected in each organization.

Sampling

Sampling choices have been made to find the optimal balance between breadth and depth, and to fit within the time and resource limit of any research. The sample is composed of four organizations. Multiple purposeful sampling methods were used to select these four organizations participating in the study (Patton, 2002) and to reinforce the research design (Eisenhardt, 1989):
- Maximum of variation, given by the industrial sector
- Homogeneous samples given by the internal clients and their innovation intensity
- Critical case referring to one organization being in a cultural multimedia context compared to a *serious* context
- Criterion sampling referring to their size, maturity in project management and the existence of a PMO

Four organizations from three economic sectors (financial services, telecommunications, and multimedia) were investigated. All the organizations in the sample do projects for internal customers; all have high levels of product innovation, and all have at least several thousand employees. All are quite mature in project management. Each set of observations includes a period prior to the implementation of the first PMO in order to understand the context that prevailed at the time. The time periods since the first PMO implementation were 12, 10, 6, and 2 years. A total of 49 persons have participated in interviews and most of them have completed questionnaires. Table 4.2 presents the profiles of respondents.

Table 4.2. Profile of the respondents

Organization identification (n=4)		COM	FIN1	MULTIM	FIN2
Economic sector		Tele-communications	Financial services	Multimedia	Financial services
Years since first PMO implementation		12	10	6	2
Number of PMOs (n= 12)		4	4	3	1
Number of interviewees (n=49)		13	16	15	5
Role	Project manager	3	3	1	1
	PMO director (idem top-level manager)	0	5	2	1
	Manager in the PMO	4	2	0	0
	Executive managers	2	1	1	1
	HR	1	0	2	0
	Financial	1	1	1	0
	Other manager	2	1	1	1
	PMO employees	0	3	7	1
Age	Mode	More than 40 years	More than 40 years	30-40 years	More than 40 years
Education level	Percent with post-graduate degree	23%	44%	40%	40%
Experience in project management	Mode	5-10 years and more than 10 years	More than 10 years	5-10 years	More than 10 years
Experience in the current job	Mode	2-4 years	2-4 years	1 year	2-4 years

Data Collection

The global strategy for data collection rests on the use of a variety of data sources on the same phenomenon. This approach by triangulation provides data that is both richer and more reliable (Patton, 2002). Table 4.3 presents the various sources of data and instruments classified under the conceptual framework. Semi-structured interviews are the major source of data. An interview guide was developed (see Appendix C). Interviews lasted for an hour. In some cases, two or three interviews were conducted, particularly with interviewees who cover a longer period of the history of their organization. The guide was adapted slightly to the role of each respondent. Interviews included the use of two questionnaires that were completed in paper format during the interview. The first questionnaire bears on the importance of the functions performed by the PMO. This questionnaire replicates question 19 from the original survey questionnaire (see Appendix A). A second questionnaire was developed to capture data on the contribution of the PMO to organizational performance (see Appendix D). Analysis of the data from this last questionnaire is presented in Section 4.5 of this chapter.

Table 4.3. Sources of data

Component of the conceptual framework	Source of the data	
Context of the organization	Internet site	Public access
	Annual reports	Public access
	Semi-structured interviews	Executives and managers
History of the organization	Annual reports	Public access
	Semi-structured interviews	Executives and managers
PMO	Organizational chart	PMO director
	Internal presentations, reports, or documents	All interviewees
	Questionnaire on functions	All interviewees except executives
	Semi-structured interviews	All interviewees
Organizational performance	Questionnaire on organizational performance	All interviewees except executives
	Semi-structured interviews	All interviewees

4.4.2 Strategy for Data Analysis

Interviews were the major source of data, with more than 700 pages of interview transcripts being analyzed. As Huberman and Miles (1991) suggested, data analysis was started during the data collection phase. There are two significant advantages to working this way. First, it allows the adjustment of instruments when encountering problems in early interviews, so the following interviews are of better quality. Second, reflection can be initiated starting with the very first interviews, and the research questions and the theoretical framework can be constructed and refined continuously. Text data from interviews and the numerical data from questionnaires went through different but parallel analysis processes.

Interviews were recorded with the permission of the interviewee, transcribed into a text format and moved to Atlas.ti (Atlas.ti Software Development, 2004) for qualitative analysis. Data from the first organization was analyzed before going to the others using a grounded theory approach leaving aside, as far as it was possible, the conceptual framework. More than 150 different concepts were identified during this first step of data analysis. In a second step, these concepts were categorized into 20 major concepts and then mapped with the concepts from the conceptual framework. All codes found their place within the framework, sometimes adding richness to the existing concept. A first theoretical model emerged from this early analysis and was presented at the European Academy of Management (EURAM) 2006 research conference, both in the doctoral forum and as a conference paper (Aubry et al., 2006a, b), where relevant feedback was received. Data collection and analysis then continued with the three other cases.

Quantitative data was transcribed into Excel (Microsoft, 2003), then moved to SPSS (SPSS, 2005). The data from questionnaires was analyzed in parallel with the text analysis. A comprehensive portrait of each organization emerged from this analysis.

Multiple strategies were used complementarily to analyze and make sense from data (Langley, 1999):

- Text coding using grounded theory approach
- Synthetic analysis making use of comparative inter-case tables
- Drawing graphics to illustrate concepts and their relations
- Counting, mostly used with data from questionnaires

Finally, data analysis included a strategy to ensure quality and a high level of confidence and credibility, which are of major importance in qualitative research (Patton, 2002). From Lincoln and Guba (1985), three techniques to enhance the quality of the research were used, as shown in Table 4.4. These quality activities produced high-level feedback and constructive criticism that improved the quality of the research results.

Table 4.4. Strategy for quality

Technique	Activity
Production of credible results and interpretation	Triangulation using multiple sources of data and multiple methods to analyze results
Validation from people participating in the research	Working sessions in organizations participating in the research
External validation	Presentations in research conferences: EURAM 2006 and 2007; PMI Research Conference 2006 and 2008; Lille Eden Doctoral Colloquium 2006, 2007 and 2008.
	Working sessions with groups of executives in Canada, Australia, and Europe

The methodological framework, data collection, and analysis strategies have been presented in this section. The following sections present empirical results starting with the description of case studies from the four organizations that participated in this research.

4.5 Case Descriptions

This section presents the results of the investigation of PMOs in the four organizations, identified by pseudonym to preserve their anonymity. The investigations show that in order to understand a PMO in the context in which it is located, the evolution of this context must be taken into account. The intention is not to delve into the details of the data analysis but rather to synthesize the history of each PMO and its organizational context and to identify major events that lead to changes in the PMO.

A total of 12 PMOs were identified in the four organizations. A detailed analysis was done of each. An attempt was made to group the PMOs into types, but significant differences among all the PMOs made the production of a typology difficult, if not impossible. Each PMO is described next in a summary fashion and has been given a name to provide an image that characterizes it in a simple manner. Table 4.5 presents an overview of the periods covered for each organization.

Table 4.5. History of PMOs in the four organizations

		Period I	Period II	Period III	Period IV
COM	Pre-PMO	Business results	Technical	Total for all periods: 12 years	
				Business unit	Consultation
FIN1	Pre-PMO	Re-engineering	Total for all periods: 10 years		
			Enterprise	Balkanization	
MULTIM	Pre-PMO	Planning	Total for all periods: 6 years		
			Allocation	Program	
FIN2	Pre-PMO	2 years			
		Major in IT			

The histories of these organizations and their PMOs are characterized by periods of relative stability punctuated by periods of rapid change. Two of the organizations studied have had PMOs for more than a decade. Each has changed their PMOs several times. The rhythm of change is approximately three to four different forms of PMO per decade, which is consistent with the survey results presented in Chapter 2.

Table 4.5 shows the 11 periods that the historical analysis revealed. In all but two periods, only one PMO was found in each organization. In COM during period III, Business unit PMO, PMOs were located in separate business units and were independent of each other. In this case, only one PMO was investigated. In FIN1 during period III, Balkanization, multiple entities that could be considered as PMOs were being created at the time the interviews were coming to a close. The situation was emerging at the time, and it was not possible to study the entire set of PMOs and the relationships among them. Two of the PMOs were, however, included in the sample of 12 case studies of PMOs. There should be no confusion as to the number of case studies: 12 PMOs in 11 periods were examined. Chapter 5 focuses on changes in PMO. There are 11 cases of a change, four cases of setting up the first PMO in the organization and seven cases of an existing PMO being transformed.

4.5.1 Organization COM

This organization is a large R&D center of an international company. The history of the PMO covers a period of 12 years, with four distinct PMO periods. The evolution of a PMO in a context of rapid economic growth during the first periods was followed by a period of downsizing.

Pre-PMO (1984-1992). This pre-PMO period started with the signature of the first important development contract in a new market and the hiring of the first project managers. The project management structure was simple: the project managers were grouped in a centralized unit working in a matrix approach with technical people. Functional units were based on the development process (conception, test, etc.), reflecting the sequential nature of the project management process at that time.

First PMO period: business PMO (1992-1996). The first PMO was implemented with a new business opportunity. Meanwhile the head office adopted a delocalization strategy concerning their R&D centers, aimed at stimulating innovation. Consequently, the business relationship with the client became the direct responsibility of the PMO, and overall the responsibilities became greater and more strategic.

Second PMO period: technical PMO (1996-1998). At this point, the head office changed its delocalization strategy to a centralized approach. Consequently, the relationship with the client went back to the head office for the business aspects of the projects. But the industry was still in a rapid growth period that saw multiple new developments entrusted to this R&D center. Thus, the center's responsibilities were focused on technology that was changing rapidly with increasing levels of complexity. The PMO became more powerful, and for the first time, project managers were part of it.

Third PMO period: business unit PMOs (1998-2004). In 1998, the industry was still growing. At the head office level as well as in this R&D center, a business unit structure was adopted. Four business units were put in place in the R&D center, each one having its own PMO. These business units were only responsible for the technical development of projects. In 2001, the technology bubble burs, creating a very difficult period for this company and more generally for the industry. But this company maintained its long-term development perspective and long-term R&D objectives, while cutting into the operations side of the business. Because of the strategy of this company to maintain its R&D activities, the economic downturn had few consequences in the short term for this local R&D center.

Fourth PMO period: consultant PMO (2004-2005). The global financial results of the company were encouraging after a three-year period of difficulties. But the organizational efficiency program was still going on and now focused on R&D activities after having optimized the operations side of the business. The organizational efficiency program globally reshaped this R&D center. This center had to prove its capacity to compete with the other centers. Business units remained in place but project management was completely centralized into a single PMO. Project managers were assigned to the projects of a business unit as consultants. The resulting structure brought two-sided management, with the business units looking after business results and the PMO looking after project processes.

4.5.2 Organization FIN I

In this company, the PMO history is spread over a period of 10 years, covering three clearly differentiated PMO periods.

Pre-PMO (1980-1995). At that time, projects were driven by the IT unit. The IT unit was literally driving the business, not only IT. When a large project was identified and funded, a specific sub-unit was usually created under its control. The rest of the organization was doing business as usual until new solutions emerged from IT. Training for the new product or processes was minimal. Project management performance was not really an issue except for the delivery date (albeit with certain limits).

First PMO period: re-engineering PMO (1996-2000). The first period corresponds to the initiation of the large re-engineering project, the largest project the company had ever undertaken, with a budget of more than 500 million dollars. The reengineering effort was motivated in part by a reaction to the situation that prevailed between 1980 and 1996. Structural changes in the banking industry, along with an intensification of competition, gave the signal within this bank to make significant improvement to its operational costs. Operational costs were an important factor the financial services company needed to improve if it was to maintain its credit rating with international rating agencies. Business managers wanted business decisions to come back to them. An executive was named specifically to manage the overall reengineering project, not only IT. A PMO was created with the mandate of realizing all sub-projects. It was positioned directly under the supervision of the reengineering project executive. This change in the organizational structure came with the integration of all the expertise required for the development of sub-projects within the reengineering project, resulting in a first matrix structure. This period also gave rise to a project management culture. After almost five years and many millions of dollars invested in the reengineering project, results were disappointing. Operational costs didn't reach the target and the risk of losing the credit rating was also present. A new strategy emerged.

Second PMO period: the enterprise PMO (2000-2004). In 2001, the company proceeded with the merger of 11 autonomous regional units within the head office. These mergers were necessary to keep operational costs at the lowest possible level in a very competitive market. The enterprise PMO arose from the awareness that a global view of all the projects of the organization was missing, as well as a view of the overall development of the company. For the first time ever, projects and strategy were under the same roof. The matrix structure was reinforced and project managers of major projects were confirmed in their positions as PMO employees. It was during this period that the concept of a portfolio of projects emerged and a project priority board (PPB) was created, so the board of directors could concentrate on its business role without having to manage projects.

However, the legitimacy of the PMO was profoundly questioned during this period. Executives were basically saying that if they were to be accountable for project results, they wanted to fully manage them. They wanted project managers to be in their units. It became obvious that the only way the PMO could survive in this business was to make a major change to its stated mission.

Third PMO period: Balkanization (2004-2005). The role of the Enterprise PMO of the previous period had now been spread among multiple units, most of which were not called PMOs. Two of them have been analyzed in detail.

What are left at the top level are the Strategy, Control, and Support PMO. Its mission concentrates on three major elements: advise the PPB, ensure the control of all projects in the organization, and support project managers throughout the organization with a standard methodology. The business units were then reinforced and redefined as accountable for the results of their project portfolios, including benefits. In each business unit, the project managers were grouped together within a PMO. Its major role is to execute projects as planned and to control them. With the role of controlling projects, the business unit PMO is on the same playing field as the central PMO. This situation leads to tensions and conflicts that become quite visible when reporting project status.

4.5.3 Organization MULTIM

Originally, this company was a family enterprise that went public in 1996. The multimedia industry is expanding very rapidly. The internal philosophy is based on strong internal development capacities. Three periods have been identified to cover the evolution of the PMO during six years in a local product development center.

Pre-PMO (1997-2000). This pre-PMO period started with the creation of the local development center, which quickly became the most important development center outside the head office country. The head office kept all the strategic issues under its own responsibility, leaving execution to the local center. The local center was organized functionally. Each project was under the responsibility of one function and the components of the project were sequentially completed, one function after the other. This center was asked to increase the number of projects and to accelerate the rhythm of delivery. The functional structure struggled to meet these new requirements.

First PMO period: planning PMO (2000-2003). The local center director saw in the project-based organization the opportunity to contribute to the growth expectations. Projects became the base of this new form of organizing, even if some general functions remained at the global level (for instances, HR and finances). A first PMO was put in place with a focus on planning issues to coordinate activities and resources for rapid delivery. The first PMO director was chosen on the basis of his great knowledge of the project management process and performance tools, which earned value among other employees. But the rigor imposed by the PMO's director in planning projects was seen as holding back the acceleration of project deliveries.

Second PMO period: allocation PMO (2003-2004). Growth was still persistent in the multimedia industry in this period. The technology infrastructure was gaining in complexity, with the arrival of new platforms year after year without removing any older ones. The industry was still driven by the time-to-market constraint. It was harder to keep up the tempo of accelerating project deliveries in this context. A new PMO director was appointed. His approach differed drastically from his predecessor in the way rigor was managed. He abandoned strict processes and permitted flexibility in planning tools. There was a great variety of tools, from Excel spreadsheets to more complex use of planning software. But there was one piece of information that must always be exact and available at strict points in time—resource utilization. The PMO director was able to prepare the global resource utilization portrait and to plan for future needs and availability for new projects.

Third PMO period: program PMO (2005-2006). The multimedia industry was still growing during this period. Complexity in the variety of the technology continued to increase, making it more difficult for the project teams to deliver on time. This period in the evolution of the PMO was in continuity from the previous one. It corresponded to adding the program management level in order to better coordinate multiple projects. Project managers were grouped by program. The PMO mirrored this change by adding a program management level in its structure.

4.5.4 Organization FIN2

This organization presents an evolution from pre-PMO to a single PMO period since the first PMO implementation in 2004.

Pre-PMO (2002-2004). This pre-PMO period in the history of the organization was marked by the arrival of a new top management team. This company suffered from the global economic context, punctuated by the technological dotcom blow-up in 2001, scandals, and bankruptcies. This new management team centered its mandate on restructuring the company to cut operating costs and initiated development activities only on essential mission-related projects. From a project perspective, they realized that outsourcing their project development had led to complete ignorance of what was going on in their IT area. IT is an important enabler for business in their context, and they became incompetent at managing it. During this pre-PMO period, an IT unit was rehabilitated at the top level with a mandate to reorganize the strategic IT activities. In 2002, all was in place for the first PMO to be created.

First PMO period: IT PMO (2005-2006). This PMO had something strange. It had in its mandate to cover all the projects of the company. But the PMO was located in a specific unit under IT and had relationships with business people for their contribution to IT projects, but also for their business non-IT projects. The decision to locate the PMO within the IT unit was based upon the importance of the IT component in most projects. The real sponsor of the PMO was the president himself. "The PMO draws its legitimacy from its sponsor," said the executive responsible for the PMO. Thus, the PMO participated in the strategic activities and was responsible for project portfolio management. This PMO had two people working in it: the director and one project management advisor. Project managers were located elsewhere in the IT unit and they worked essentially with external consultants for IT development.

4.6 Multiple Views on PMO Organizational Performance

Earlier in this chapter, the PMO was positioned as an entity within organizational project management. Performance is embedded in the proposed definition in terms of value creation. Section 4.1 concluded that current literature in the project management field suggests a narrow view of performance limited to financial terms and falls short in providing a theoretical foundation for PMO performance. In Section 4.2.3, the concept of organizational performance with the competing values framework was introduced. This framework allows for the coexistence of multiple views on organizational performance within the organization. It is based on communication and dialogue between stakeholders from different parts of the organization. The PMO is often at the heart of such paradoxes on organizational performance. The competing values framework is also part of the dynamic characteristics of the PMO. PMOs change over time, so do the organizational values and the way performance is assessed. The competing values model has been proposed to build the foundations that are missing in the project management field, and more specifically in the PMO literature.

In this section, the competing values model is explored in more detail. First, the competing values approach is elaborated in the context of PMO organizational performance. This is followed by a presentation of the empirical results from the four case study organizations.

4.6.1 The Competing Values Framework in Detail

Organizational performance was the object of worldwide study for a nucleus of researchers (Cameron & Whitten, 1983; Quinn & Rohrbaugh, 1983) toward the end of the 1970s and at the beginning of the 1980s. Quinn and Rohrbaugh (1983) were, however, the first to have proposed the competing values approach. This approach came out of a research program over a period of several years and was intended to evaluate performance in the public sector. This sector is enormously complex and at a time when the economy was affected by strong inflation, it was important to ensure the best possible use of public funds in all public institutions (Rohrbaugh, 1981).

The theoretical basis of the competing values approach rests on the following assumption: tensions exist in all organizations where needs, tasks, values, and perceptions must compete (Thompson et al., 1981). These authors continue: "The model was designed to help people graph their perceptions of these tensions within their own organizations" (p. 193).

Rather than imagine a new model, Quinn and Rohrbaugh approached the problem in a highly original way by undertaking research based on criteria already identified by Campbell (1976, as cited in Quinn & Rohrbaugh, 1983). They treated these criteria using a combination of the Delphi approach and statistical modeling, with the participation of a group of very reputable researchers in two panels. The research identified a set of 17 unique criteria grouped in three significant dimensions: the structure dimension (paradox between flexibility and control), the focus dimension (paradox between internal and external), and the dimension of purpose and orientation.

These dimensions formed three sets of values that explicitly expressed the dilemmas or paradoxes present in the organizations (see Figure 4.2). These values are in constant competition in the organizations, and to succeed, the organization must reach good overall results, without necessarily seeking a balance! In this context, organizational performance depends on the values of those who are evaluating (Cameron, 1986). The following are the value dimensions and the dilemma associated with them (Quinn & Rohrbaugh, 1983).

- The *focus* of the organization, internal vs. external: the internal focus is directed toward people (person-oriented), whereas the external focus is turned toward the organization itself and its external environment (organization-oriented). The values are, on the one hand, market competitiveness and, on the other hand, socio-technical balance and employee wellbeing.
- The structure of the organization, between flexibility and control: it refers to preferences of the organizations in relation to the structure by presenting the contrast between the interest in stability and control on the one hand, and flexibility and change on the other hand. Values relative to stability are at one end while flexibility and innovation are at the other.
- The orientation and purpose of the organization: refers to the degree of proximity to organizational results and the contrast between a concern with results and a concern with orientation. The dilemma can present itself as a conflict between timelines, short term versus long term.

The third dimension (orientation and purpose) was not often used in empirical research based on the competing values approach, including research by Cameron and Quinn (1999). In a fashion consistent with this stream of research only the structure dimension (paradox between flexibility and control) and the focus dimension (paradox between internal and external) have been employed in this research. Figure 4.2 presents the competing values framework.

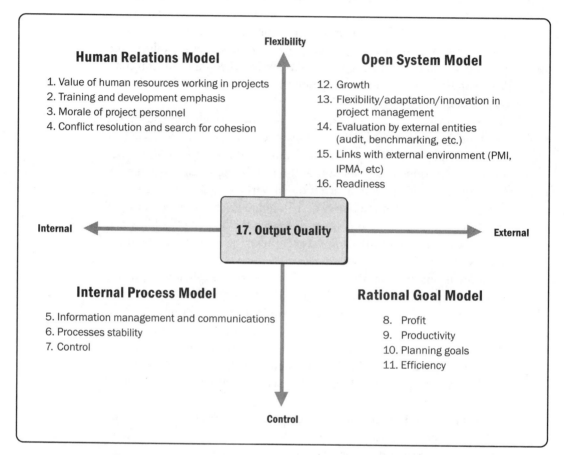

Figure 4.2. The competing values framework

The research of Quinn and Rohrbaugh (1983) thus led to the formulation of a framework that presents 17 criteria and their dimensions in four quadrants, each associated with a specific pre-existing model of organizational performance: the open system model, the human relations model, the internal process model, and rational goals model. Sixteen of the 17 criteria are associated with one of the four models, each representing a different conception of organizational performance. The seventeenth criterion, output quality, was not associated specifically with any of the models.

A precision must be made to differentiate between open systems and rational goal models. The open systems model values effectiveness. On the other hand, the rational goal model values efficiency, profitability, and ROI.

The development of the competing values approach partly resolves the broader question of the theoretical and empirical organizational performance construct.

From the theoretical viewpoint, in an organization considered to be a set of open systems, the construct covers the conceptual space from four entirely different perspectives on the organization and on the relations between them. It allows for exchange within the organization and the evaluation of its organizational performance. In this way, the organization influences the way organizational performance is evaluated but also, the evaluation of performance influences the constantly evolving organization. From the empirical point of view, it has been an object of research to which many researchers have contributed (Quinn & Rohrbaugh, 1983). This approach, because it contains multiple conceptions, sheds light on the importance of flexibility between different perspectives that exist simultaneously.

The competing values approach has been applied to a variety of areas. Originally, it was the public sector that saw the emergence of the competing values approach in the first studies of Rohrbaugh (1981), but several sectors are represented today: higher education (Pounder, 2002), manufacturing (McDermott & Stock, 1999), R&D (Jordan et al., 2003), banking (Dwyer et al., 2003), and cross-sector (Stinglhamber et al., 2004). Moreover, Cameron and Quinn (1999) accounted for more than 1,000 interventions in organizations from several industrial sectors as diversified as agriculture, insurance, and construction. This wide empirical base confirms the applicability of this approach in various organizational contexts.

4.6.2 The Model of Competing Values Applied in the Context of the PMO

Organizational performance is a subjective construct because it exists in the minds of those who are evaluating. The organizational performance of PMOs will vary depending on who is the evaluator. A construct is not directly observable. It can be evaluated through the variables that form it.

The justification of the PMO remains a recurring problem in organizations. From the results of the survey presented in Chapter 2, more than 40% report that the existence of their PMO has been recently questioned. A PMO should be legitimate if it can convincingly demonstrate its contribution to organizational performance. However, the evaluation of organizational performance is a complex question that could have as many variations as the PMO itself. What could be of value for the chief executive officer might not be the same as for the chief information officer. One could argue that the PMO's ultimate contribution to the organization should be measured against the strategic objectives.

Organizational performance is anchored in the values and preferences of the stakeholders. In the context of the PMO, the stakeholders are the people and the groups who have a substantial interest in the management of the overall projects of the organization. These people can be identified as those who must make decisions about the content of the projects as well as about the management process of the projects. Other important stakeholders are the users of methodologies, standards, tools, reports, and so forth produced by the PMO. The stakeholders could include the business unit manager, the PMO director, the project portfolio managers, the functional managers, project managers, project controllers, and so on. As the PMO is part of the global organizational project management, other stakeholders take the form of groups, boards, or committees, such as the project governance board, the functional management committee, the PMO as an autonomous unit, and different ad hoc committees created to follow or coordinate one or more projects. They often have a crucial role associated with one or more PMO functions. Yet most of these stakeholders belong to different units that have different cultures and different values.

Furthermore, as was shown in Chapter 2, PMOs perform all of the 27 functions to different degrees. Are these different functions regarded with the same value by different stakeholders? The PMO's contribution to organizational performance seems to take different forms. And it should be distinguished from the project's own contribution. The PMO's contribution lies behind the total performance of each individual project. This context of diversity supports the definition proposed for the organizational performance of PMOs based upon the competing values framework.

The model is now applied in examining the two dimensions and the paradoxes that these dimensions give rise to in the context of the PMO.

The structure dimension: paradox between flexibility and control. The PMO usually belongs to the hierarchy and as such, participates in maintaining stability. One of the most important roles for the PMO is to monitor and control the performance of projects. Another important role is the standardization of methods and processes. At the same time, the PMO is part of multiple project management networks where projects and ad hoc committees are created, dissolved, and recreated according to project management needs. Projects are temporary organizations often associated with innovation and change, disruptive or incremental, as each project brings a new and unique solution to a particular problem. In this context, the PMO supports creativity and innovation, or at the very least should not impede it! The PMO participates in the line of control, giving the necessary stability while at the same time encouraging innovation and change with flexibility. In this sense, the PMO can be said to be an ambidextrous entity in developing ability in both control and flexibility (Tushman & O'Reilly, 1996). These examples illustrate the paradox between control and flexibility as it applies in the context of PMOs.

The focus dimension: paradox between internal and external. The PMO adopts an outright external focus when, to measure project and project management results, it looks at quantitative financial indicators and compares itself to other organizations or industries. Kendall and Rollins (2003) suggested that the main indicators for measuring the value-added of a PMO are related to three major elements:

- The reduction of the life cycle of projects
- More projects completed during the fiscal year with the same resources
    - A tangible contribution for reaching organizational goals in terms of cost reduction, revenue increase, and a better ROI

The professionalization of project management also contributes to the fact that organizations want to compare and share their best practices. The PMO has an active role to play relative to the internal focus through the development and dissemination of project management methodology, the fostering of internal communication, including the presentation of project results to upper management, and the development of competencies. The PMO is often responsible for creating the common language relative to project management. At the same time, the PMO is connected to the external world by means of consultant firms and project management associations. When a PMO is asked to benchmark the internal project management processes, the internal common language must be translated to a universal common language. The PMO is an entity in which there exists a permanent arbitrage between internal and external focuses.

The examination of the two dimensions in the specific context of the PMO confirms the existence of paradoxes identified by the competing values framework within a project management context. The evaluation of the organizational performance of the PMO can shed light on the different perspectives from which organizational performance can be examined based on the values of those evaluating. The competing values framework represents a means to make these values explicit, which will then lead to an understanding of what constitutes a contribution to the organizational performance of the PMO and of the entire organization.

The competing values framework has the advantage of integrating the financial perspective of performance with the other conceptions to form a multidimensional perspective. Indeed, the four conceptions of the framework provide a multi-faceted representation of the performance of organizational project management. The rational goals (efficiency) conception integrates the economic value to measure profit, project management efficiency, and ROI. The open systems (effectiveness) conception includes variables that measure growth and take into consideration innovation and effectiveness of projects. The human relations conception emphasizes the development of human resources, cohesion, and personnel morale, which are often absent from the evaluation of organizational performance. The internal processes conception captures measurements related to corporate processes tied to project management such as project realization processes, and knowledge management processes. Overall, the competing values model bears directly on the performance (objective variables) instead of bearing on success factors (explanatory variables).

Organizational performance must therefore be examined from different viewpoints surrounding the PMO and be scrutinized from several loci of analysis. PMOs are positioned at the interface of several entities, some of which belong to project networks and others to operational organizations (Lampel & Jha, 2004). They are in touch with the projects, program, project portfolios, corporate strategy, and business units. The PMO is therefore at the center of numerous perspectives on organizational performance.

4.6.3 The Contribution of PMOs to Organizational Performance: Empirical Results

This section presents the empirical results on the PMOs' contribution to organizational performance. First, the specific methodology for this part of the research is presented. Empirical results are then presented in two parts. The first part bears on making sense of the historical data on PMOs relative to paradoxes along the two dimensions from the competing values framework, which are control versus flexibility and internal versus external focus. The second part proposes a pragmatic list of criteria for each of the four conceptions within the competing values framework.

Methodology

From a methodological perspective, the study of organizational performance was based upon two types of data: interviews and a questionnaire. The most important data come from interviews, where open-ended questions were asked specifically on the organizational performance of the PMO. As detailed in Section 4.3, interviews were codified and analyzed using Atlas.ti software (Atlas.ti, 2004). In the specific case of the organizational performance of PMOs, transcripts were coded using the 17 criteria from the competing values framework. Respondents were chosen to represent different roles, leading potentially to different conceptions of the PMO's contribution to organizational performance (see Table 4.2 for the profile of the respondents for each organization). All periods of the PMO's history have been taken into consideration with the exception of the period before the first PMO implementation. While the pre-PMO period may represent great interest, it is not the focus of this research.

In addition to interviews, a questionnaire was built with the objective of capturing the different conceptions of the PMO's contribution and its underlying values (see Appendix D). The questionnaire contains 17 criteria from the original list of the competing values framework (Quinn & Rohrbaugh, 1983) grouped into the four conceptions. They have been adapted to the particular context of the PMO. For this specific analysis, the output quality criterion has been included within the process criteria. Respondents were asked to assess the importance of each of the criteria in their current context using a 5-point Likert scale. The scale was the same as for the questionnaire on the importance of the functions: 1, not important at all, to 5, very important. Criteria with a score of 4 or 5 were considered important. The number of important criteria was calculated for each PMO.

A Typology of PMOs Based on Organizational Performance Criteria

Chapter 3 presented a search for typologies based on the survey data. Here, a typology based on organizational performance criteria is presented. As previously pointed out, the competing values framework takes into account the values within organizations, and provides an instrument that helps highlight paradoxes between values. The diagram shown in Figure 4.2 forms a typology based upon four different conceptions of organizational performance. Interestingly, some PMOs are in balance between extreme positions of the dimensions. This is presented in the middle row and middle column of Table 4.6. Each square is identified by a single letter to facilitate interpretation. In this section, the distribution of 11 of the 12 PMOs positioned in the competing values framework is presented and discussed. The PMO from the second financial services organization, FIN2, is not shown or discussed here.

Table 4.6. PMOs classified by the importance of their organizational performance criteria

	Internal focus	Equilibrium internal / external	External focus
Flexibility	**A** MULTIM period III	**B** FIN1 period II	**C** COM period I COM period IV MULTIM period I
Equilibrium flexibility/ control	**D** FIN1 period I	**E** *none*	**F** COM period II MULTIM period II
Control	**G** COM period III FIN1-central period III	**H** FIN1-business period III	**I** *None*

From this perspective, PMOs can more easily be compared with each other. Each square from A to I is first described. The MULTIM PMO in period III, where human factors were valued while maintaining a high degree of flexibility, is found in A. This PMO was internally focused. Emphasis was placed on the development of people working in projects and their wellbeing. It might not be surprising to find under human relations a PMO from the multimedia industry. In its third period, this growing company had to take action to recruit new employees and retain the ones already on the job.

The FIN 1 PMO in its second period is found in B. It is a good illustration of the balance between human relations and open system models. In this period, projects within the PMO's scope were expected to deliver business results, so it can be valued using the open system model. During the same period, the role of project manager was officially recognized after the PMO had strongly pushed for it.

Three PMOs fall in C. COM period I and MULTIM period I were both in a period of exponential growth at that time, which is in line with the open system model. Curiously, COM in period IV is also part of this square, but this period took place after a rationalization plan. It indicates a turn to the external market after having passed a difficult time with the bursting of the dotcom bubble.

FIN1 period I is found in D. This first implementation of a PMO coincides with a first project management methodology and standards without heavy control. Many consultants were hired, leaving time for internal project managers to develop their skills. No PMO from our sample is found in E. COM and MULTIM in their second period are found in F. They both moved from the open system model of their first period. It might be interpreted as a natural move following a period of rapid growth. These PMOs have to manage their projects in a way to be not only effective, but also efficient.

Two PMOs are found in G: COM and FIN1-central in their third period. In the case of FIN 1, this corresponds to a major change of its mandate. At that period, this central PMO saw itself as the controlling entity for project management processes of other PMOs in business units. In the COM case, this PMO was situated in a business unit without any central PMO. It implemented its own processes and methodology and controls its use. In H, there is the PMO from FIN1-business unit, in period III. Positioned in a business unit, this PMO had to deliver results in terms of profit, but at the same time, it offered project managers a loose project management framework. In I, there is no PMO. This result has been explained by several respondents in the interviews, as they do not see the PMO as a pure profit-oriented entity.

When considering Table 4.6 globally, several observations can be made. First of all, no PMO is perfectly balanced on both axes (E). Square E is situated at the middle point on both dimensions, control/flexibility and internal/external. It can be said to be in a total equilibrium between the extreme positions of these dimensions. Remembering what has been said earlier, the competing values framework does not envision the equilibrium as a target position. To the contrary, different points of views are encouraged. It might not be surprising that no PMOs fall in this square. It confirms the presence of multiple values around PMOs. This result supports the use of the competing values approach as a pertinent way of opening up the dialogue between individuals having different views on the PMO's contribution to organizational performance.

Second, on the flexibility/control dimension, 5 of the 11 PMOs (45%) emphasize flexibility (A, B, and C). It is therefore not rare that a PMO shows flexibility, and this, in spite of its sometimes important role as methodology and standards guardian. Three of them have an external focus at the same time (C). These are PMOs that are flexible and open to the external environment. Noticeably, PMOs from different industries are in the same situation: telecommunications and multimedia. We saw in Chapter 3 that the sector of activity is not a variable that explains the variety of PMOs. However, we find only one PMO, FIN1, among those that show flexibility, while two PMOs are among those that value control. The sector of financial activities is usually associated with tighter control because of the nature of financial activities.

Third, only three PMOs emphasize control. The focus of two of them (G) is turned inward. In these conditions, the PMO is focused on the adherence to processes and standards. We also note changes in the situation, notably for the COM case where the PMO of period I, strong in flexibility and focused on the outside (C), later loses in flexibility during period II (F); then it takes a diametrically opposed position during period III, with a strength in control and a focus on the inside (G); it finally comes back to its initial position in period

III, where flexibility and openness toward the outside are valued once again (C). This coming back to the original position is an illustration of the general lack of a pattern that could be assimilated with a life cycle or a general progression to a more mature state that was found throughout the data analysis.

In all, the purpose behind the competing values framework is not to aim for perfect balance but rather to show the values underlying what organizational performance represents in organizations (Cameron, 1986). The *competing values* approach results from the integration of the four most popular models for evaluating organizational performance (Cameron & Whetten, 1983). This model allows for a plurality of perspectives within a single organization. The results presented here show that certain perspectives prevail at certain times and evolve with the context without having a predetermined life cycle in the evolution of their contribution to the organizational performance.

The following section continues the presentation of results related to the contribution of the PMO to organizational performance with the identification of indicators borne out of the qualitative analysis.

4.6.4 The Identification of Indicators of the PMO's Contribution to Organizational Performance

The PMO's contribution to organizational performance was the object of a quantitative evaluation based on a questionnaire, the results of which were presented in the previous section. This section aims to identify specific indicators for the PMO and in doing so, enriches the thinking about the PMO's contribution to organizational performance. In this section, specific indicators are identified that complement and complete the four conceptions and the 17 generic criteria initially proposed within the competing values framework (Quinn & Rohrbaugh, 1983). The original 17 criteria can be applied in different contexts (Cameron & Quinn, 1999). For this reason they are at a more abstract level. Cameron and Quinn (1999) recognize that the four models and the 17 criteria are quite abstract and recommend that sets of criteria be developed that are specific to a particular use. In a manner consistent with this recommendation, specific sets of indicators were developed for each of the four models and the 17 criteria. The sets of indicators create value in two ways. First, they enrich the understanding of the PMO's contribution to organizational performance by providing detail that is meaningful in this context. Second, they provide the basis for instruments to measure the presence of the models in real organizational settings.

The goal here is to be more specific and to identify relevant concrete indicators in the context of PMOs. Transcripts of the interviews have first been coded using the 17 criteria. Then excerpts have been scrutinized for their meaning to group multiple variations under a common indicator. From this second step, a list of 79 unique indicators was produced. Table 4.7 presents the overall results.

Table 4.7. Number of indicators within the competing values framework

Human Resources	Open Systems
4 criteria	4 criteria
25 indicators	14 indicators
Internal Processes	**Rational Goals**
4 criteria	5 criteria
23 indicators	14 indicators
Output Quality	
1 criteria	
3 indicators	

Indicators illustrate the variety of possible measurements in the different PMOs. An advantage of this exercise is to render explicit notions about the contribution of the PMO to organizational performance that, until now, may have remained abstract. As can be seen from Table 4.7, a greater variety exists in the human relations and internal processes conceptions of organizational performance than in open systems and in rational goals conceptions.

Indicators within Human Resources Conception

The indicators related to human resources improve the understanding of the role that the PMO can play in this area (see Table 4.8). A great variety of indicators was found from one organization to the next. It appears that each of the four organizations has a different flavor in the way it values the human resource contribution of the PMO.

For example, the organization in the multimedia industry stands out for the large number of indicators in human resources. The scope of these indicators often covers all the resources working in projects rather than only PMO employees. In this case, the PMO plays a direct role in the development of competencies of personnel, according to the needs of upcoming projects and employee wishes. It is unusual that an organization structured by project (which is the case here) stresses personnel contribution to projects and intensifies the role of the PMO in HR management. But management of human resources, in this organizational context is a particularly critical function. The personnel are exceedingly young; the average age is less than 30 years old. This fact accounts for the strength of the company at the same time as it has its own nightmares. These "teenagers" require a considerable amount of supervision to respect the project constraints and the never-ending challenges. There is an important shortage of qualified personal in this high technology sector. This company has invested massively in training in conjunction with local governments. It has also implemented an internal school to provide skilled workers for its own development needs. Furthermore, personnel turnover is significant. Altogether, the management of human resources is an important function and the PMO plays an active role in this organization.

Table 4.8. Indicators within human resources conception

Criteria	Indicators
Value of human resources working in project	1. Empowerment
	2. Stimulating projects (participate in something big)
	3. Visibility for good work in projects
	4. Individual assessment
	5. Internal recruitment is privileged over external
	6. Teamwork valued
	7. Trust in PMO
Training and emphasis on development	8. Training in project management
	9. Level of experience of the personnel working in PMO
	10. Encouragement for PMP
	11. Individual development plan for project management competencies
	12. Diversity in competencies
	13. Coaching
	14. Organization of events - knowledge transfer
	15. Change management in project management
Morale on project's personnel	16. Pleasure in working
	17. Career job security
	18. Employees' satisfaction in project
	19. Work-family equilibrium
	20. Number of overtime hours
Conflict resolution and search for cohesion	21. Conflict prevention
	22. Resolution of conflict in HR management
	23. Negotiation on progress report (e.g., color code)
	24. Negotiation on actions to be taken from progress report
	25. Negotiation on project selection in portfolio

The significant number of indicators identified within the human relation conception shows that underlying values exist in organizations to assess the contribution of the PMO to the organizational performance regarding the human resources. A PMO manager confirms the impact of his entity on the degree of satisfaction of project managers: "Well, we took it all [multiple PMOs] and centralized it; it [the degree of satisfaction of employee] went from 0 to 24 in 12 months. The energy, the empowerment there was a huge improvement."

It is also notable that the PMO plays a social role and that it has an influence on the work-family balance; an indicator allows us to grasp this dimension (number 19 in Table 4.8). Analysis also reveals that the capacity for negotiation is a competence essential to the resolution of conflicts surrounding the state of advancement of a project.

The role of PMOs within HR management is often neglected in the literature on PMOs, with the exception of a few authors who dedicated their efforts to emphasizing this role (Crawford & Cabanis-Brewin, 2006; Huemann, Keegan, & Turner, 2007). From the qualitative analysis, we see that the PMO can make a significant contribution to organizational performance regarding the human resources, and that concrete indicators can be used to assess it.

Indicators Within Internal Processes Conception

Table 4.9. Indicators within internal processes conception

Criteria	Indicators
Information and communication management	1. Accuracy of information in progress report
	2. Transparency of information in progress report
	3. Circulation of the information on projects (transverse role)
	4. Keeping the memory of projects for forecasting (historical statistics)
	5. Existence of project documentation
	6. Capacity to absorb a lot of information (project managers and coordinators)
	7. Creation of open places for people to discuss
	8. Politics – visibility of the CEO
	9. Learning from errors
Stability in processes	10. Standardization in the way things are done
	11. Importance of the resource appointment process
	12. Existence and stability of project management processes
Control	13. Rigor in the project management process
	14. Control of the appointment process to avoid thieving
	15. Capacity to act (difference between monitoring and controlling)
	16. Control of project delivery date
	17. Control of costs
	18. Control of scope
	19. Control of earned value
	20. Ratio number of changes/respect of cost
	21. Equilibrium between time and budget
	22. Control of risks
	23. Percent of precision in control data

The internal processes conception of organizational performance shows the largest number of individual indicators of the four conceptions (see Table 4.9). This emphasizes the position of project management and the PMO in their traditional roles of process management.

Many indicators bear on the criteria of information and communication management. The PMO seems to collaborate in many networks and plays a central role in the circulation of information. A respondent emphasizes this role:

"I think that the PMO has an important role in the sense that they have a vision of what is going on elsewhere in the organization. [...] Normally, the PMO has antennae in each portfolio [...] I think it could have a unifying role."

Indicators also reflect both quality of information and the ease of its flow throughout the organization. The criteria dedicated to the stability of processes pinpoints more specifically the traditional role of PMOs in standardizing project management. The criteria of control included of course meeting costs, deadline, and project scope. However, PMO control is getting increasingly diversified and is often exercised on the processes themselves.

Of particular interest is the situation with multiple PMOs where the values given to indicators are quite different. Two PMOs were observed within the organization FIN1, the central one and the business one. These two PMOs don't value the same elements as far as the quality of deliverables and communications management is concerned. This is understandable in complementary but paradoxical terms. For example, the business unit PMO values product quality and business results, while the central PMO values process maturity and project performance in terms of cost, schedule, and the project requirements. As can be seen from this example, two PMOs in the same organization may have complementary but conflicting priorities.

Indicators Within the Rational Goals (Efficiency) Conception

Table 4.10. Indicators within the rational goals conception

Criteria	Indicators
Profit	1. Profit from projects
	2. Benefits planning within project business case
Productivity	3. Order in productivity
	4. Best use of resources in project management (leave fewer people on the bench)
	5. Index of productivity
	6. Bureaucracy
	7. Internal competition (e.g., between units in different countries
	8. Existence of an organizational structure to deliver projects
Planning in goals to reach	9. Importance of the strategic dimension in the selection of the "good" projects
	10. Equilibrium in projects of a portfolio (risk, benefits on the short, medium, and long terms, value)
	11. Prediction of the delivery capabilities (resource allocation)
	12. Alignment of enterprise objectives with the employees ones
Efficiency	13. Efficiency in the relations between PMO and functional or business units – negotiation on projects
	14. Project success (PMO impacts on projects)

The number of indicators is lower on both external models: rational goals and open system. However, those on the rational goals (efficiency) conception shown in Table 4.10 are the most frequently cited indicators. The presence of indicators for profit is not surprising; they reflect the current interest in contributing to the business's bottom line. Looking at the productivity criterion, the contribution of PMOs could be significant, particularly in the allocation of resources. This point highlights an important issue for organizations having multiple highly specialized expert profiles working on multiple projects. In the case studies this issue was of prime importance in two organizations having projects where 200 to 300 staff work in parallel. In those two organizations, PMOs centralize the allocation of HR. The idea here is to not leave anyone "on the bench." The director of a PMO pinpointed his role in the allocation of project managers:

> "We wanted to use project management resources in a better way so that, for example, if a project manager was freed up in one product line, and there was a need in another product line, we could move that person over if the competence and the profile both matched the requirements."

Productivity in project management is a constant challenge. The challenge is even more evident in international organizations where there is competition between different offices in different locations. Productivity in project management becomes an important factor for deciding where projects will be realized. The role of PMOs in project management productivity is often recognized in the literature (Kendall & Rollins, 2003). These authors directly link productivity and performance on projects to the legitimacy of the PMO.

The criterion of planning in the PMO context mostly refers to their strategic and multi-project functions. The contribution of the PMO to organizational performance is recognized through its involvement in portfolio and program management. Indicators proposed by respondents give some idea of the concrete outcomes that relate to the strategic action of PMOs in selecting the right projects. Indicators also emphasize the role of the PMO in balancing the portfolio relative to risks, their benefits in short and long terms, and their value for the organization. The capacity planning indicators recognize the PMO's role in allocating resources in the long run, the capacity to deliver, and the capacity for internal resources to absorb changes from projects. Alignment of employees' objectives to the organization's is also found under the planning criterion. This indicator recognized that PMOs are involved in the appraisal process for individuals working in projects.

Two indicators are under the efficiency criterion. The one refers to the relationship that a PMO has with other parts of the organization. From interviewees it is clear that this refers to the perception of numerous inefficient meetings with PMO employees or managers. PMOs often perform a monitoring and controlling function on the performance of projects. To do this, information in additional to that available on reports or website is needed. Different committees or meetings are then called to share information. People working on projects repeat the same information in their functional unit in addition to the PMO unit. This may result in inefficiency. But at the same time it recognizes the role of the PMO in negotiations when it comes the time to decide on the status report color. The second indicator mentioned is project success, and more specifically, the role of the PMO in project success.

Indicators Within the Open System (Effectiveness) Conception

Table 4.11. Indicators within the open system (effectiveness) conception

Criteria	Indicators
Growth of the organization	1. Sales results
	2. Qualitative element from business case (business positioning)
	3. Effectiveness
Flexibility/adaptation/ innovation in project management	4. Innovator, creator, and good at conflict or problem resolution
	5. Hiring of project management personnel having creation skills
	6. Existence of initiatives in project management methodology (sometimes being delinquent)
	7. PMO product a variety of reports
	8. Hiring of external consultants who know the best practices in project management
	9. Evolution in project management process and tools
	10. Participation of stakeholders in the development and evolution of project management processes.
Assessment by external entities	None
Link with external environment	11. Link with the local PMI chapter (sometimes too much!)
	12. Benchmarking
Responsiveness	13. Being agile
	14. Responsiveness in appointment when urgent need

As previously mentioned, the number of indicators is lower on both external models: rational goals and open system (see Table 4.7). The open system effectiveness indicators shown in Table 4.11 deal mostly with flexibility, adaptation, and innovation in project management. The first criterion, growth of the organization, refers directly to the business side of the organization, taking into account sales, qualitative result, and effectiveness. These elements relate to the benefits from projects. It emphasizes that the PMO could be involved in a wider project life cycle, covering the benefits from projects. According to PMI (2006a), benefits management is associated with program management. Nonetheless, it stretches project management toward the product life cycle (Jugdev & Müller, 2005).

The criterion of flexibility, adaptation, and innovation shows numerous indicators. They are rarely shared from one case to another, except for delinquency in relation to methodology. One respondent stated, "A lot of flexibility, what matters to me is the result; I couldn't care less if we used a saw or a screwdriver to get there." This highlights the fact that the contribution of the PMO to organizational performance is not limited to the establishment of a methodology in project management (from internal processes conception), but also the flexibility in use that the PMO encourages. While no indicators were mentioned in the evaluation by external entities criterion, respondents mentioned some for the criteria of having links with external environment. Links with PMI are not always valued. It appears sometimes that it is too much. Benchmarking was mentioned often in a context of justification of the PMO, particularly to justify the number of staff working in it. The criterion of responsiveness included two indicators that were mentioned quite often by respondents. The PMO should be able to respond quickly to make projects succeed and to adapt to different situations.

Indicators in this open system conception contrast quite well with the ones included in the internal processes conception. This confirms that paradoxes exist in the PMO context. There are individuals who will value the respect of project management processes while, at the same time in the same organization, others will value exactly the contrary and will encourage delinquency.

Indicators Within the Output Quality Conception

Table 4.12. Indicators of output quality

Criteria	Indicators
Quality of deliverables	1. Quality of the product
	2. Satisfaction of the sponsor
	3. Satisfaction of clients

The output quality criterion includes three indicators, as shown in Table 4.12. First, the quality of the product has been included here, as many interviewees mentioned this element in relation with the PMO's contribution to overall quality performance. Second and third, we find indicators on satisfaction of the PMO sponsor and clients of the PMO. These indicators are quite usual when assessing quality.

The competing values framework offers an opportunity to acknowledge these paradoxes and from there to open up a dialogue to develop a common basis for organizational performance. This work supports the recognition of the diversity of the contributions a PMO can make to an organization. And it should also help to develop the awareness of the PMO managers and their employees of the paradoxes that are at work in their organizations regarding their performance. This approach brings a valuable instrument to initiate a dialogue and come to a common understanding of what is valued. PMO actions should then be aligned on this common understanding of organizational performance.

To the best of our knowledge, this is the first time the competing values framework has been used in the field of project management. It is also the first time that concrete indicators of performance within the four models have been identified. The indicators presented here are expressed in terms very close to those used by the interviewees. In this respect, they are *in vivo* indicators, or citations drawn directly from the interview transcripts. They are therefore neither complete nor perfectly articulated and coherent. However, they are a good starting point for developing a more complete and better refined set of indicators.

4.7 Conclusion

The first part of the qualitative approach of this research program on PMOs has been presented in this chapter. After having presented the results from the literature review, the conceptual and methodological frameworks have been presented. Empirical results from 12 PMOs in four organizations were then presented in two distinctive parts. The first part aimed at telling the story of PMOs within these organizations. The second part focused on the contribution of PMOs to organizational performance.

Until now in this book, the individual PMOs have been the focus of the empirical results from quantitative data (Chapters 2 and 3) as well as qualitative data (Chapter 4). The survey results presented in Chapter 2 showed that most PMOs are temporary structural arrangements that can be expected to change within a few years. The retrospective histories of PMOs in the three case study organizations that have had PMOs for several years confirmed and illustrated the temporary nature of PMOs. These two important findings have led to the development of an alternative way of conceptualizing the PMO, to new research questions, "Why do PMOs change so often?" and "What processes are at play?" and to an alternative method of analysis. In Chapter 5, PMOs are conceived as being the product of a dynamic process of transformation. The object of investigation is their transformations over a period of time instead of snapshots of PMOs frozen in time. The next chapter aims at understanding PMO through this process full of events, tensions, and sometimes, conflicts.

CHAPTER FIVE: THE PROCESS SIDE OF PMOs

5.1 Introduction

Until now, results from the research have described the structural characteristics and functions of PMOs (Chapter 2), their typologies (Chapter 3), and their historical path (Chapter 4). The survey results presented in Chapters 2 and 3 are based on the synchronic description of a large number of PMOs and their organizational contexts. They have shown the extreme variety in both the form and function of PMOs. Chapter 4 presents a diachronic description of PMOs in four organizations based primarily on data from interviews. These approaches have provided a rich description of the great variety found in the population but have not provided a comprehensive understanding of the ever-changing PMOs.

Both the survey results and the case studies showed that in the majority of cases, PMOs are unstable structures: organizations most often reconfigure their PMOs every few years. This instability can be interpreted in many ways. It could be an illustration of structuring as an ongoing organizational process (Pettigrew, 2003). It could also be interpreted as an illustration of organizational experimentation as organizations search for an adequate structural arrangement (Midler, 1994). The PMO can be seen as an organizational innovation and the frequent changes as processes of variation and selection (Hobbs, Aubry, & Thuillier, 2008). Half of the respondents to the survey report that the legitimacy of their PMO in its present form is being questioned. This is consistent with both the interpretation in terms of experimentation and a search for best practices, and with the interpretation as an instance of the inherent instability of an ongoing process of structuring. This chapter investigates the organizational processes that transform PMOs, with the aim of coming to a better understanding of PMOs. It is based on a process approach, using the in-depth investigation of the cases presented in Chapter 4. But rather than examining the PMOs, this chapter focuses on the transformations of the PMOs from one period to the next. There are 11 cases, four cases of setting up the first PMO in the organization and seven cases of an existing PMO being transformed. These transformations are the object of investigation in this chapter.

5.2 The Literature on Organizational Innovation

One of the possible interpretations of the PMO transformation is that of an organizational innovation. The innovation literature has, therefore, been reviewed for relevant concepts and theories. Four subsets of the literature on innovation are examined to identify alternative approaches relevant to the examination of PMOs as organizational innovations. First, the general literature on innovation is examined. This is followed by an examination of the literature based on evolutionary, coevolutionary and institutional isomorphism approaches. All are sensitive to evolution over time.

5.2.1 The General Literature on Innovation

Early research on innovation operated mostly from an economic perspective and a general assumption of growth (Chandler, 1962). The interdisciplinary curriculum has developed over time with the contribution of new knowledge stemming from a variety of sources: economics (Cohen & Levinthal, 1990; Penrose, 1959; Schumpeter, 1950), organizational management (Dougherty, 1992), sociology (Robert & Barley, 1996), and social ecology (Bijker, 1989). Others provide a categorization of innovation based on product, process, or architecture (Abernathy & Utterback, 1988; Henderson & Clark, 1990). In this perspective, organizations are considered to be very similar, responding to the same incentives.

Innovation theory has shifted to a social innovation approach, broadening the concept of technological innovation to a social system.

> "[…] the sociological crucial point is that organizations have not only become prominent actors in society, they may have become the only kind of actor with significant cultural and political influence. Yet, recent organization theory has surprisingly little to say about how organizations affect the society." (Robert & Barley, 1996, p.148)

New questions have emerged that lead to motivation theory and to the context of innovation that rehabilitates history along with innovation, thus introducing the temporal element to the social innovation system (Barley, 1998; Graham & Shuldiner, 2001). This historical perspective was a natural step after the ecological model that demonstrated the usefulness of the biological metaphor with the concepts of evolution and coevolution (Massini et al., 2002). This social approach paved the way for looking at organizations as part of the social innovation system and new forms of structure as innovations. Along this line of thought, innovation is viewed as an art or, more exactly, as a craft (Graham & Schuldiner, 2001). Innovation then becomes a creative act, the dynamic construction of something new in which it can be difficult to discern any regular pattern[5] (Dooley & Van de Ven, 1999).

---

5 Dooley and Van de Ven have been working on what is called complexity theory. This theory says that more complex tools are needed to understand the complex reality of today's organization. Changes in organization could follow three different dynamic types (from less to more complex):

5.2.2   From Evolutionary Theory to Coevolution

The evolutionary theory was developed in the theory of organizations based on a biological metaphor. A basic evolutionary model of an organization envisions it as a collection of routines or stable bundles of activities. With time, variation occurs within these routines, with the result that any given set of routines evolves, whether intentionally or not. A certain number of new routines are then adopted as temporarily permanent practices. This simple "variation – selection – retention" repeats itself continuously (Miner, 1994).

Evolutionary theories are made up of two major groups: contingency theories and social theories. Contingency theories consider technological change as an exogenous phenomenon, which triggers organizational evolution (Chandler, 1962; Rosenkopf & Tushman, 1994). This deterministic approach makes structural arrangements predictable from variables such as complexity, uncertainty and interdependency, which can be integrated into a single dimension, the ability to treat information (Scott, 1990).

Social theories view organizations as technological social constructions in which the community of organizations determines the nature of technological evolution (Rosenkopf & Tushman, 1994). In this approach, organizational structures are seen as processes in action, which are continuously built and rebuilt (Scott, 1990). Scott argued that these approaches are two sides of the same coin (1990). On the one hand, technology can be considered the causal agent that shapes the structure of organizations; while on the other hand, to reverse this causal effect, organizations influence the innovation process with either the creation of a new technology or its early adoption (Scott, 1990).

This complementarity is recognized in the coevolution theory in which technological innovations are believed to give the impetus that initiates new cycles of variation – selection – retention and in which a dynamic process of evolution with innovation constantly feeds organizations (Rosenkopf & Tushman, 1994; Van de Ven & Garud, 1994).

Massini et al. (2002) confirmed that evolutionary theory is capable of explaining changes in organizational structures and routines. They concluded that organizational adaptation is a consequence of changes related to the adoption of technological innovations. Looking at large Western and Japanese firms at two different periods in time (1992, 1996), their research confirms both the progressive adaptation over time and the tendency to adopt organizational routines associated with a higher capacity for flexibility. This also confirms the selection and emergence of dominant routines suggested by the evolutionary theory. They also confirm that these changes are context-dependant: the institutional context in which organizations are embedded defines patterns of organizational structures and strategies.

---

periodic, chaotic, or random time series (colored noise: white, pink, or brown) (Dooley & Van de Ven, 1999).

5.2.3 Coevolution

In biology, coevolution is defined as evolution involving successive changes in two or more ecologically interdependent species (as of a plant and its pollinators) that affect their interactions. (*Merriam-Webster Collegiate Dictionary*, 2007, p. 240) The relation could be of a predator-prey nature or of a symbiotic nature. Coevolution is also used in a narrower context when it refers to a specific form of relation (inside or outside of a company). Eisenhardt and Galunic (2000) referred to coevolution (of a symbiotic nature) when they argue that multi-business corporations are coevolving ecosystems. From this viewpoint, collaboration occurs only when it gives a positive performance result in terms of growth, market share, and profits.

Coevolution helps the understanding of the evolution of complex systems. At a macro-level[6], Rosenkopf and Tushman (1994) proposed a framework to examine various stages of coevolution of organizational and technological forms. The object of their analysis is the technological community[7]. These authors argue that there are two different interlinked processes: the evolution of community organization and the evolution of technology within one cycle of variation – selection – retention. Organizations are part of their community and they contribute to the evolutionary process of community organization that simultaneously drives and is driven by cyclical technological progress through eras of ferment followed by eras of incremental change.

At a micro level, there are numerous technological (variation) events, rule-making (selection) events, and institutional rule-following (retention) events that occurred and coevolved over time to facilitate and to constrain the development and commercialization of an innovation. Van de Ven and Garud (1994) analyzed the case of cochlear implant development within this perspective. They scrutinized this innovation for 35 years to identify events and found that they can be grouped into three time periods: initiation, expansion, and stabilization. The initiation period was marked by technological events originating in basic research, while both rulemaking and rule-following events were important in the expansion period. Not surprisingly, during the stabilization period, rule-following events were dominant.

It is also worth noting that the evolutionary theory suggests a progression toward some more evolved state. Evolution provides regularity and a certain form of predictability. In complexity theory, this could be associated with random time series of longitudinal data in which there is no pattern such as life cycle, but rather a tendency to "follow itself," to repeat a movement toward the same direction, for example. This randomness is associated with brown noise (Dooley & Van de Ven, 1999) and is different from a periodic pattern. In conclusion, technology and organization are parts of a common social system in which innovation breaks a

---

6   Their level of analysis is the organizational community, which they define as the set of organizations that are stakeholders for a particular technology (Rosenkopf & Tushman, 1994).

7   The technological community is defined as the set of organizations that are stakeholders for a particular technology (Rosenkopf & Tushman, 1994).

temporary equilibrium and launches an unpredictable journey through a process of variation – selection – retention.

Some criticisms have been aimed at the evolutionary theory in relation to its inability to provide an appropriate analysis of the context of technological evolution. De Bresson (1987) suggested turning to the historical perspective to get the broader picture of technological evolution. This implies that researchers have to look at processes rather than ad hoc events. One good example of looking at the innovation process is Van de Ven (1999), who concluded that what is encountered in the life of an organization does not match any regular pattern.

5.2.4 Institutional Isomorphism

Institutionalism theories propose to understand changes at the organizational field level, where the evolution of a population of organizations can be observed (DiMaggio & Powell, 1983; Hannan & Freeman, 1977). In this perspective, organizational survival is based upon the capacity to adapt to the environment through the evolutionary process of variation – selection – retention, forming what has been called the *Population Ecology of Organizations* (Hannan & Freeman, 1977). Some authors have worked to explain the diversity of organizations and to identify criteria that make some survive while others disappear (Pettigrew, 2003). Based on this biological metaphor, DiMaggio and Powell (1983) observed instead a tendency toward greater homogeneity and asked a basic question from this perspective, "What makes organizations so similar?" (p. 147). Their research leads to a questioning of rationality in decision-making processes related to organizational structure. They argued that the resulting organizational structure has not so much to do with market competition and efficiency. They found instead that institutional isomorphism could better explain the form organizations take on. The level of analysis is the organizational field, defined as a dynamic network of organizations that is recognized as having an institutional life. DiMaggio and Powell (1983) identified three mechanisms of institutional isomorphic change: coercive isomorphism, mimetic processes, and normative pressures. This thinking sheds light on the discussion around the PMO as an isomorphism mode or as a rational entity within organizations aiming at being more efficient in project management.

5.2.5 Organizational Innovation in the Project Management Literature

The mainstream literature on innovation approaches organizational innovation as organizing for innovation (Burns & Stalker, 1961; Massini et al., 2002). Innovation is often defined in a product or process view, and is opposed to invention. Innovation confirms the commercial success of an invention: "an invention that has found a useful and commercially viable application" (Granstrand, 1999, p.479). Ironically, organizational innovation could better be defined as an invention: "[…] those works of mind which are new, novel, non-obvious, and useful" (Granstrand,

1999, p. 479). A patent can be obtained to protect an invention, but not for innovation or *a fortiori* for organizational innovation.

Innovation in the project management literature refers most often to product and process innovation and is often classified using the bipolar model of radical and incremental (Kenny, 2003; Shenhar & Dvir, 1996) using the typology from Nelson and Winter (1982). Turner and Keegan (2004) suggested that product and process innovations require a creative environment with specific characteristics. Elsewhere, Duggal (2001) proposed a next-generation PMO, where a R&D function exists for specific purposes of project management innovation.

Organization itself is worth considering as the object of innovation and not only a means for product or process innovation (Schumpeter, 1934, as cited in Drejer, 2004). Organizational innovation has been explored in the field of project management (Martinsuo et al., 2006). Building on institutional isomorphism, Martinsuo et al. (2006) explored project-based management as an organizational innovation. The aim of this research was to understand the adoption of project-based management as an organizational innovation. More specifically, it aimed to identify the drivers that lead to adoption of project-based management and the results from adopting it in terms of changes and benefits. Their research on 111 companies from different industries revealed that context-related elements, such as external pressure and internal complexity, play a role as drivers for introducing project-based management.

For the purpose of this research, organizational innovation is defined as a new, non-obvious and useful set of rules, processes, and structure that has found viable application in organizations.

5.3 Modeling the PMO Transformation Process

Implementing a PMO or reconfiguring an existing PMO is an important organizational change. This change is often part of a wider organizational reconfiguration. A methodology and an interpretive framework are needed to capture the dynamic complexity of organizational change. The approach that has been adopted investigates the PMO embedded in its organizational context. The approach can be related to a long tradition of contextual studies in the literature on project organizations, from Midler (1994) to Pellegrinelli et al. (2007). History and context are essential to understanding what is observed at any one point in space and time in complex systems such as organizations (Engwall, 2003). The theoretical foundations of the social innovation system framework take into account the context in which such organizational innovations take place (Hughes, 1987). Social innovation builds also on a bi-directional relation that conceptualizes organizational innovations as socially constructed and society-shaping (Bresnen et al., 2005). Organizational innovations are produced by the interplay between actors in structures and the organization as a whole. The PMO is seen as a socially constructed entity that in turn shapes the organization. The PMO and its host organization coevolve.

Organizational change occurs in a political environment. Changes to PMOs are both caused by political forces and shape a new political environment. Tensions within the organization play an important role in determining the path that an organization's development will follow. In turn, each new structural arrangement realigns the power structure and creates new tensions. The investigation of the creation or restructuring of PMOs needs to integrate the political dimension of organizational change.

The organizational transformations have been modeled using a framework based on conditions, action/interaction, and consequences proposed by Strauss and Corbin (1998, p. 167). These three elements form a process that repeats itself, consequences becoming the conditions for the next iteration. In this approach, the PMO in one period is seen as a temporary state resulting from previous conditions and generating new consequences.

This sequence constitutes the PMO structuring process, which is illustrated in Figure 5.1.

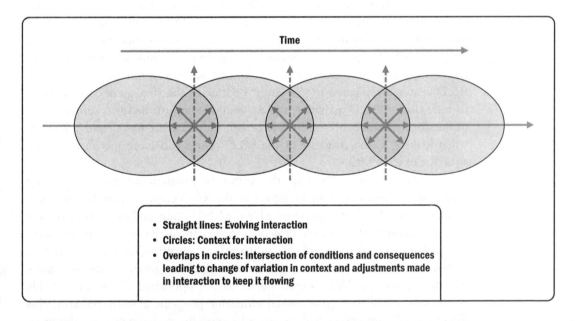

Figure 5.1. The PMO structuring process, based on Strauss and Corbin (1998, p. 167)

The conditions that lead to an organizational transformation have been grouped under four themes: events from the surrounding social system, internal events, the philosophy of management, and tensions to be resolved. The action/ interaction element corresponds to the structuring itself. New tensions are among the consequences of the restructuring. Other consequences exist but the focus here is on the new tensions that are created. This framework for modeling the process of structuring PMOs is presented in Table 5.1.

Table 5.1. The framework for data collection and analysis

Conditions	Project management structure	Consequences
Social system events		
Internal events	Resulting structure	New tensions
Philosophy of management		
Tensions to be resolved		

5.3.1 Conditions

The four conditions that give rise to a specific structure are listed on the left side of Table 5.1. The first two, social system events and internal events, are themes drawn from the social innovation framework presented in Section 4.2. A good example of conditions related to the social system can be found in the telecommunication case study, with the major turbulences caused by the bursting of the dotcom bubble in 2001. An example was presented in Chapter 4, where major turbulence in this industry did not immediately impact the R&D center that was part of our study. This company maintained its long-term development perspective and long-term R&D objectives while cutting into the operations side of the business. R&D activities were concentrated in a limited number of centers, including the R&D center investigated in this study. Because of the strategy of this company to maintain its R&D activities, the economic downturn had few consequences in the short term for this local R&D center. Indeed, there was a relative stability when looking at the structure of the R&D center and more specifically at the structure of the PMO.

It was only in 2004 that the company program aimed at increasing organizational efficiency had an impact on the R&D centers. With this program, major organizational changes occurred in the R&D center and the PMO structure with the centralization of all project management activities within one unit. The global financial results of the company were encouraging after a three-year period of difficulties. But the organizational efficiency program was still going on and focused on R&D activities after having optimized the operations side of the business. The organizational efficiency program globally reshaped this R&D center. This center had to prove its capacity to compete with the other centers and, more importantly, regain the trust of the head office, among others, on respecting delivery dates. Business units remained in place with even more accountability to deliver solutions to internal clients. As can be seen from this example, events from the external environment have observable consequences on companies. Their responses to these events may involve the remodeling of their strategies and structures. In this example, an event from the external environment has effects over many years, three years after the economic event in this case. Thus, the example also illustrates the mediating effect of management action on the impact of external events and the indirect or delayed effects that external events can have.

For all of the seven transformations found in the case study organizations, change in the structure corresponds to a change in the philosophy of management. This expression *philosophy of management* was used by interviewees. It can be associated to a particular philosophy of life defined as an overall vision of or attitude toward life and the purpose of life (*Merriam-Webster Collegiate Dictionary*, 2007, p. 930). The concept of philosophy of management is used here to group together the set of values and elements of a cultural nature that form a global entity capable of orienting decisions and actions of people in the organization. The philosophy of management can be related to that of one individual, of the top management team, or of the whole organization. A new philosophy of management usually initiates a new restructuring process, the current structure not being coherent with the new philosophy of management. Continuing with the example of the telecommunication company, the philosophy changed from one supporting entrepreneurship to one supporting tight controls and improved performance, particularly on schedule. The PMO manager who was put in place in 2004 had a vision of the PMO as exercising strong centralized control. This approach had an influence on the role and the mandate of this PMO at the time: project management was completely centralized in one PMO. All project managers were part of this PMO and were assigned to the projects of a business unit as consultants. The resulting structure brought two-sided management: one side looking after business results and the other looking after the project processes. It recognized the importance of both and each project had to find its own equilibrium to deliver project results. This situation imposed strict control in the management of projects, where project managers were playing the role of controller. A high value was placed on transparency. Any deviation from plans should be reported and corrective action immediately identified and applied. The personal incentives of the PMO manager were linked to this: no project was allowed to pass directly from green to red!

Tensions (between individuals, between sub-structures, etc.) emerge generally from discomforts that get constructed over time within a specific structure. The word *tension* is used here in its abstract sense to describe a state of latent hostility or opposition between individuals or groups (*Merriam-Webster Collegiate Dictionary*, 2007, p. 1288). In the context of project management organizational structures, tensions often build up slowly until a breaking point is reached, at which time a change in the structure will take place, modifying or eliminating the source of tension. From the previous example, one of the consequences of implementing the new centralized PMO was the creation of tension related to transparency and the information provided by the product line manager:

> "It actually goes against the goals of most people in positions of authority in the various product units because they are held accountable for every decision, all the time, all the projects. If you're comfortable with that you have no ability to bend the truth or mask any information or try to fix something quietly for a week or two. Now everything is always posted on the website, it's updated every week. The track of projects is always there." (Verbatim from an interview.)

Another tension from the same example relates to the trade-offs between quality and schedule. Project managers push to implement as planned even if quality problems persist. Once the project is completed, problem solving is under the responsibility of the product manager. As can be seen from these examples, tensions bring the political dimension of organizations into play. In some cases, a tension leads to open conflict and almost all actors will recognize it and will name such a situation as a tension or conflict. However, in some organizational and/or nation cultures, the terms tension and conflict are too strong. In these cultures, the term "issue" can often be used to refer to this same reality.

5.3.2 Resulting Structure

The resulting PMOs have been described using variables measuring their structures, the importance of functions performed, and their resulting contributions to organizational performance as defined in the descriptive model of PMOs presented in Section 1.3 and further developed in Chapter 2. The object of this chapter is not to focus on PMO structures as such, but to examine the processes that transform them. The focus here is on identifying patterns in the change process when going from one PMO to the next within a dynamic context.

5.3.3 Consequences

There are many consequences that can be identified from changes to organizational structure. The focus here is on the tensions that are created following a restructuring of a PMO. Tensions are present at the two ends of the structuring process: they serve as a set of conditions, and once a new structure is put in place, new tensions emerge as consequences of the new structure. As such, tensions offer an opportunity to understand the dynamics of coevolution between the PMO and its environment.

5.4 The Empirical Study

The empirical study aims at obtaining data that will then enable a process analysis. In this view, PMOs are changing through a process of transformation. The empirical study should provide data on such transformation. A constructivist epistemology has been adopted, meaning that the phenomenon, here the PMO, is a complex object evolving in interaction within a context. In other words, the PMO and its context construct themselves overtime. To capture the construction over a period of time, it is essential to get historical data. Data from in-depth case studies presented in Chapter 4 was used in this part of the research. Please refer to Section 4.3 for the methodological details.

When taking a process view, the focus is no longer on the description of each individual PMO, but rather on the transformation. Therefore, the unit of analysis is the organizational transformation around an implementation or a reconfiguration of a PMO. The sample is made up of 11 organizational transformations: four cases of implementing first PMOs and seven cases of reconfiguring existing PMOs. Table 5.2 presents a summary of the data.

Table 5.2. Summary of the data

Organization	Number of PMO transformations		Number of years
	First PMO	**From existing PMO**	
Telecommunication	1	3	12
Financial 1	1	2	10
Multimedia	1	2	8
Financial 2	1	0	4

The same data is being used in Chapters 4 and 5. In this chapter, data from verbatim interview transcriptions has been codified and analyzed using the conditions, structure, and consequences model as shown in Table 5.1. From this analysis, a typology of tensions emerges, which is the subject of the following section.

5.5 A Typology of Organizational Tensions

An analysis of the 11 transformations revealed that the organizational tensions, conflicts, or issues contribute significantly to making sense of PMO transformations. Five categories of tensions have been identified: economic, political, customer relationship, standardization versus flexibility, and controlling the project machine.

5.5.1 Economic Tension

There are two sources of economic tension: project performance and PMO cost. Project performance is often questioned inside organizations. Tensions emerge when projects do not meet their objectives. This is true with or without the presence of a PMO, but when a PMO exists it is often recognized as having a role to play in project performance. The performance of projects is often used as a key performance indicator for PMOs (Kendall & Rollins, 2003). Several scenarios have been observed. In some cases, project performance remains poor, bringing the PMO's legitimacy into question. In other cases, project performance is seen as improving independently of the efforts deployed by the PMO. In yet other cases, a pattern was observed where an organization implemented a PMO to improve performance and when performance improved, the PMO was no longer seen as useful. Following the dismantling of the PMO, performance declined and a new PMO was created to improve project performance once again. Pellegrinelli and Garagna (2009) described this phenomenon as "emptying the PMO." More generally, those responsible for PMOs are often under pressure to show value for money. It is usually within this pattern that the second source of economic tension emerges. In some of the case studies, the cost of the PMO appears as a tension when overall project performance improves significantly following the efforts of the PMO. PMO costs seem to be superfluous, because there is a belief in the organization that the level of project management maturity has increased to the point that the PMO is no longer necessary. This leads to both constantly documenting the value of PMOs and to PMOs being the victims of frequent attacks on their legitimacy.

5.5.2 Political Tension

Political tensions emerge around issues of power and control. The power to manage projects seems to be the most important tension, the one that gives rise to the most important issues and the one that has the greatest influence on decisions related to organizational structure. Who is going to manage projects? Answering this question determines the location of project managers. Accountability is closely related to the issue of control. Who in the organization will be accountable for project management results? If the attainment of business objectives relies to a large extent on projects, the key to power and influence in the organization relates to having power and influence on projects. If senior managers are to be accountable for business results, they want to have the means to attain them; they want to have control over project management.

Tension emerges naturally on the issue of control of projects. In some organizations a distinction is introduced between monitoring and controlling. Many PMOs monitor project progress and performance. Some are limited to the monitoring function, while others have a role to play in controlling projects. Tensions emerge when PMOs exert control over projects for which they do not have primary responsibility. In some situations, PMOs are allowed to report information on projects, to ask questions, to integrate information by portfolio, but are not allowed to make judgments and even less to dictate actions on projects. This leads to a paradox where a PMO cannot take action but at the same time can be criticized for its inability to affect project performance.

Many PMOs have in their mandate to control projects either managed internally or managed by other entities. The situation is more conflicting when a project is in difficulty; nobody appreciates diffusion of bad news on his or her project. Judgment on the project's health depends upon the perception and the position of the individual. People from the PMO or from the business unit do not have the same point of view, as they are not pursuing the same objectives and do not have the same incentives. Each may have his or her own criteria for reporting the project status as green, yellow, or red. Discussion on the color of the project status is a widespread phenomenon and involves much debate and negotiation among people at all levels of the organization. These discussions come back periodically, often monthly. They provide an opportunity to observe the tensions that emerge around the management of the project and its status.

Another source of tension related to control of projects is the issue of transparency. Discussions on the color of the project status may be avoided by giving inaccurate or incomplete information. PMOs sometimes play a detective role to make sure that no information is hidden by other managers. In this situation, a climate of trust is difficult to establish and tensions can become very apparent.

5.5.3 Client Relationship Tension

From the PMO's perspective there are two types of clients: their own clients for their deliverables and the clients of projects that are realized in the organization. The tensions are related primarily to the second type of client, usually represented internally by an organizational entity. This relationship seems sensitive as it provides legitimacy. Some business and IT entities attempt to retain exclusive responsibility for customer relationships and to push the PMO outside of this relationship. Not being in a close relationship with an internal client can have important consequences with respect to having knowledge of the projects. A PMO can easily be discredited when it has poor information on projects. In one of the cases, a PMO was dismantled because of its inability to help project managers due to a misunderstanding of projects' needs.

5.5.4 Standardization/Flexibility Tension or Business Versus Process Orientation

The standardization of project management methodology and process is often in opposition to the flexibility needed in the execution of a project in real life. On one side, PMOs often have the responsibility for developing and standardizing methodologies. The development of these tools is very often participative, with contributions from all entities involved in project deliverables. But when it is time to put the methodology into application, confrontations are rather the norm. The tension between standardization and flexibility is closely related to issues of power and control. Standards are followed or not, depending on who has the power to decide.

Project owner and project sponsor roles are determinant in project governance (Cooke-Davies, 2005). An opposition often emerges between a business and a process orientation in decision making. Tension is created between business managers demanding flexibility to meet business needs and those who are responsible for the project management process. In certain circumstances, business managers encourage delinquency in the pursuit of business objectives, while in others the emphasis is placed on respecting the project management process. Tensions also emerge with respect to the profile of the project manager, should he or she be a process, technical or business manager. Changes in structures often require project managers to develop new competencies, which takes time.

5.5.5 Controlling the Project Machine Tension

The expression "controlling the project machine" was used by several interviewees. This expression is used to evoke two versions of the same tension: either the machine should be upgraded or it races out of control. Raising the organizational capacity to deliver projects brings up problems around resource allocation. But reducing this capacity is more subtle and brings tension between PMOs and functional or business units. A good example can be drawn from one of the case studies in which a PMO was given the responsibility to align projects to the business strategy while project managers were under the responsibility of business units. Managers in business units wanted their entity to succeed and flourish. One way of doing this is to initiate new projects and to increase human resources working on them, or at least to maintain them at present levels. Under good portfolio management, such behavior should not be permitted if projects are not required to reach business objectives. In this case, the PMO was at the heart of a conflict resulting from an attempt to reduce the project portfolio being opposed by business units that wanted to increase it.

5.6 The Most Important Drivers of PMO Transformation

Conditions act as drivers for a PMO transformation, which in turn contains within itself tensions that may be the ingredients for the next transformation. When looking in more detail at the conditions as drivers of change, not all of them have the same degree of importance. In each case, significant conditions for a PMO change have been codified in a grounded theory approach, letting categories emerge from the analysis of the interview transcripts. The qualitative analysis of PMO transformations includes a quantification strategy when appropriate (Langley, 1999). Table 5.3 presents the number of elements grouped in two integrative types: external and internal environments. Events from the social system come from the external environment of the organization. Altogether, internal events, philosophy of management, and tensions to be resolved are part of the internal context specific at each organization.

Results show evidence of the prevalence of internal drivers. Three factors can lead to an underestimation of the importance of external drivers. First, events from the external environment that had an impact on the PMO have been selected. The numbers reflect only a partial view of the global external environmental analysis. Second, interviewees in higher management positions often linked external events to a PMO transformation, while project managers generally focused on their project and were unaware of the global external environment. Third, an external event can have numerous impacts on the internal context of an organization during a long period of time. Despite these qualifying remarks, it is clear that most people interviewed attributed the changes in PMOs to conditions that are internal to the organization.

Table 5.3. Importance of different conditions

	EXTERNAL	INTERNAL		
	Social system events	Internal events	Philosophy of management	Tensions to be resolved
Telecommunication	2	8	6	10
Financial 1	4	6	3	15
Multimedia	4	4	4	7
Financial 2	2	2	4	13
Subtotal	12	20	17	45
TOTAL	**12**	**82**		

Table 5.4 presents the list of drivers ordered by their frequency in the 11 PMO transformations. The first four elements of Table 5.4 refer to the human side of the PMO transformation. The first two elements refer directly to the individual level. A change of CEO and of PMO director are the most frequent drivers associated with a PMO transformation. The third element, philosophy of management, is also associated with people, either at the individual or group level. Organizational politics, the fourth element, refers also to people within an internal political system. The importance of these drivers related to human factors might not significantly different from any other transformation within an organization. A new manager will align the organization under his or her control with his or her values, culture, and globally to his or her philosophy of management. It should be noted that there are usually multiple interwoven forces at play at the same time. One condition may be more powerful, but alone, it may not lead to a PMO transformation. Less visible drivers may play an important role in certain circumstances.

Table 5.4. Most frequent drivers from case studies

Number	Name of the driver
The most frequent drivers	
1	CEO or business unit manager change
2	PMO director change
3	Change in the philosophy of management
4	Organizational politics
5	Economic tension on the cost of PMO
6	Standardization versus flexibility
7	Business or process orientation
The most infrequent drivers	
1	Controlling the project machine
2	Client relationship

Several executive workshops have been held using this interpretation of PMO changes in Canada, Australia, and Europe. The feedback from participants confirmed not only the way the PMO transformation process has been modeled but the relative importance of the drivers as well. Nevertheless, some executives expressed some reserve regarding the word transformation. They argued for an "evolution" instead of a "transformation." The drivers may stay the same, but it is acknowledged in the organization that the PMO will evolve and it is managed that way. In such organizations, the change process is seen as an evolution. It is difficult to know whether the organizational realities being described are different or whether the organization or national culture may not accept that there are transformations in the same way that some cultures do not recognize the existence of conflicts. The 11 changes from the qualitative case studies were all recognized as transformations. However, there are certainly variations in the degree of change; they may vary from evolutionary to radical and disruptive. This should be taken into account in future research.

5.7 Two Alternative Interpretations

The great variety of PMOs found in organizations at the present time and the frequent creation and restructuring of PMOs can be interpreted in two ways. These observations can be seen as illustrations of the early phase of an organizational innovation. This is the era of ferment, the variation stage that will be followed by selection and institutionalization. Alternatively, these observations can be seen as illustrations of the unstable nature of organizations as they undergo continuous restructuring.

5.7.1 The PMO as an Organizational Innovation

The prevalence of PMOs is an important and relatively recent phenomenon. The great variety and lack of any obvious pattern can easily be interpreted as illustrating the era of ferment. The selection process may have already begun but it is not yet clearly visible. Ad-hoc conversations with many different people reveal that a considerable amount of mimicry is taking place. The PMO has become a very widespread and well-known organizational phenomenon. In many organizations, people are being given the mandate to implement a PMO without a clear image of what this might entail. The difficulty stems from the great variety of PMOs presently in place and the lack of consensus as to their value. For one organization to mimic another, there must be a relatively clear perception of the phenomenon to be reproduced (DiMaggio & Powell, 1983). This is often lacking with PMOs. Therefore, mimicry may partially explain the initial drive to set up a PMO, but it does not provide an adequate explanation of the structure that is implemented. In addition, it cannot explain the instability observed among the population of PMOs.

5.7.2   PMOs as Manifestations of Organizational Instability

PMO structures alternate between periods of tension and periods of a relative stability. This alternating can be interpreted as "waves of rationality." Hatchuel (1995) depicted the history of modern organizations as a cyclical effort to rationalize. In this perspective, rationalization is a myth, a figure of progress; each new managerial technique bringing a concrete portrait of rational management that is valid for a limited time. Scientific management, operational research, total quality management, business process reengineering, and expert systems are all archetypes of a rational wave. Their typical life cycle begins with a blend of enthusiasm and reluctance that is fed with confused images describing progress or calamities resulting from them. After a few years, first passions are followed by caution and often disillusion. Elements of the new managerial technique survive but are used much more selectively. These authors interpret the history of changes in organizations through the myth of rationality, where actors play a central role, the philosophy espoused by senior management playing a central role in shaping the evolution of the organization. The cases examined in this study provide many illustrations of the role played by the philosophy of management in regulating organizational behavior.

From this perspective, implementing a PMO can be seen as a rational effort to implement new managerial techniques. The 11 examples of the structuring of PMOs examined during this study can be interpreted as 11 waves of rationality or attempts to introduce rationality in the management of projects. Tensions emerging from each new structure slowly erode the rationale upon which the change was based, leading to a new wave of rationality implemented through a new organizational arrangement, including a new structure for the PMO.

Hatchuel (1995) considered organizations as fundamentally irrational. It is not necessary to adopt this point of view to conceive of organizations as constantly restructuring. Pettigrew (2003) proposed a conceptualization of organizations as continuously going through processes of strategizing and structuring. The constant change is being driven in part by the internal political dynamics of the organizations. It is also being driven by the need to adapt to dynamic environments (Brown & Eisenhardt, 1997). The cases examined in this study provide many illustrations of constantly shifting structures driven both by organizational politics and by adaptation to contextual changes.

The data analyzed in this study track the evolution of PMOs in four organizations that are very mature in project management. It is reasonable to think that the processes of selection and retention of "better" PMO structures would be more visible in organizations that have considerable expertise in project management. One of the organizations has had four different PMOs over a 12-year period. Two others have had three PMOs over eight- and 10-year periods. Yet no discernable pattern was found. This may be because the sample is small or because the processes of selection and retention require more time. This may also illustrate the unstable nature of organizational structures.

5.8 Conclusion

The analysis presented here makes several contributions to the study of organizations and organizational innovation. It confirms that the PMO is deeply embedded in its host organization, and that the two coevolve. The study also shows that organizational tensions are among the primary drivers behind the implementation and reconfiguration of PMOs. The playing out of these tensions brings into focus the importance of organizational politics. The analysis shows that PMOs and more generally the structures put in place to manage multiple projects are part of a political system that plays an important role in organizations (Morgan, 1986). In the project management literature, power and politics are often treated with an instrumental approach through risk management and stakeholder management (Magenau & Pinto, 2004). The analysis here shows that power and politics should be examined at the organizational level and integrated into organizational project management.

The PMO is an organizational innovation in the sense that it is a recent and important phenomenon. But if it is an innovation, it is unstable and still evolving, both in individual organizations and in the population of organizations as a whole. If the institutionalization process is at work, the results are not yet visible. Given the ever-changing nature of organizations, it may take considerable time before a discernable pattern emerges, if it emerges at all.

CHAPTER 6: CONCLUSION

This book presents the results of a multi-year, multi-method research program aimed at developing a better understanding of PMOs. The detailed conclusions have been summarized and commented upon in the final section of each chapter. The multi-method approach combined with multiple opportunities to present and discuss preliminary or partial results in several forums with both researchers and practitioners over a period of several years has proved to be very fruitful. It has provided cross-fertilization between survey and case study methodologies, frequent rethinking of both the preliminary results and the approach, and opportunities for sense-making and partial validation. This general conclusion examines what was learned and the significance of what was discovered for practitioners, professional organizations, researchers, and the field of project management as a whole.

A PMO can be described by answering the following two questions, "How are PMOs structured?" and "What functions do they fill?" Responses to these two questions form the two major groups of variables in the model of PMOs that emerged from this research as shown in Figure 1.1, which is reproduced here.

The goal of this research program is to develop a better understanding of PMOs. The authors' understanding of PMOs has been both improved and transformed. At the outset, the PMO was conceptualized and studied as if it were an isolated and stable organizational entity. The first project in the research program was a survey to describe the population that collected the descriptions of 502 PMOs worldwide. The most important and influential finding from the analysis of the survey data was possibly one of the simplest and most obvious in retrospective: most PMOs change every few years. This simple fact has profound consequences for practitioners, professional organizations, and researchers.

6.1 The Demand for Guidelines

The professional-practitioner community has been demanding best practices, guidelines, and eventually a standard on PMOs since the turn of the century. Practitioners are often asked to give advice within their organization on the implantation or renewal of a PMO. Their underlying questions are, "How should PMOs be structured?" and "What functions should they fill?" If PMOs are temporary arrangements, it is impossible to answer these questions, at least as they are presently conceptualized. The answer might be, "It depends." The best way to set up a PMO is context-specific. This is the concept behind contingency

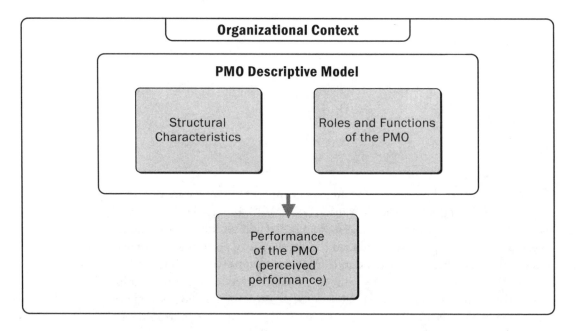

Figure 1.1. A model of the PMO in its context

theory, a very well-established school within the field of organizational studies, and an idea well-accepted by practitioners.

The second most important finding from the analysis of the survey data was that PMOs do not vary systematically according to the classic organizational contingency factors. PMOs in different industries, different geographic regions, in large and small organizations, and in public and private organizations do not vary systematically in either the way they are organized or the functions they fill. Because these contingency factors are quite stable and PMOs change quickly, it is normal that no relationship exists between them.

6.2 How PMOs are Structured

The analysis of the survey data did identify some project management-specific organizational characteristics that are associated with the structural characteristics of PMOs. And both are associated with the performance of the PMO. These are presented in Figure 3.5, which is reproduced here.

The most important organizational contextual factor is the organization's level of project management maturity. However, considerable caution must be exercised in interpreting this result. First, the association only describes a state of nature; it does not directly answer the normative question as to how things "should be." Second, an association does not identify the causal relationship; A might influence B or vice versa, or both might be under the influence of a third variable. Third, if project management maturity is the "cause," this cause can only be changed very slowly and with considerable investment.

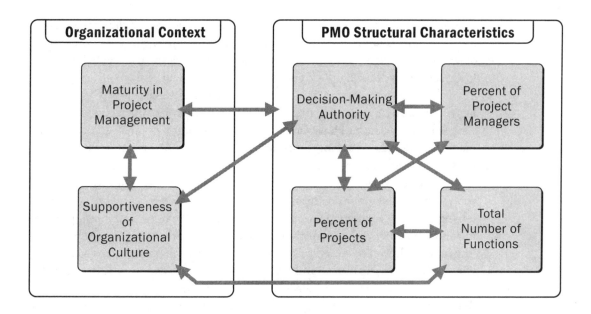

Figure 3.5. The augmented cluster of organizational contextual variables and PMO characteristics

A plausible interpretation is that organizations that value project management have invested in getting better at it, which is captured in the measure of their project management maturity. Being valued means that management has invested both financially and symbolically in project management and that the organizational culture supports and values project management. A PMO in this situation would likely also be valued because it is part of the organization's implementation of project management. The perceived value of the PMO could be both a favorable perceptual bias and a measure of the organizational reality. An organization that values project management and sees itself as mature in project management may be more likely to set up a higher performing PMO. If this interpretation holds true, it begs the question, "How can an organization develop a culture that supports project management and become mature in project management?" Is there a role for the PMO in developing the culture and the level of maturity? Most probably, "Yes." If so, this becomes a chicken-and-egg problem. It is also a warning to those trying to set up a PMO in an organization that does not value project management or is not mature in project management; the PMO may lack legitimacy and need extra support and even protection.

The three structural characteristics of the PMO shown in Figure 3.5 are more readily amenable to management influence. The most important of these and the most difficult to manipulate directly is the level of authority or influence of the PMO. The influence of a small organizational entity such as a PMO is largely determined by its credibility. The support and the decision-making authority given by upper management are important determinants of both credibility and authority. The competency of the PMO manager and staff are also important. However, the results indicate that the competency of the personnel is critical.

This research did not investigate the human resource policies of the organizations in which PMOs are found, so any conclusion is tentative. But based on ad hoc observation, it seems that few organizations have policies that make being in the PMO a career-advancing position. This observation is certainly worth pursuing.

As shown in Figure 3.5, the analysis also identified that PMOs with a higher proportion of the organization's projects and project managers were more successful on average. However, in a particular organizational context, there may be good reasons for not putting all the projects or project managers in a PMO. For example, following the presentation of these results at a practitioner conference, a manager of an apparently very successful PMO said, "We have 600 project managers in our organization and I don't want them all reporting to me!" Giving the PMO the mandate to be involved in all the organization's projects may not be in line with the mission that management wants to give to the PMO. The result is, however, an indication that a PMO with no project managers is less likely to be seen as legitimate and is likely to need more support. The issue may be just a question of perception; PMOs with project managers may be seen as busy doing important work, while those that do not may be seen as a visible overhead expense. The question as to what projects and project managers, if any, are put in a PMO is an important organization design issue that is likely to have important consequences for the PMO and the organization.

Analysis of the survey data also revealed that PMOs have many meaningful characteristics and that the variance on most is high. In addition, there are few strong associations among these structural characteristics in the overall population of PMOs. This means that when designing a PMO, an organization has a large number of choices as to how to organize the PMO, and that the choice on one characteristic does not constrain the choice on other characteristics. The result for one organization designing its PMO is that there are many options. The result for the entire population of PMOs is extreme variety.

6.3 The Roles of PMOs

PMOs can fill many roles or functions. The research investigated 27 functions and showed that all 27 are important for large numbers of PMO and that PMOs generally fill multiple functions, an average of 12.7. The analysis reduced the number of functions to eight independent underlying groups of functions. The independence of the groups is important. It means that an organization designing a PMO has eight groups to choose from and that the choice of one group does not constrain the choice of other groups. The result for one organization designing its PMO is that there are many options. The result for the entire population of PMOs is extreme variety.

This information on functions filled by PMOs is strictly descriptive. But what functions should a PMO fill? This question is difficult to answer, partly because some to the most import functions are filled by almost all PMOs. This means that these functions are unlikely to discriminate among successful and unsuccessful PMOs. In addition, all of the eight groups of functions are weakly correlated with

PMO performance. The total number of functions filled by the PMO is more strongly correlated with PMO performance than any of the individual functions. PMOs that fill multiple functions that are in line with management's vision are more likely to be better perceived.

6.4 Types of PMOs

The population of PMOs is thus characterized by extreme variety in both their structural characteristics and the functions they fill. This variety could be reduced and better managed if PMOs could be grouped into homogeneous groups or types. Given the finding previously discussed, it is unlikely that clearly discriminated types can be found in the population, but meaningful groups do exist. Several strategies were deployed in search of such types.

The choice of the proportion of projects and project managers to include in a PMO can be used to create four types of PMOs that are significantly different on all the organizational contextual and PMO structural characteristics, as shown in Figure 3. 4. The four types are:
- Type 1: A small percentage of the organization's projects and project managers
- Type 2: A small percentage of the organization's projects and a large percentage of its project managers
- Type 3: A large percentage of the organization's projects and a small percentage of its project managers
- Type 4: A large percentage of the organization's projects and a large percentage of its project managers

The functions filled by PMOs can also be used to identify types, but for the reasons stated, attempts to identify types by function were less fruitful and did not identify true types.

An alternative means of conceptualizing the role of PMOs in an organization is to examine the aspects of organizational performance to which the PMO contributes. This novel way of approaching the issue of the contribution of project management to organizational performance was developed in Chapter 4. One of the results was a typology of PMOs based on the model of organizational performance to which the PMO contributes. The framework identifies the following four concepts of organizational performance, each with a different focus. The framework is presented in Figure 4.2, which is reproduced here.

The use of this framework to address the question, "What should the role of the PMO be?" reframes the issue as one of strategic choice.

6.5 PMO Embedded in Organizational Dynamics

PMOs are extremely varied and they are changed frequently. It is highly plausible that it is the internal dynamics of the organization that are driving the implementations and frequent reconfigurations of PMOs. The second major

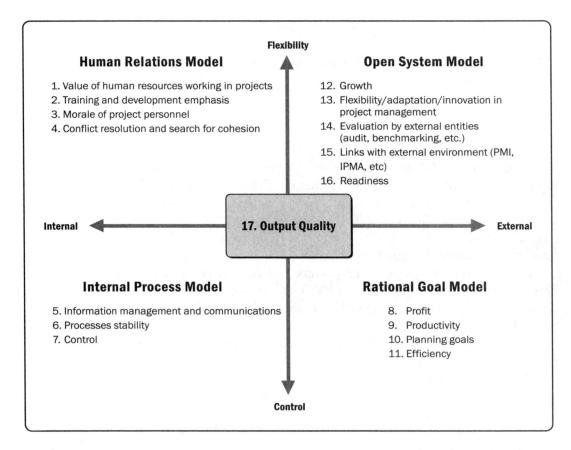

Figure 4.2. The competing values framework

project in this research program was set up to investigate PMOs within their organizational context. PMOs in four organizations were examined in in-depth qualitative case studies using a retrospective historical approach. The aim of the case studies was to answer the question, "How and why do organizations implement their first PMO or reconfigure existing PMOs every few years?" The qualitative study provides a rich description of PMOs embedded in their organizational context. Rather than examining the PMO as a static and isolated organizational entity, the PMO is conceptualized as an entity that plays multiple roles in multiple organizational processes.

The historical account of the PMOs showed periods of relative stability and periods of significant change. PMOs can thus be examined within different timeframes. In a narrow timeframe, a PMO can be examined during a period of relative stability to better understand how it was structured and the role it played in the organizational context. In a wider timeframe, the PMO can be examined as it went from a period of relative stability through a period of important change to another period of relative stability. In this latter timeframe, the focus becomes the process that transformed the PMO. In the examination of this process, one of the central questions is, "What was driving the change?" The results show that the most important drivers in decreasing order are:

1. CEO or business unit manager change
2. PMO director change
3. Change in the philosophy of management
4. Organizational politics
5. Economic tension on the cost of PMO
6. Standardization versus flexibility

The four most important drivers are elements of the organizational context in which the PMO is embedded. The fifth is related to challenges to the legitimacy of the PMO because of the overhead expense incurred by the organization. This challenge to its legitimacy may be related to the first four drivers. The only driver in this list that is related to the role played by the PMO is the last one. This is related to the project management processes, which can be either too ad hoc and flexible, or too standardized and rigid. The answers to the questions, "How is the PMO structured?" and "What functions does it fill?" are being driven primarily by changes in the organization in which the PMO is embedded and by the political agenda within this context.

To understand PMOs, particularly during periods of change, it is important to understand the organizational dynamics in which they are embedded. These dynamics have rational, political, and human dimensions. There is a business rationale behind the change. There is a political rationale because all organizational change mobilizes political forces and reconfigures the political landscape. There is a human dimension both because the changes are being driven by individuals, particularly people in positions of authority, and also because organizational change impacts the work and working environment of many people.

The PMO is not an inanimate object. By engaging with the organization, the PMO, and particularly the PMO manager, influence the destiny of both the PMO and the organization. The PMO and the organization influence each other in a relationship that can be usefully conceptualized as coevolution. However, the PMO is a small fish in a big pond with some much bigger fish.

The examination of the processes that transform PMOs is based on a small sample of 11 such transformations. A follow-up study is underway to further examine these processes and to extend the study to a larger sample.

6.6 Theoretical Foundations

The study of the PMO is clearly situated at the organizational level of analysis. The concept of organizational project management, a concept that has emerged in recent years within the project management practitioner literature (PMI, 2003, 2008b), is clearly also situated at the same level of analysis. Recent empirical work has confirmed that the PMO is often a central element of the implementation of project management in organizations (Thomas & Mullaly, 2008). However, there has been almost no work to link the study of either organizational project management or the PMOs to existing theoretical frameworks.

The concept of project-based organization, under several related labels, has received considerable attention within the more theoretical literature in project management. This concept has been linked to theoretical frameworks in organization theory and innovation management. However, this stream of literature has not focused on the PMO as an object of study and has not integrated the concept of organizational project management.

It is important to provide a theoretical basis for any object of study. Within the present research program an effort has been made to do so. More work to this end is needed. A fruitful path for doing so is to situate the PMO within organizational project management and the project-based organization, and to situate both of these within organization theory and innovation management. The authors are currently pursuing this path in other work.

6.7 Changing Organizational Myths

For several years the authors have given and listened to many presentations on PMOs and discussed PMOs with many practitioners and researchers. This has provided an opportunity to be both a participant in and an observer of the collective discourse on PMOs. A change seems to have occurred in the dominant myth within the practitioner community. In 2005, the belief was that it is possible to have one best practice for PMOs. This was captured in a limited number of types of PMOs, of which one type was obviously better. In 2008, it is more common to hear that PMOs are quite varied and change quite a bit. The current myth is that as they change, PMOs are becoming more mature. There is nothing particularly scientific about these observations, but possibly offer some food for thought.

The question, "Are PMOs becoming more mature?" was not one of the research questions investigated here. However, the retrospective histories of three of the organizations that participated in the qualitative research covered three or four successive PMOs in each organization. No pattern of increasing maturity was observed and none of the people interviewed said that the PMOs were being changed to make them more mature. The forces driving the changes had little to do with becoming more mature. Because the sample is small and because the question of increasing maturity was not the focus of the investigation, it is not possible to reach a conclusion on this question based on the research presented here.

APPENDICES

A   Original survey questionnaire

B   Follow-up survey questionnaire

C   Case study interview guide

D   Case study questionnaire on the PMOs contribution to organizational performance

Appendix A

General Information on the Organisation

In compliance with the policies of the Research Ethics Committee of the UQAM, all the information provided will remain strictly confidential.

1. What is your present position?

○ Project Manager
○ Manager in the PMO (Director or middle manager)
○ Executive
○ Manager elsewhere in the organisation
○ Professional in the PMO
○ Professional elsewhere in the organisation
○ Consultant
○ Other (Please specify)

2. The organisation is of which type?

○ Private enterprise
○ Public sector organisation
○ NGO or a not-for-profit organisation

3. The primary activities of the organisation are in which economic sector?

4. What is the total number of employees?
(For large organisations including multi-nationals, please indicate the total number of employees.)

○ Less than100   ○ 101 to 500   ○ 501 to 1000   ○ 1001 to 10,000   ○ 10,001 to 30,000   ○ More than 30,000

5. Which of the follow categories best describes the level of project management maturity of the organisation?

○ Initial Level - ad hoc and chaotic; relies on the competence of individuals not the organisation's.
○ Repeatable Level - there is a project management system and plans are based on previous experience.
○ Defined Level - common, organisation wide understanding of project management activities, roles and responsibilities.
○ Managed Level - stable and measured processes against organisational goals; variations are identified and addressed.

○ Optimising Level - the entire organisation is focused on continuous improvement.

6. In which country does the PMO operate primarily?

○ Canada

○ USA

○ Other (Please specify)

[   ]

Identification and Location of the PMO

☒

PMOs can take many forms in different organisations. Several organisations have more than one PMO, e.g. a central PMO and PMOs in Business Units. Your responses for the rest of this survey must describe only one PMO. If you are able to describe more than one, we invite you to fill-out a survey for each PMO.

7. Which of the following situations best describes your PMO and its position in the organisation?

○ The only PMO in the organisation and it is central

○ The only PMO in the organisation, located in a business, functional or regional unit

○ More than one PMO in the organisation. This PMO is central.

○ More than one PMO in the organisation. This PMO is located in a business, functional or regional unit and has no relationship with a more central PMO.

○ More than one PMO in the organisation. This PMO is located in a business, functional or regional unit and has a relationship with a more central PMO.

8. What name is given to this PMO?

○ Project Management Office (PMO)

○ Project Support Office

○ Programme Office

○ Center of Excellence

○ Other (Please specify)

[   ]

9. How long has this PMO been in existence?

○ Less than 1 year

○ 1 to 2 years

◯ 3 to 5 years
◯ More than 5 years

☒

For the three following questions please respond in relation to the organisational entity in which the PMO is active. This may be the entire organisation, a division, a department or any other part of the organisation.

10. How many projects are executed simultaneously in this entity?

◯ Less than 10
◯ 11 to 50
◯ 51 to 100
◯ 101 to 500
◯ More than 500

11. In what percentage of these projects does the PMO play an active role?

◯ Less than 20%   ◯ 21% to 40%   ◯ 41% to 60%   ◯ 61 to 80%   ◯ More than 80%

12. What percentage of Project Managers in this entity report to the PMO?

◯ None
◯ Less than 25%
◯ 26% to 50%
◯ 51% to 75%
◯ More than 76%
◯ All report to the PMO

13. In addition to any Project Managers, how many people, expressed in fulltime equivalents, work in the PMO? (Including the person responsible for the PMO.)

◯ Less than 1   ◯ 2 to 3   ◯ 4 to 7   ◯ 8 to 12   ◯ 13 to 18   ◯ More than 18

14. On the average, how many people are actively involved in a typical project in the PMO?

◯ Less than 10   ◯ 11 to 25   ◯ 26 to 50   ◯ 51 to 75   ◯ 76 to 100   ◯ 101 to 200   ◯ More than 200

15. What is the average duration of projects in the PMO, expressed in months?

◯ 1 to 3   ◯ 4 to 8   ◯ 9 to 12   ◯ 13 to 18   ◯ More than 18

16. Primarily, the projects in which the PMO is involved are for:

◯ Several customers internal to the organisation
◯ One customer internal to the organisation
◯ Several customers external to the organisation
◯ One customer external to the organisation

17. What is the PMO's level of decision-making authority?

◯ No authority
◯ Little authority
◯ Some authority
◯ Considerable authority
◯ Very significant authority

18. The manager to whom the person responsible for the PMO reports has authority over what percentage of the human resources that work on the PMO's projects?

◯ Less than 20%   ◯ 21% to 40%   ◯ 41% to 60%   ◯ 61 to 80%   ◯ More than 80%

19. At the present time, how important are the following roles or functions in the PMO's mandate?

	Not important at all	Of little importance	Of some importance	Of considerable importance	Very important
Develop and implement a standard methodology	○	○	○	○	○
Supply a set of tools without an effort to standardize	○	○	○	○	○
Develop the competency of project personnel, including organising training	○	○	○	○	○
Provide mentoring for Project Managers	○	○	○	○	○
Recruit, select, evaluate and determine salaries for Project Managers	○	○	○	○	○
Promote project management within the organisation	○	○	○	○	○
Organise environmental scanning and networking	○	○	○	○	○
Execute specialised tasks for Project Managers, e.g. preparation of schedules	○	○	○	○	○
Identify, select and prioritize new projects	○	○	○	○	○
Manage one or more programmes	○	○	○	○	○
Manage one or more portfolios	○	○	○	○	○
Coordinate between projects	○	○	○	○	○
Manage benefits	○	○	○	○	○
Allocate resources between projects	○	○	○	○	○
Monitor and control project performance	○	○	○	○	○
Implement and operate a project information system	○	○	○	○	○
Develop and maintain a project scorecard	○	○	○	○	○
Report the status of projects to upper management	○	○	○	○	○
Provide advice to upper management	○	○	○	○	○
Participate in strategic planning	○	○	○	○	○
Conduct project audits	○	○	○	○	○
Conduct post-project reviews or post mortems	○	○	○	○	○
Implement and manage a database of lessons learned	○	○	○	○	○
Implement and manage a risk database	○	○	○	○	○
Manage archives of project documentation	○	○	○	○	○
Manage customer interfaces	○	○	○	○	○
Monitor and control the performance of the PMO	○	○	○	○	○

20. Does this PMO fill other roles or functions? Please specify.

Implementation of the PMO

The questions in this section refer exclusively to the period during which the PMO was implemented. If you did not participate in the implementation or do not otherwise have access to information necessary to answer the following questions, please jump to question 24.

21. In your opinion, to what extent did the organisational culture support the implementation of the PMO?

○ Not at all
○ Very little
○ Somewhat
○ Considerably
○ Very much

22. In your opinion, what was the most important obstacle to implementation of the PMO?

23. The implementation of the PMO was carried out over what period of time? If the implementation is not yet complete, how much time do you think it will take?

○ Less than 6 months
○ 6 months to a year
○ 1 to 2 years
○ 2 to 3 years
○ More than 3 years

Conclusion

24. Has the relevance or even the existence of the PMO been seriously questioned in recent years?

◯ Yes   ◯ No

25. Indicate to what extent you agree with the following statements.

	Total disagreement	More or less in disagreement	Neither in agreement or disagreement	More or less in agreement	Total agreement
The PMO's mission is well understood by those that deal with the PMO.	◯	◯	◯	◯	◯
The PMO works in close collaboration with other project participants.	◯	◯	◯	◯	◯
Those that deal with the PMO recognize the PMO's expertise.	◯	◯	◯	◯	◯
The PMO is perceived as having a significant impact on the performance of projects and programmes.	◯	◯	◯	◯	◯
The PMO's reporting level is too low in the organisation.	◯	◯	◯	◯	◯
The PMO is fully supported by upper management.	◯	◯	◯	◯	◯
The PMO is relatively useless and costly.	◯	◯	◯	◯	◯
The PMO is perceived as controlling too much.	◯	◯	◯	◯	◯

26. In your opinion, what are the PMO's strong points?

27. In your opinion, what are the areas the PMO needs to improve?

28. If you wish to receive a copy of the results of this survey, please provide your e-mail address.

e-mail address

29. Would you agree to participate in an individual interview to go more deeply into some of the issues raised by this study?

◯ Yes   ◯ No

Description of another PMO
If you are able to describe another PMO, we invite you to record your data by selecting Finish below and restarting the survey from the site www.pmo-survey.esg.uqam.ca/

Sending the survey to another person
If you know someone who could describe a different PMO, please invite him or her to do so and provide him or her with the address www.pmo-survey.esg.uqam.ca/

The survey results accumulate automatically. You can access the results by clicking on Finish below.

You can save the address of the results page in order to access the results at a later date.

Thank you for your collaboration.

Appendix B

Ethics Statement

This follow-up survey is meant only for those that have already responded to the survey on the "Reality of PMOs." It is designed to gather additional information on the same PMOs that were described in the original survey. Please answer the questions below with respect to the same PMO at the time of your original response. Each data set is a photograph of one PMO at a particular time.

We use the e-mail address used to send you the survey results to link the answers to these additional questions to your original responses. Please provide this e-mail address below.

1.

Your e-mail address:

2. What is the background of the personnel of the PMO other than the project managers?

○ IT professionals

○ Finance or accounting

○ Other professionals or technical specialists

○ Operations

○ Business

○ Other (please specify)

3. What is the average number of years of experience of PMO personnel other than project managers in positions of project or program manager?

years as project or program managers

4. Are there business analysts or business architects among the PMO staff?

○ Yes   ○ No

5. Is the project methodology supported by the PMO homegrown?

If the PMO doesn't support any methodology, write N/A.

Percentage of the methodology that is homegrown

6. Is compliance with the PMO's methods, policies or recommendations compulsory or discretionary?

○ Entirely discretionary

○ Encouraged but not enforced

○ Compulsory but weakly enforced

○ Compulsory and strongly enforced

○ Compulsory and unavoidable

7. Are the PMO's methods, policies or recommendations followed?

○ Never

○ Occasionally

○ Regularly

○ Almost always

○ Always

8. Is the PMO more process driven or business driven?

○ exclusively process driven

○ more process driven than business driven

○ as much one as the other

○ more business driven than process driven

○ exclusively business driven

9. In some contexts, projects end with the delivery of the final product. In other contexts, project scope includes post-delivery activities. What is the scope of your PMO's projects?

☐ Projects end with delivery of the final product

☐ Responsibility for the following post-delivery activity is an important part of project scope: Communication

☐ Responsibility for the following post-delivery activity is an important part of project scope: Commercialization

☐ Responsibility for the following post-delivery activity is an important part of project scope: Integration into operations

☐ Responsibility for the following post-delivery activity is an important part of project scope: Organizational change

☐ Other important post-delivery responsibilities (please specify)

[   ]

10. The funding for the PMO is:

◯ clearly insufficient

◯ less than adequate

◯ adequate

◯ more than adequate

◯ overly generous

11. The PMO bills for its services:

◯ Yes   ◯ No

12. The PMO's involvement in outsourcing contracts is:

◯ not involved

◯ only very indirectly involved

◯ important responsibility on supplier side

◯ important responsibility on customer side

13. The PMO reports to which part of the organization:

◯ Top executive

◯ IT

◯ Finance

◯ Human Resources

◯ Other functional unit

◯ Operations

◯ Business unit

◯ Other (please specify)

14. The PMO's projects deliver primarily which type of products or services:

◯ Tangible products

◯ IS/IT

◯ Intangible products or services

15. The primary performance criteria for the PMO's projects is:

◯ Respect of schedule

◯ Respect of budget

◯ Meeting technical specifications

◯ Realizing business benefits

Thank you for your participation. As soon as you have finished this questionnaire, you will have access to results as they accumulate. We suggest that you save the address of the site on which results are accumulated in order to be able to return to this page.

Appendix C

Initial Question
What is your career path within this company?

Questions on specific themes

1. Theme Social Innovation System
1.1 When was your first project managed within a PMO?
1.2 From your point of view, why is there a PMO in your company?
1.3 Were there changes in the life of the PMO at your company? Why?

2. Theme Project Management Office
2.1 Complete the questionnaire on the Reality of the PMO, for the present situation.
2.2 Who are the people with which you are mostly in relation, in your job of project manager?
2.3 What are your most important deliverables for the PMO?
2.4 From where is the information coming?

3. Theme Organizational Performance
3.1 What are the most important performance criteria for PMO?
3.2 Complete the questionnaire on PMO performance.

Socio-demographic questions

Group of age: ___less than 30 years   ___30 - 40 years   ___ mote than 40 years

Academics: ___College   ___Under graduate   ___ Master   Other: ___

Domain of the academic formation: _____

Actual Position: _____

Number of years of experience in project management: _____

Number of years in the actual position: _____

Closure

1. Are there any others items that have not been mentioned yet in relation to the PMO, or PMO performance?
2. Can you provide internal documents that would help to understand the PMO context of your organization?

Appendix D

Case study questionnaire on the PMO contribution to organizational performance

PMO contributes to the organization performance by:

No	Criteria	Degree of importance				
		1 Not important at all	2 Some importance	3 important	4 Very important	5 Very much important
1	Value of human resources – project					
2	Training and development emphasis					
3	Moral on project's personnel					
4	Conflict resolution and search for cohesion					
5	Output quality					
6	Information management and communications					
7	Processes stability					
8	Control					
9	Profit					
10	Productivity					
11	Planning goals					
12	Efficiency					
13	Growth					
14	Flexibility / Adaptation / Innovation in project management					
15	Evaluations by external entities (audit, benchmarking)					
16	Links with external environment (PMI, etc.)					
17	Readiness					

REFERENCES

Abernathy, W. J., & Utterback, J. (1988). Patterns of industrial innovation. In M. L. Tushman, & W. Moore (Eds.), *Readings in the management of innovation* (pp. 25-36). Dunmore, PA: Harpercollins.

Aczel, A. D. (1996). *Complete business statistics* (3rd ed.). Chicago, IL: Irwin.

Andersen, E. S. (2006). Toward a project management theory for renewal projects. *Project Management Journal, 37*(4), 15-30.

Archibald, R. D. (1992). *Managing high-technology programs and projects* (2nd ed.). New York, NY: John Wiley & Sons, Inc.

ATLAS.ti Software Development. (2004). ATLAS.ti (version 5.0) [Computer software]. Available from Atlas.ti's Web site: http://www.atlasti.com

Aubry, M. (2006, May). Making sense: A question of focus. *Doctoral Colloquium of EURAM 2006.* Oslo: European Academy of Management.

Aubry, M. (2007). *La performance organisationnelle des Bureaux de projet: Une analyse intersectorielle.* Université du Québec à Montréal, Montréal.

Aubry, M., Hobbs, B., & Thuillier, D. (2006, May). Organisational project management: A new approach to the PMO. *EURAM 2006.* Oslo: European Academy of Management.

Aubry, M., Hobbs, B., & Thuillier, D. (2007). A new framework for understanding organisational project management through PMO. *International Journal of Project Management, 25*(4), 328-336.

Aubry, M., Hobbs, B., & Thuillier, D. (2008). Organisational project management: An historical approach to the study of PMOs. *International Journal of Project Management, 26*(1), 38-43.

Barley, S. R. (1998). What can we learn from the history of technology? *Journal of Engineering and Technology Management, 15*(4), 237-255.

Benko, C., & McFarlan, F. W. (2003). *Connecting the dots: Aligning projects with objectives in unpredictable times.* Boston, MA: Harvard Business School Press.

Bijker, W. E. (1989). The social construction of Bakelite: Toward a theory of invention. In W. E. Bijker, T. J. Pinch et P. T. Hughes (Eds.), *The social construction of technological system: New directions in the sociology and history of technology* (pp. 159-151). Cambridge, MA: MIT Press.

Blomquist, T., & Müller, R. (2006). Practices, roles, and responsibilities of middle managers in program and portfolio management. *Project Management Journal, 37*(1), 52.

Boyne, G. A. (2003). What is public service improvement? *Public Administration, 81*(2), 211-227.

Bredillet, C. N. (2004). From the editor. *Project Management Journal, 35*(2), 3-4.

Bredillet, C. N. (2006, October). *Investigating the future of project management: A co-word analysis approach.* Paper presented at the International Research Network on Organizing by Projects Conference, Xi'an, China.

Bresnen, M., Goussevskaia, A., & Swan, J. (2005). Organizational routines, situated learning and processes of change in project-based organisations. *Project Management Journal,* 36(3), 27.

Bridges, D. N., & Crawford, K. J. (2001). *A project office: Where and what type.* Paper presented at the Project Management Institute Annual Seminars & Symposium, Nashville, TN.

Brown, S. L., & Eisenhardt K. M.. (1997). The art of continuous change: Linking complexity theory and time-paced evolution in relentlessly shifting organizations. *Administrative Science Quarterly, 42*(1), (1-34).

Burns, T., & Stalker, G. M. (1961). *The management of innovation.* London, UK: Tavistock Publications Limited.

Cameron, K. S. (1981). Construct space and subjectivity problems in organizational effectiveness. *Public Productivity Review* (June), 105-121.

Cameron, K. S. (1986). Effectiveness as paradox: Consensus and conflict in conceptions of organizational effectiveness. *Management Science, 32*(5), 539-553.

Cameron, K. S., & Quinn, R. E. (1999). *Diagnosing and changing organizational culture: Based on the competing values framework.* Reading, MA: Addison-Wesley.

Cameron, K. S., & Whetten, D. A. (1983). Organizational effectiveness: One model or several. In K. S. Cameron & D. A. Whetten (Eds.), *Organizational effectiveness: A comparison of multiple models* (pp. 1-24). New York, NY: Academic Press Inc.

Canadian Oxford Dictionary. (2004). Toronto, Ontario, Canada: Oxford University Press.

Chandler, A. D. Jr. (1962). *Strategy and structure.* Cambridge, MA: MIT Press.

Cohen, W. M., & Levinthal, D. A. (1990). Absorptive capacity: A new perspective on learning and innovation. *Administrative Science Quarterly, 35*(1), 128-152.

Cooke-Davies, T. J. (2001). *Towards improved project management practice: Uncovering the evidence for effective practices through empirical research.* Leeds, UK: Leeds Metropolitan University.

Cooke-Davies, T. J. (2004). Project management maturity models. In P. W. G. Morris & J. K. Pinto (Eds.), *The Wiley guide to managing projects* (pp. 1234-1264). Hoboken, NJ: John Wiley & Sons, Inc.

Cooke-Davies, T. J. (2005, May). The executive sponsor – Hinge upon which organisational project management maturity turns? Proceedings from the EMEA Project Management Institute Global Congress, Madrid, Spain.

Cooke-Davies, T. J., & Arzymanow, A. (2003). The maturity of project management in different industries: An investigation into variations between project management models. *International Journal of Project Management, 21*(6), 471-478.

Cooper, R. G., Scott, J. E., & Kleinschmidt, E. J. (1997a). Portfolio management in new product development: Lessons from the leaders - I. *Research Technology Management, 40*(5), 16-28.

Cooper, R. G., Scott, J. E., & Kleinschmidt, E. J. (1997b). Portfolio management in new product development: Lessons from the leaders - II. *Research Technology Management, 40*(6), 43-52.

Cosgrove Ware, L. (2003). Best practices for project management offices, Consulted on 2007/01/15 from http://www2.cio.com/research/surveyreport.cfm

Crawford, K. J. (2002). *The strategic project office.* New York, NY: Marcel Dekker.

Crawford, K. J., & Cabanis-Brewin, J. (2006). *Optimizing human capital with a strategic project office: Select, train, measure, and reward people for organization success.* Boca Raton, FL: Auerbach.

Crawford, L. (2002, April). *Developing individual and organizational project management competence.* Paper presented at the Project Management Institute of South Africa, Johannesburg, South Africa.

Crawford, L., Hobbs, B., & Turner, R. J. (2005). *Project categorization systems: Aligning capability with strategy for better results.* Newtown Square, PA: Project Management Institute.

Crawford, L., Hobbs, B., & Turner, R. J. (2006). Aligning capability with strategy: Categorizing projects to do the right projects and to do them right. *Project Management Journal, 37*(2), 38.

Dai, C. X. Y., & Wells, W. G. (2004). An exploration of project management office features and their relationship to project performance. *International Journal of Project Management, 22*(7), 523-532.

De Bresson, C. (1987). The evolutionary paradigm and the economics of technological change. *Journal of Economic Issues, 21*(2), 751-762.

DeFillippi, R. J., & Arthur, M. B. (1998). Paradox in project-based enterprise: The case of filmmaking. *California Management Review, 40*(2), 125-139.

Dietrich, P., & Lehtonen, P. (2004, August). *Successful strategic management in multi-project environment: Reflections from empirical study.* Paper presented at the International Research Network on Organizing by Projects Conference, Turku, Finland.

DiMaggio, P. J., & Powell, W. W. (1983). The iron cage revisited: Institutional isomorphism and collective rationality in organizational fields. *American Sociology Review, 48*(April), 147-160.

Dinsmore, P. C. (1996). Toward corporate project management: Beefing up the bottom line with MOBP. *PM Network* (June), 10-13.

Dinsmore, P. C. (1999). *Winning in business with enterprise project management.* New York, NY: AMACOM.

Donaldson, L. (2001). *The contingency theory of organizations.* London, UK: Sage Publications.

Dooley, K. J., & Van De Ven A. H. (1999). Explaining complex organizational dynamics. *Organization Science, 10*(3), 358.

Dougherty, D. (1992). Interpretative barriers to successful product innovation in large firms. *Organization Science, 3*(2), 179-202.

Drejer, I. (2004). Identifying innovation in surveys of services: A Schumpeterian perspective. *Research Policy, 33*(3), 551-562.

Duggal, J. S. (2001, November). *Building a next generation PMO.* Paper presented at the PMI 2001 First to the Future. Nashville, Project Management Institute.

Dwyer, S., Richard, O. C., & Chadwick, K. (2003). Gender diversity in management and firm performance: The influence of growth orientation and organizational culture. *Journal of Business Research, 56*(12), 1009-1019.

Eisenhardt, K. M. (1989). Building theories from case study research. *Academy of Management Review, 14*(4), 532-550.

Eisenhardt, K. M., & Galunic, C. D. (2000). Coevolving: At last, a way to make synergies work. *Harvard Business Review*, 91-101.

Englund, R. L., Graham, R. J., & Dinsmore, P. C. (2003). *Creating the project office: A manager's guide to leading organizational change.* San Francisco, CA: Jossey-Bass.

Engwall, M. (2003). No project is an island: Linking projects to history and context. *Research Policy, 32*(5), 789-808.

Fernez-Walch, S., & Triomphe, C. (2004). Le management multi-projets, définitions et enjeux. In G. Garel, V. Giard & C. Midler (Eds.), *Faire de la recherche en management de projet* (pp. 189-207). Paris, France: Vuibert.

Galbraith, J. R. (1995). *Designing organizations: An executive briefing on strategy, structure, and process.* San Francisco, CA: Jossey-Bass Publishers.

Gareis, R. (2002, July). *Management in the project-oriented society.* Paper presented at the Project Management Institute Research Conference, Seattle, WA.

Gareis, R. (2004). Management of the project-oriented company. In P. W. G. Morris & J. K. Pinto (Eds.), *The Wiley guide to managing projects* (pp. 123-143). Hoboken, NJ: John Wiley & Sons.

Gareis, R., & Huemann, M. (2003). Project management competences in the project-based company. In R. J. Turner (Ed.), *People in project management.* Aldershot, UK: Gower.

Garfein, S. J. (2005, September). *Strategic portfolio management: A smart, realistic and relatively fast way to gain sustainable competitive advantage.* Paper presented at the Project Management Institute Global Congress North America, Toronto, Canada.

Graham, M. B. W., & Shuldiner, A. T. (2001). *Corning and the craft of innovation.* Oxford, UK: Oxford University Press.

Granstrand, O. (1999). *The economics and management of intellectual property: Towards intellectual capitalism.* Cheltenham, UK: Edward Elgar.

Hagström, P., Sölvell, Ö., & Hedlund, G. (1999). A three-dimensional model of changing internal structure in the firm. In A. D. Chandler, Jr., P. Hagström, & O. Solvell (Eds.), *The dynamic firm: The role of technology, strategy, organization, and regions* (pp. 166-191). New York, NY: Oxford University Press.

Hannan, M. T., & Freeman, J. (1977). The population ecology of organizations. *American Journal of Sociology, 82*(5), 929-964.

Hatchuel, A. (1995). *Experts in organizations: A knowledge-based perspective on organizational change.* (L. Libbrecht, Trans.). Berlin, Germany: Walter de Gruyter.

Hedlund, G. (1994). A model of knowledge management and the N-Form Corporation. *Strategic Management Journal, 15*(special issue Summer), 73-90.

Henderson, R. M., & Clark, K. B. (1990). Architectural innovation: The reconfiguration of existing. *Administrative Science Quarterly, 35*(1), 9.

Henrie, M., & Sousa-Poza, A. (2005). Project management: A cultural literature review. *Project Management Journal, 36*(2), 5.

Hobbs, B., (2007). *The multi-project PMO: A global analysis of the current state of practice.* Newtown Square, PA: Project Management Institute.

Hobbs, B., & Aubry, M. (2007). A multi-phase research program investigating project management offices (PMOs): The results of phase 1. *Project Management Journal, 38*(1), 74-86.

Hobbs, B., & Ménard, P. M. (1993). Organizational choices for project management. In P. C. Dinsmore (Ed.), *The handbook of project management,* (pp. 81-108). New York, NY: Amacom.

Hobbs, B., Aubry, M., & Thuillier, D. (2008). The project management office as an organisational innovation. *International Journal of Project Management, 26*(5), 547-555.

Hobday, M. (2000). The project-based organisation: An ideal form for managing complex products and systems? *Research Policy, 29*(7-8), 871-893.

Huberman, A. M., & Miles, M. B. (1991). *Analyse des données qualitatives: Recueil de nouvelles méthodes.* Bruxelles, Belgium: De Boeck - Wesmael.

Huemann, M., & Anbari, F. T. (2007). Project auditing: a tool for compliance, governance, empowerment, and improvement. *Journal of the Academy of Business and Economics, 7*(2),

Huemann, M., Keegan, A. E., & Turner, J. R. (2007). Human resource management in the project oriented company. *International Journal of Project Management, 25*(3), 312-320.

Hughes, P. T. (1987). The evolution of large technological systems. In W. E. Bijker, T. P. Hughes, & T. J. Pinch (Eds.), *The social construction of technological systems: New directions in the sociology and history of technology,* 51-81. Cambridge, MA: MIT Press.

Ibbs, C. W., Reginato, J., & Kwak, Y. H. (2004). Developing project management capability: Benchmarking, maturity, modeling, gap analysis, and ROI studies. In P. W. G. Morris & J. K. Pinto (Eds.), *The Wiley guide to managing projects* (pp. 1214-1233). Hoboken, NJ: John Wiley & Sons, Inc.

Interthink Consulting. (2002). *State of the PMO 2002.* Report published by Interthink Consulting, Calgary, Alberta, Canada.

Jamieson, A., & Morris, P. W. G. (2004). Moving from corporate strategy to project strategy. In P. W. G. Morris, & J. K. Pinto (Eds.), *The Wiley guide to managing projects* (pp.177-205). Hoboken, NJ: John Wiley & Sons, Inc.

Jelinek, M. (1993). The innovation marathon: Lessons from high technology firms. *The Innovative Marathon* (pp. 469). San Francisco: Jossey-Bass Publishers.

Jordan, G. B., Streit, D., & Binkley, S. J. (2003). Assessing and improving the effectiveness of National Research Laboratories. *IEEE Transactions on Engineering Management, 50*(2), 228-235.

Jugdev, K., & Müller, R. (2005). A retrospective look at our evolving understanding of project success. *Project Management Journal, 36*(4), 19.

Kaplan, R. S., & Norton, D. P. (1996). Using balanced scorecard as a strategic management system. *Harvard Business Review, 74*(1), 75-85.

Kendall, G. I., & Rollins, S. C. (2003). *Advanced project portfolio management and the PMO: Multiplying ROI at warp speed.* Boca Raton, FL: J. Ross Publishing.

Kenny, J. (2003). Effective project management for strategic innovation and change in an organizational context. *Project Management Journal, 34*(1), 43.

Lampel, J., & Jha, P. P. (2004). Models of project orientation in multiproject organizations. In P. W. G. Morris & J. K. Pinto (Eds.), *The Wiley guide to managing projects* (pp. 223-236). Hoboken, NJ: John Wiley & Sons, Inc.

Langley, A. (1999). Strategies for theorizing from process data. *Academy of Management Review, 24*(4), 691-710.

Larson, E. (2004). Project management structures. In P. W. G. Morris & J. K. Pinto (Eds.), *The Wiley guide to managing projects* (pp. 48-66). Hoboken, NJ: John Wiley & Sons, Inc.

Light, M. (2000). *The report office: Teams, processes, and tools.* Stamford, CT: Gartner Group.

Lincoln, Y. S., & Guba, E. (1985). Establishing trustworthiness. *Naturalistic Inquiry* (pp. 289-331). Thousand Oaks, CA: Sage Publications.

Lindkvist, L. (2004). Governing project-based firms: Promoting market-like processes within hierarchies. *Journal of Management & Governance, 8*(1), 3-25.

Lundin, R. A., & Söderholm, A. (1995). A theory of the temporary organization. *Scandinavian Journal of Management, 11*(4), 437-455.

Magenau, J. M., & Pinto, J. K. (2004). Power, influence, and negotiation in project management. In P. W. G. Morris, & J. K. Pinto (Eds.), *The Wiley guide to managing projects* (pp.1033-1060). Hoboken, NJ: John Wiley & Sons, Inc.

Marsh, D. (2000). The programme and project support office. In R. J. Turner & S. J. Simister (Eds.), *Handbook of project management* (pp. 131-144). Aldershot, UK: Gower.

Martinsuo, M., Hensman, N., Artto, K. A., Kujala, J., & Jaafari, A. (2006). Project-based management as an organizational innovation: Drivers, changes, and benefits of adopting project-based management. *Project Management Journal, 37*(3), 87-97.

Massini, S., Lewin, A. Y., Numagami, T., & Pettigrew, A. M.. (2002). The evolution of organizational routines among large Western and Japanese firms. *Research Policy, 31*(8-9), 1333-1348.

Maylor, H., Brady, T., Cooke-Davies, T., & Hodgson, D. (2006). From projectification to programmification. *International Journal of Project Management, 24*(8), 663-674.

McDermott, C. M., & Stock, G. N. (1999). Organizational culture and advanced manufacturing technology implementation. *Journal of Operations Management, 17*(5), 521-533.

Merriam-Webster Collegiate Dictionary. (2007). 11th ed. Springfield, MA: Merriam-Webster Inc., p. 1623.

Microsoft. (2003). Microsoft Office Professional Edition [Computer software]. Available from Microsoft Web site : http://www.microsoft.com

Midler, C. (1994). *L'auto qui n'existait pas.* Paris, France: InterÉditions.

Midler, C. (1995). Projectification of the firm: The Renault case. *Scandinavian Journal of Management, 11*(4), 363-375.

Miles, R. E., Snow, C. C., Mathews, J. A., Miles, G., & Coleman, H. J., Jr. (1997). Organizing in the knowledge age: Anticipating the cellular form. *The Academy of Management Executive, 11*(4), 7-21.

Miller, D., & Freisen, P. H. (1984). *Organizations: A quantum view.* Englewood Cliffs, NJ: Prentice-Hall.

Miner, A. S. (1994). Seeking adaptive advantage: Evolutionary theory and managerial action. In J. A. C. Baum, & J. V. Singh (Eds.), *Evolutionary dynamics of organizations* (pp. 76-89). New York, NY: Oxford University Press.

Mintzberg, H. (1979). *The structuring of organizations: A synthesis of the research.* Englewood Cliffs, NJ: Prentice-Hall.

Morabito, J., Sack, I., & Bhate, A. (1999). *Modeling organization: Innovative architectures for the 21st century.* Upper Saddle River, NJ: Prentice Hall.

Morgan, G. (1986). *Images of Organization.* Beverly Hills, CA: Sage.

Morin, E. M., Savoie, A., & Beaudin, G. (1994). *L'efficacité de l'organisation: Théories, représentations et mesures.* Montréal, Québec, Canada: Gaëtan Morin éditeur.

Mullaly, M. E. (2006). Longitudinal analysis of project management maturity. *Project Management Journal, 37*(3), 62.

Nelson, R. R., & Winter, S., G. (1982). *An evolutionary theory of economic change* (p. 437). Cambridge, MA: Belknap Press.

Nobeoka, K., & Cusumano, M. A. (1997). Multiproject strategy and sales growth: The benefits of rapid design transfer in new product development. *Strategic Management Journal, 18*(3), 169.

Nonaka, I., Sasaki, K., & Ahmed, M. (2003). Continuous innovation in Japan: The power of tacit knowledge. In L. V. Shavinina (Ed.), *The International Handbook on Innovation* (pp. 882-889). Oxford, UK: Elsevier Science Ltd.

Norrie, J., & Walker, D. H. T. (2004). A balanced scorecard approach to project management leadership. *Project Management Journal, 35*(4), 47-56.

Partington D., Pellegrinelli, S., & Young, M. (2005). Attributes and levels of programme management competence: An interpretative study. *International Journal of Project Management, 23*(2), 87-95.

Patton, M. Q. (2002). *Qualitative research & evaluation methods.* Thousand Oaks, CA: Sage Publications.

Pellegrinelli, S. (1997). Programme management: Organising project-based change. *International Journal of Project Management, 15*(3), 141-149.

Pellegrinelli, S., & Garagna, L. (2009). Towards a conceptualisation of PMOs as agents and subjects of change and renewal. *International Journal of Project Management, 27*(7), 649-656.

Pellegrinelli, S., Partington, D., Hemingway, C., Mohdzain, Z., & Shah, M. (2007). The importance of context in programme management: An empirical review of programme practices. *International Journal of Project Management, 25*(1), 41-55.

Penrose, E., T. (1959). *The theory of the growth of the firm.* Oxford, UK: Oxford University Press.

Pettigrew, A. M. (2003). Innovative forms of organizing: Progress, performance and process. In A. M. Pettigrew, R. Whittington, L. Melin, C. Sanchez-Runde, F. A. J. Van den Bosch, W. Ruigrok, & T. Numagami (Eds.), *Innovative forms of organizing* (pp. 331-351). London, UK: Sage Publications.

Pounder, J. S. (2002). Public accountability in Hong Kong higher education: Human resource management implications of assessing organizational effectiveness. *The International Journal of Public Sector Management, 15*(6/7), 458.

Powell, W. W. (1990). Neither market nor hierarchy: Networks forms of organizations. *Research in Organizational Behavior, 12*, 295-336.

Project Management Institute. (2003). *Organizational project management maturity model: OPM3 Knowledge Foundation.* Newtown Square, PA: Project Management Institute.

Project Management Institute. (2004). *A guide to the project management body of knowledge* (3rd ed.). Newtown Square, PA: Project Management Institute.

Project Management Institute. (2006a). *The standard for portfolio management.* Newtown Square, PA: Project Management Institute.

Project Management Institute. (2006b). *The standard for program management.* Newtown Square, PA: Project Management Institute.

Project Management Institute. (2008a). *A guide to the project management body of knowledge* (4th ed.). Newtown Square, PA: Project Management Institute.

Project Management Institute. (2008b). *Organizational project management maturity model: OPM3 Knowledge Foundation – Second edition.* Newtown Square, PA: Project Management Institute.

Quinn, R. E., & Cameron, K. S. (1983). Organizational life cycles and shifting criteria of effectiveness: Some preliminary evidence. *Management Science, 29*(1), 33-51.

Quinn, R. E., & Rohrbaugh, J. (1983). A spatial model of effectiveness criteria: Towards a competing values approach to organizational analysis. *Management Science, 29*(3), 363.

Robert, N. S., & Barley, S. R. (1996). Organisations and social system: Organization theory's neglected mandate. *Administrative Science Quarterly, 41,* 146-162.

Rohrbaugh, J. (1981). Operationalizing the competing values approach: Measuring performance in the employment service. *Public Productivity Review* (June), 141-159.

Rosenkopf, L., & Tushman, M. L. (1994). The coevolution of technology and organization. In J. A. C. Baum, & J. V. Singh (Eds.), *Evolutionary dynamics of organizations* (pp. 403-424). New York, NY: Oxford University Press.

Savoie, A., & Morin, E. M. (2002). Les représentations de l'efficacité organisationnelle: développements récents. In R. Jacob, A. Rondeau & D.

Luc (Eds.), *Transformer l'organisation: La gestion stratégique du changement* (pp. 206-231). Montreal, Quebec, Canada: Revue Gestion.

Schumpeter, J. (1950). *Capitalism, socialism, and democracy.* (p. 431) New York, NY: Harper & Row Publishers.

Scott, W. R. (1990). Technology and structure: An organizational-level perspective. In Paul S. Goodman, & Lee S. Sproull (Eds.), *Technology and organizations* (pp. 109-143). Oxford, UK: Jossey-Bass Publishers.

Shadish, W. R., Cook, T. D., & Campbell, D. T. (2002). *Experimental and quasi-experimental designs for generalized causal inference.* Boston, MA: Houghton Mifflin Company.

Shenhar, A. J., & Dvir, D. (1996). Toward a typological theory of project management. *Research Policy, 25*(4), 607.

Shenhar, A. J., Dvir, D., Levy, O., & Maltz, A. C. (2001). Project success: A multidimensional strategic concept. *Long Range Planning, 34*(6), 699-725.

Singleton, J., Royce A., & Straits, B. C. (2005). *Approaches to social research* (4th ed.). New York, NY: Oxford University Press.

Söderlund, J., & Bredin, K. (2006). HRM in project-intensive firms: Changes and challenges. *Human Resource Management, 45*(2), 249.

SPSS Inc. (2005). SPSS (Version 14.0) [Computer software]. Available from SPSS Web site: http://www.spss.com

Stanleigh, M. (2005). *The impact of implementing a project management office: Report on the results of the on-line survey.* Business Improvement Architects.

Stewart, W. E. (2001). Balanced scorecard for projects. *Project Management Journal, 32*(1), 38-53.

Stinglhamber, F., Bentein, K., & Vandenberghe, C. (2004). Congruence de valeurs et engagement envers l'organisation et le groupe de travail. *Psychologie du Travail et des Organisations, 10*(2), 165-187.

Strauss, A., & Corbin, J. (1998). *Basics of qualitative research: Techniques and procedures for developing grounded theory* (2nd ed.). Thousand Oaks, CA: Sage Publications.

Thamhain, H. J. (2004). Linkages of project environment to performance: Lessons for team leadership. *International Journal of Project Management, 22*(7), 533-544.

Thiry, M. (2004). Program management: A strategic decision management process. In P. W. G. Morris & J. K. Pinto (Eds.), *The Wiley guide to managing projects* (pp. 257-287). Hoboken, NJ: John Wiley & Sons, Inc.

Thiry, M. (2006, July). *A paradoxism for project-based organizations.* Paper presented at the Project Management Institute Research Conference 2006, Montréal, Canada.

Thiry, M., & Matthey, A. (2005, February). *Delivering business benefits through projects, programs, portfolios and PM's.* Paper presented at the Project Management Institute Global Congress, Singapore.

Thomas, J. L., & Mullaly, M. E. (2008). *Researching the value of project management.* Newtown Square, PA: Project Management Institute.

Thompson, M. P., McGrath, M. R., & Whorton, J. (1981). The competing values approach: Its application and utility. *Public Productivity Review* (June), 188-200.

Turner, R. J., & Keegan, A. E. (1999). The versatile project-based organization: Governance and operational control. *European Management Journal, 17*(3), 296-309.

Turner, R. J., & Keegan, A. E. (2001). Mechanisms of governance in the project-based organization: Roles of the broker and steward. *European Management Journal, 19*(3), 254-267.

Turner, R. J., & Keegan, A. E.. (2004). Managing technology: Innovation, learning, and maturity. In P. W. G. Morris & J. K. Pinto (Eds.), *The Wiley guide to managing projects* (pp. 567-590). Hoboken, NJ: John Wiley & Sons Inc.

Tushman, M. L., & O'Reilly, C. A., III. (1996). Ambidextrous organizations: Managing evolutionary and revolutionary change. *California Management Review, 38*(4), 8-30.

Van de Ven, A. H. (1999). *The innovation journey.* New York, NY: Oxford University Press.

Van de Ven, A. H. (2007). *Engaged scholarship: Creating knowledge for science and practice.* Oxford, UK: Oxford University Press.

Van de Ven, A. H., & Garud, R. (1994). The coevolution of technical and institutional events in the development of an innovation. In J. A. C. Baum, & Jitendra V. Singh (Eds.), *Evolutionary Dynamics of Organizations* (pp. 425-443). New York, NY: Oxford University Press.

Van den broecke, E., De Hertogh, S., & Vereecke, A. (2005, September). *Implementing strategy in turbulent environments: A role for program and portfolio management.* Paper presented at the Project Management Institute North America Congress 2005, Toronto, Ontario, Canada.

Whitley, R. (2006). Project-based firms: New organizational form or variations on a theme? *Industrial and Corporate Change, 15*(1), 77-99.

Williams, T. (2005). Assessing and moving on from the dominant project management discourse in the light of project overruns. *IEEE Transactions on Engineering Management, 52*(4), 497-508.

Williams, T. (2007). *Post-project reviews to gain effective lessons learned.* Newtown Square, PA: Project Management Institute.

Winch, G. M. (2004, July). *Rethinking project management: Project organizations as information processing systems?* Paper presented at the Project Management Institute Research Conference 2004, London, UK.

Winter, M., Smith, C., Morris, P., & Cicmil, S. (2006). Directions for future research in project management: The main findings of a UK government-funded research network. *International Journal of Project Management, 24*(8), 638-649.